KU-131-063

Contemporary American Fiction

Editors: Malcolm Bradbury and Sigmund Ro

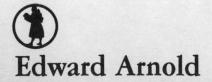

Edward Arnold

813.5409
CON

© Edward Arnold (Publishers) Ltd 1987

First published in Great Britain 1987 by
Edward Arnold (Publishers) Ltd, 41 Bedford Square, London WC1B 3DQ

Edward Arnold (Australia) Pty Ltd, 80 Waverley Road, Caulfield East,
Victoria 3145, Australia

Edward Arnold, 3 East Read Street, Baltimore, Maryland 21202, U.S.A.

British Library Cataloguing in Publication Data

Contemporary American fiction.——(Stratford-upon-Avon studies.
  Second series)
  1. American fiction——20th century——History and criticism
  I. Bradbury, Malcolm, *1932–* II. Ro, Sigmund III. Series
  813'.54'09   PS379

ISBN 0–7131–6469–7

All rights reserved. No part of this publication may be reproduced, stored
in a retrieval system, or transmitted in any form or by any means, electronic,
photocopying, recording, or otherwise, without the prior permission of
Edward Arnold (Publishers) Ltd.

286293

Index compiled by Jennifer Kane
Text set in 10/11pt Garamond
by Colset Private Limited, Singapore.
Made and printed in Great Britain by Richard Clay Ltd., Bungay, Sufflok.

23190

Contents

Preface

Malcolm Bradbury

I

The problems of mapping contemporary American fiction are enormous, and not entirely remote from those the first explorers and discoverers found as they faced the task of mapping the shapeless great American continent itself, before they were entirely sure it was a continent, or even on what part of the map of the world it lay. Let us suppose that the 'contemporary' period of the American novel is that since 1945 – a long period in writing, of some 40 years, during which the nature of fiction has evidently changed a great deal and its styles and manners altered and proliferated. In the 1940s and 1950s we thought we knew what a national tradition was, and in important books like Richard Chase's *The American Novel and Its Tradition* (1957) and Leslie A. Fiedler's *Love and Death in the American Novel* (1960) it seemed that much of the modern terrain and its history had been mapped and that, perhaps for the first time, there was a discernable and usable American past for the novel which was available to the contemporary writer. Yet it was just as that past, with its romance tradition and its gothic features, its distinctive preoccupations and myths, was being constructed that signs were growing of an extraordinary new variety and heterogeneity in American fiction. And so it has been since. The 40 years since the end of the Second World War, a war that in many ways brought American writing and culture to a central place in the history of the contemporary arts, have indeed been years of extraordinary versatility, variety and multiplicity, the writing reflecting and refracting a nation itself multi-ethnic and multidox, extraordinarily mixed in its cultural roots and its cultural levels, and showing the complexities and cultural variation of an immigrant land spread across a vast continental land-mass that faces both toward Europe in the east and the Pacific in the west.

It is not surprising that the fiction that comes from it is multiform, in regional characteristics, ethnic sources and cultural levels. It is a fiction that has grown in ethnic variety – thus the dominance in the 1950s and 1960s both of the Jewish-American novel and the black novel, and the contemporary growth of hispanic fiction – and in regional variation, a good deal of the best current writing in fact displaying the characteristics and contours of the region in which it is set. It has been a fiction that has manifested both the complex stratifications of American culture – from the high cultural to the pop, from the academic to the populist, from the avant garde to the generic – and indeed the cultural variation has been fed by its own intersections, so that play with cultural cliches and generic forms has been a way of fictional development; Kurt Vonnegut interplaying popular science fiction and wartime reportage in *Slaughterhouse-5*, Richard Brautigan parodying and interfusing the types in his fictions, so that *The Hawkline Monster* is subtitled 'A Gothic Western'. In the period we can call 'contemporary', then, a wide variety of traditions exist, themselves displaying the varieties of a culture that is both populist and profoundly assimilative of the culturally new. Moreover 40 years in the modern arts is a long time – long enough for forms that seemed innovative to become exhausted, original developments to become backwards, major careers to fall into silence, new generations to grow and die. It is therefore a period in which several different generations exist, often overlaying each other, adding new variation or commentary to what has shortly gone before. John Barth once proposed, indeed, that the age was one of the 'literature of exhaustion,' its literary arts displaying the 'used-upness' of fiction, so parodic and intertextual did much of the writing of the time become. Yet, he suggested in a later essay, it was also a time of 'the literature of replenishment', when the conventions and constraints of discourse fractured, the multiplying of types developed, and late twentieth-century fiction became a fiction of playful seductions quoting the past and constructing the indeterminacies of the present with a new buoyancy. This playfulness acquired a handy name, 'postmodernism', to account for it; the term, which has had much currency in contemporary architecture, where the same sense of exuberant and random quotation has come to be laid over modernist principles, has a fairly vigorous life in this book. It certainly bears some relation to the Byzantine and plural nature of contemporary American society; the multiple nature of the texture of American life, its driving search for a hyper-modernity, its rapid and ever-accelerating consumption of styles, its cultural eclecticism and its culturelessness, is constantly noted by those who visit the United States for the first time, as well as of course by its own social commentators and its novelists. Modern American fiction thus seems to display the late modern energy, plurality, cultural diversity, and of course the political and economic power of an immigrant and polyglot nation in its condition as a great continental superpower whose experience has been transformed by its late entry into a major role in global history. And perhaps it is this mixture of modernity and power, the assimilative energy of a late imperial fiction, that helps explain the dominant role the contemporary American novel has played in guiding the direction and shaping the prospects for the late twentieth-century novel at large. But its variety and assimilativeness are precisely what makes it hard for us to map, while at the same time they indicate some of the fundamental energies underlying the contemporary evolution of fiction.

The question of whether the energy and innovation remains as strong as it was is important, though perhaps hard to judge, for the nearer we come to the present the harder we find it to sense shapes and directions of promise and importance. It may well be that the enormous moral vigour of the 1940s and the 1950s and the experimental excitements of the 1960s and early 1970s have largely given way to more modest circularities and repetitions, and that Latin American and once again European fiction now has stronger excitements. But there can be no doubt at all that from the 1940s to the 1970s American fiction did play a dominant role in the international direction of the novel, and that the combination of economic and political power and major talent was an international force. It gave us many authors of major gifts, from the less than completely American Isaac Bashevis Singer and Vladimir Nabokov to Bellow and Updike, Mailer and Salinger, Pynchon and Hawkes. In many of its fundamental preoccupations – with the future of humanism and the collapse of the subject, with the power of reportage and the fictive text, with the recovery of realism and the advance of avant gardism – it pointed to many of the main artistic issues of the times. In recent years a number of very distinctive newer talents have emerged, a number of them considered in this book (which, like the parallel British volume, *The Contemporary English Novel*, is especially concerned with more recent developments and approaches to those developments). But what is striking is that in the 1940s and early 1950s this sense of variety and innovation was not generally felt, and that the assumption that postwar American fiction was a major power in the modern novel was not widespread. For the beginnings of the change into late twentieth-century achievement were, as in European countries, slow to come and when they did come they did not take the forms that many critics and commentators expected. The late twentieth-century mood in American fiction has its own strong character, and it is worth considering just how it developed.

II

Great expectations have, of course, been central to modern American experience. The coming of the twentieth century generated many myths of American influence, potency and modernity, and these flourished in the arts as well as in social and political life. But the struggles and the disappointments that troubled the life of the world in the twentieth century had their profound impact in the United States. The two major world wars both started in Europe, but they had great impact on the United States, and brought about their central involvement. The Great Depression of the 1930s was also a world event, though it had particular roots in the American economy, and challenged the entire direction of national development. It was the recovery of the American economy after 1945, as well as the growth of global strategic and political responsibilities, that made the United States a postwar superpower, different in character from what it had been before. In the arts too we can see something of the same change. By the 1920s Americans could claim to be powerful figures in the development of artistic modernity, and in the 1930s the movement of emigrés from Europe increased the cosmopolitanism of artistic culture. But the experience of war, the impact of the holocaust, and the emergence of the atomic era transformed national awareness, and, as has been observed by a number of critics, American writing like Americans themselves seemed shaken into a consciousness of history which questioned and transformed many of the fundamental American myths. The spirit of writing changed with the spirit of the culture, and in the United States as in the economically or physically shattered countries of Europe awareness of the need to reconstruct artistic and intellectual life was clear. It was an existentialist season, and Jean-Paul Sartre's quest for a new intellectual responsibility helped shape the mood of the times: sombre, much concerned with moral recuperation, and with the destructive forces of totalitarian regimes – even those of life in the armies of those who had been fighting against totalitarianism – his influence was strong.

The postwar scene, in the United States as in Europe, was not marked by that sense of experimental excitement that passed through all the western arts after the First World War, when the movement of Modernism reached its peak. It was muted, cautious, and historically anxious, generally lacking in aesthetic flamboyance. Thus many critics in the late 1940s and early 1950s felt less that a whole new era was starting than that one was ending, as the great novelists who had given America its modern novel – Hemingway, Faulkner, Dos Passos, Steinbeck – came toward the end of their careers, received their Nobel Prizes, and moved toward the end of *oeuvres* that now seemed not so much contemporary as eminently classical and teachable. As for successors, they seemed hard to discern, and the tradition seemed to some degree to have fractured. Looking around the new America of the 1950s, of new affluence and new conformity, new cold war conservatism and caution, critics like Malcolm Cowley and John Aldridge were disposed to consider that the great era of American fictional experiment was over, along with the bohemianism and expatriation, the modernism and the confident American mythologies that had made it. Indeed it came to seem that the American arts were in a post-modern time – and that phrase did not contain the affirmative and experimental association that we give to it today. It meant to suggest that the contemporary American writer wrote in late days, in the shadow of great predecessors, and without strong orientations and directions. The positive if critical myths of the great American moderns – the buoyancy of Scott Fitzgerald, who may have sensed that the American dream was lost but kept on trying to redeem it, displacing money into beauty and vulgarity into myth, the experimental rhetoric of William Faulkner, attempting to mythicize the past and give America a timeless history even if he knew the taint in the land and the power of history to defeat, the tight existential economy of Ernest Hemingway, which spread outward into metaphorical certainty and a faith in attainment and mastery – apparently no longer offered confident guidance to authors who belonged to the age after

Auschwitz and Hiroshima, the age of the modern lonely crowd, the disorienting city, of new material dreams and psychic needs. 'Let us assume for a moment that we have reached the end of one of those recurrent periods of cultural unrest, innovation and excitement that we call "modern",' Irving Howe wrote in a famous essay of 1959, 'Mass Society and Post-Modern Fiction', going on to say that, if one wants to consider the fiction written in America since 1945, 'there is a decided advantage in regarding them as 'post-modern', significantly different from the kind of writing we usually call modern.' If we read the postwar writers in this way, Howe says, we will notice their distinctive qualities, the things that make them new but less heroic and demanding than their predecessors: 'It tunes the ear to their distinctive failures. And it lures one into patience and charity.'

Clearly Howe's definition of the postmodern condition by no means matches those which are several times explored, in different ways and from different standpoints, in the following book. Nonetheless it shares with them several features, including the most obvious, the general assumption that Modernism has come to an end, become historical. Howe explains this by discerning amid the plurality and multivalency of modernist fiction a basic sense of there being a stable reality, historical and social, from which the political and social instincts of Modernist fiction derive; and suggesting that it is this sense of the historically real which has collapsed. Again, this view diverges from a good deal of more recent criticism, which assumes that the postwar period was a time of a return to social and moral realism. For Howe, the force that has produced the change is the coming of modern mass-society, 'a relatively comfortable, half welfare and half garrison society in which the population grows passive, indifferent and atomized', materially satisfied but historically unalert, physically pleased but spiritually bereft. It is a society still to be fully grasped by the sociologist and the novelist, though many of them see 'the hovering sickness of soul, the despairing contentment, the prosperous malaise'. Surveying the work of writers like Bernard Malamud, Herbert Gold, J.D. Salinger, Nelson Algren, Wright Morris and Saul Bellow, what Howe discerns is an oblique approach to social existence, a feeling that experience can only be taken on the sly, and a quality of being novels of the will, improvising the life of self against the life of society. Hence they concentrate on an old American subject, the search 'for personal identity and freedom. In their distance from fixed social categories and their concern with the metaphysical implications of that distance, these novels constitute what I would call "post-modern" fiction.'

What is clear is that Howe felt that a new sense of alienation and extremity was entering American fiction, dissolving its sense of reality and therefore the power directly to confront history. And this view of the postwar American novel was to be developed by many of the writers themselves. So Saul Bellow, perhaps the most important of all the new writers, was to say himself in an essay a little later, 'Some Notes on Recent American Fiction' (1963), that he was struck by the theme of 'the loss of self' in modern American writing, and the instinctive parallelism between the reports of American authors into the violent and arbitrary nature of existence and contemporary French philosophy. So, he suggests, many of his best contemporaries – and he adds to names mentioned previously those of James Baldwin, J.F. Powers, John Updike, Philip Roth, J.P. Donleavy and Vladimir Nabokov – seem to feel 'the pressure of a vast public life, which may dwarf him as an individual while permitting him to be a giant in hatred or fantasy'. Bellow suggests that the twin images of the sovereign self and the self absented or deprived, as in existentialist or absurdist philosophies, consort with each other, depriving the novel of the dense private life that was once essential to it. Indeed, he says, we have so debunked the idea of the Self that we cannot continue in the same way: 'Undeniably the human being is not what he was commonly thought a century ago. The question nevertheless remains. He is something. What is he?' This is the question, Bellow maintains, that contemporary writers have answered poorly. Yet his own splendid novels display the anxiety, struggling from an existential alienation toward a civil contract which will not readily yield itself in the age of anonymity and mass. In another influential and much quoted essay, 'Writing American Fiction' (1961), Philip Ròth made a very similar point, arguing that the American actuality was continually outdoing the talents of any novelist, that it sickened and infuriated, and left the imagination bereft. The balanced equivalence of realism was clearly hard to achieve in the postwar American novel, and from Bellow's *Dangling Man* (1944) the underlying strong influence seems to be Kafka, with his sense of consciousness overwhelmed by the modern massing of power and authority, driven into fantasy and those anxieties of self that are expressed in the existential novel of Sartre and Camus, which clearly had potent influence on the American writers of the 1950s.

No doubt it is true that the American writers of the immediately postwar period, during the 1940s and 1950s, shared with their European contemporaries a reaction against the experimentalism of Modernism and a spirit of return to a relative realism. Yet in a sense this was a way of acquainting themselves with a history and a social reality dark, oppressive and disorienting, and the spirit was less one of simple realism than realism intensified on the one hand by a hard naturalism and on the other by fantasy. In this sense they did indeed lack the experimental verve of the writers who transfigured the arts after World War I, and when a more experimental spirit came back into writing during the 1960s some of their achievement appeared modest. Yet the view does little justice to some of the very finest of them; Bellow, Roth, Updike, and to some degree Mailer and Salinger seem among the great American twentieth-century novelists. They were indeed writing a fiction different in spirit from their predecessors, and in many ways far more Europeanized and cosmopolitan. The war novels they wrote – Norman Mailer's *The Naked and the Dead* (1948), John Hawkes's *The Cannibal* (1949), James Jones's *From Here to Eternity* (1951) and then the bleaker, more absurdist works of the 1960s like Joseph Heller's *Catch-22* (1961) and Kurt Vonnegut's *Slaughter-*

house-5 (1969) – portrayed a time envisioned in terms of mass armies and corrupt military relations, with the adversary as often the American Army itself as the Nazi enemy. War was an aspect of a totalitarianism which had not died and still persisted in the social institutions and the moral oppressions of the age; the era of humanism seemed threatened, if not drawing to an end, in the random violence of the age, the harsh relations, the social massing. Sometimes highly naturalistic, sometimes drawing on elaborate forms of comic or grotesque fantasy, these books often appeared parables not simply of wartime life but of life in postwar American society itself. And when it came to portraying that society in its contemporary existence, similar themes returned, in the bleak naturalistic novels of Nelson Algren and John Horne Burns, or in the more grotesque and extreme writing of the new Southern novelists – Eudora Welty, Carson McCullers, Flannery O'Connor, Truman Capote – who revived Gothic forms from the past to deal with the prevailing sense of evil and extremity.

Thus the spirit of realism may, as Keith Opdahl's essay on Updike here proposes, have been important in postwar American fiction, but it was realism in complex and modern forms: Updike's high aestheticism, shading into myth and fantasy, Salinger's mannered, fragile portrait of a world of love and squalor, or the urgent moral realism of the Jewish-American novelists, who had every reason for bringing the postwar novel back to its humanistic, moral and metaphysical potential in the wake of the holocaust and the totalitarian threats of fascism to language; their work, concerned with social and historical experience but informed with a dark sense of modern alienation and bleak if not black comedy, had much to do, as Paul Levine argues, with the destiny of the postwar American novel. Fed by consciousness of the immigrant experience and the European backgrounds of American life, alert to the conditions of modern urban existence and the sufferings of victimization, it bore some relation to the development of black fiction, also discussed later in this book by Robert Stepto, and which, on from Richard Wright's *The Outsider* (1940), captures the sense of namelessness and exposure that marks much modern black life. Ralph Ellison's *Invisible Man* (1952), which suggests that 'Who knows but that, on the lower frequencies, I speak for you?', and the 1950s novels of James Baldwin indeed carry into lower frequencies the sense of existential extremism in modern American experience, while raising many of the moral and social preoccupations we associate with a realistic fiction. The painful world of Southern Gothic fiction also carried that haunting sense of alienation and that awareness of historical anxiety that seemed such a strong feature of the newer American novel, and the realism of the period – much as with similar realistic tendencies in Europe – was heavily marked by a moral urgency and a sense of absurdism that passed onward into the fictional tradition.

Certainly this made the direction of the postwar American novel hard to judge. Critical interpretation divided, sometimes emphasizing the return to traditionalism, sometimes emphasizing the dark, troubled, experimental nature of the new vision. Edmund Fuller, looking at the writing of the period in his *Man and Modern Fiction* (1958), found it filled with a portrait of the individual as 'an ironic biological accident, inadequate, aimless, meaningless. . . . His uniqueness as a person is denied or suppressed. He inhabits a hostile universe.' Ihab Hassan, writing in *Radical Innocence* (1961), read matters differently, discerning a spirit of radical recovery at work, and the persistence of the anarchic hero who refuses to accept the rule of modern reality in the determination to find more transcendent and radical meanings in experience. Marcus Klein, in *After Alienation* (1964), considered that a central subject in the new American fiction was the desire to transcend the alienated self, and hence there was a general spirit of accommodation – if cautious and oblique, comic and absurd. Such divisions were understandable, given both the various nature of the new writers now emerging, and the fact that a good deal of the new fiction in a time of the new liberalism was marked by a sharp tension, by which the claims of alienation and accommodation, of isolated individual and massed social system, of a comically absurd self struggling with an anarchic process of history, combine and re-combine, generating fresh types of fictional structure. This allows for a re-apprehension of realism, and certainly for a marked change of spirit in postwar American fiction, away from the strong and modernism and American mythicism of the great novelists of the 1920s, toward a more anguished, urban, immigrant and often cosmopolitan vision. It was part of the Existentialist spirit of the time that the endeavour was made to draw humanist conclusions from potentially totalitarian situations, moral judgement from a world of cold war politics and often narrow national ideology.

Yet the position was hard to maintain, and from early in the postwar period we can find a more experimental, avant garde and politically radical spirit emerging in American fiction. John Hawkes published his gothic and experimental *The Cannibal* in 1949, and William Gaddis's great novel of art as counterfeiting, *The Recognitions*, came out in 1955. In the same year Vladimir Nabokov, an old Modernist hand who had published fiction in Russian and German, turned to the English language and an American subject to write his highly reflexive novel *Lolita*, which was sufficiently outrageous in its theme of the American as nymphet to be published in Paris. So was William Burroughs's *The Naked Lunch* (1959), a work which was to some a novel of virulent political satire, and to others of drug-induced hallucination, but which certainly helped familiarize the spirit of random and aleatory construction – the cut-up, fold-in method of writing – which helped justify a good deal of expressive practice in the 1960s. But in the American context Burroughs appeared part of a move-ment or tendency which had been developing right through the 1950s, the movement of the 'Beat' generation. Its romantic-radical bohemianism and its 'spontaneous bop prosody' found its fictional expression in the novels of Jack Kerouac, most famously in *On the Road* (1957), though the book to my taste acquired its reputation far more from the life-style it celebrated than from the creative depths of its prose. John Barth's *The Floating*

Opera, a work of modern absurdism about a nihilist who sees no sense in life but none in suicide either, came out in 1956; the book showed strong existentialist influence but, like Nabokov's novel, a strong sense of fiction's own self-referentiality, its inherent 'fictiveness'. It was clear that a new experimental mood was growing, developing from the new radicalism apparent in political and social culture that was to flower in the 1960s, but also from the late Modernist developments initiated by writers who had been shaped by prewar experimentalism, like Beckett, Borges and Nabokov. Thus the new spirit that came to preoccupy the 1960s was made of a number of strands, from the post-existentialist and absurdist spirit that fed the black humour mood of the early 1960s in the work of authors like Joseph Heller and Kurt Vonnegut to the textual experimentalism of authors like Gaddis and Thomas Pynchon, and from the intertextual, fictive mood of the work of Barth, Nabokov and others to the self-conscious new reportage of the non-fiction novel and the 'new journalism'. It is out of these rather various funds that there came into being that tendency which we have chosen nowadays to describe as 'postmodernism'.

III

It is perhaps not surprising that the usefulness and the limitations of that term 'postmodernism' have been the concern of several of the contributors to this book, including Peter Currie, Allan Lloyd Smith and Jerome Klinkowitz, who has written extensively on the matter. It is a term that has, as we have seen, been widely and variously used, transformed, and in some quarters seriously despised. It has not always given great comfort to those writers who have been enrolled in its membership. It is a term that has largely arisen in criticism, rather than out of the movement identification of authors themselves, and like most critical terms it is far from pure, implying a history, a function and a philosophical approach to writing. It has been variously applied to a good many experimental writers whose work is therefore assumed to share much in common, writers who in various ways seem to have been redefining, recategorizing and deconstructing the practice of fiction and the nature of the fictional tradition. It has also done much to give us a vocabulary of understanding and a contemporary critical perspective. Beyond that, it has often been used as part of an endeavour to define the stylistic character and condition, the dominant aesthetic and epistemological tendency, of the arts of the age. Many of the assumptions surrounding it therefore derive from *post facto* definitions of the character, importance and implied legacy of the Modernist movement, which was itself remarkably various and constructed out of contention. The result of this is that the term amounts to a troubled but now strongly forged alliance between the practice of fictional writing, and the criticism of it. Thus, where novelists have indeed been willing to talk of 'surfiction', 'metafiction', and so on, critics have supplemented practice with theory, and often aligned the fictional practice with critical developments in the area of Post-Structuralism and Deconstruction.

'Metafiction' has been twin-towned with 'Paracriticism', 'discontinous fiction' with 'Deconstruction', and those conditions of linguistic slippage and aporia which have engaged contemporary philosophers and literary theorists have been given analogues or paradigms in the often randomizing, deferring, self-parodying, intertextual practices of many of the more experimental new novelists.

Similarity between philosophical theory and fictional practice should not surprise us; it has always been characteristic of the arts, and an appropriate aspect of their interpretation. But philosophy and fiction or poetry are far from being analogous modes of enquiry, and the theoretical interest of part of modern fiction – its status as anti-text, its resistance to referentiality, its sense of the disappearance of the subject, its use of randomness as a generative principle, its emphasis not so much on the iconic nature of the art object but its multiple use and its plurality – is not an outright proof of its importance as art. The temptation to see synchrony between the direction of philosophy and that of fiction has proved strong. Thus in Ihab and Sally Hassan's invaluable collection of essays on postmodernism, *Innovation/Renovation* (1983), one of a good many important books that have appeared on innovative American writing and its cultural context over the last few years, the French philosopher J.-F. Lyotard writes: 'A postmodern artist or writer is in the position of a philosopher; the text he writes, the work he produces, are not in principle governed by pre-established rules, and they cannot be judged according to a determining judgement, by applying familiar categories to the text or to the work . . .'. The modern writer shares the condition of expressive indeterminacy of which philosophers have grown profoundly conscious. And yet this statement might be applied to the work of any artist or writer, or to none. The prevalence of postmodern theoretics has perhaps been not so much the cause of or the explanation for contemporary American writing, but a visible and powerful intellectual context surrounding it. It is one of the interests of this present book that its essays look predominantly at the fiction of a time after postmoderism, acknowledging, as Jerome Klinkowitz does, that the spirit of experiment the term designates has by no means died, but has changed in flavour and taken on new casts and preoccupations. And as several of these essays suggest, there is not only evidence in current American fiction, the fiction of the 1980s, of a new assessment of the importance of realism, a realism undoubtedly questioned and challenged by what has gone before, but some use in looking back and reading the works of the writers who have been called 'postmodern' in a more open and historically attentive way. This revision is understandable. The temptation to give canonical status to the postmodern has not only sometimes limited the way in which some of the best writers have been read, but narrowed the span of American fiction and led to neglect of other important writers and tendencies, some of them given their due attention in this book.

The spirit of American fiction in the 1980s has indeed changed, and not only in the work of newer writers – the important new black writers, the major work of new women writers, the newer, exacting experiments of authors like Walter Abish or Raymond Carver – but in that of well-established figures like William Gaddis or Robert Coover. Both have recently published very important novels – Gaddis's *Carpenter's Gothic*, Coover's *Gerald's Party* – which are written in modes a good deal closer to realism, though with a strong sense of the parodic and the power of the American Gothic tradition to which Gaddis's title directly alludes. They retain a strong sense of textual self-examination, and possess an habitual virtuosity, a great sense of performance always strong in the greatest American fiction. They also possess a strong sense of political and historical urgency, someting that indeed has never been far from a good deal of American experimental writing. Today American writing seems to show less a clear aesthetic direction than a general versatility, founded in part on its lively postwar heritage. The essays in this collection show the mood, looking from a variety of perspectives on the mixed directions of current American fiction, and at its intersections with other forms and other genres – so Warren French looks at fiction and film, and Ihab Hassan, one of the most interesting critics of postmodernism, at forms beyond conventional fiction, autobiography and adventure. If, once again, in the middle of the 1980s, American fiction, always changeable, seems to have chosen multi-directionality and variety over strong aesthetic definition, it needs a similar range of mapmakers, a plurality of perspectives.

Note

Select critical bibliography: realism

Robert Alter, 'The Self-Conscious Moment: Reflections on the Aftermath of Modernism', *Triquarterly* 33 (Spring, 1957), pp. 209–30.

John Barth, 'The Literature of Replenishment', *The Atlantic* 246 (Jan. 1980), pp. 65–71.

Gerald Graff, 'Babbitt at the Abyss', *Triquarterly* 33 (Spring, 1975), pp. 305–36.

Gerald Graff, 'The Myth of the Postmodernist Break-through', *Triquarterly* 26 (Winter, 1973) pp. 383–417.

Alfred Kazin, *Bright Book of Life* (Boston: Little, Brown & Co., 1973).

Hugh Kenner, *A Homemade World*, 1975: The American Modernist Writers (New York: Alfred A. Knopf, 1975).

Jerome Klinkowitz, *Literary Disruptions* (Urbana, Ill: University of Illinois Press, 1975).

Harold H. Kolb, Jr, *The Illusion of Life* (Charlottesville: The University Press of Virginia, 1969).

George Levine, *The Realistic Imagination* (Chicago: The University of Chicago Press, 1981), pp. 3–22.

Janet Holmgren McKay, *Narration and Discourse in American Realistic Fiction* (Philadelphia: University of Pennsylvania Press, 1982).

Raymond M. Olderman, *Beyond the Wasteland: A Study of the American Novel in the Nineteen-sixties* (New Haven: Yale University Press, 1972).

Donald Pizer, *Realism and Naturalism* (Carbondale: Southern Illinois University Press 1966).

Tony Tanner, *The Reign of Wonder* (Cambridge: Cambridge University Press, 1965).

Victor Shklovsky, 'Art as Technique', in *Russian Formalist Criticism: Four Essays*, trans. and ed. by Lee Lemon and Marion J. Reis (Lincoln: University of Nebraska Press, 1965), pp. 3–57.

Select critical bibliography: The Centaur

Robert Detweiler, *John Updike* (New York: Twayne, 1972).

Alice and Kenneth Hamilton, *The Elements of John Updike* (Grand Rapids, Michigan: Wm. B. Eerdman's Publishing Co., 1970).

George W. Hunt, *John Updike and the Three Great Secret Things* (Grand Rapids, Michigan: Wm. B. Eerdman's Publishing Co., 1980).

Joyce B. Markle, *Fighters and Lovers: Themes in the Novels of John Updike* (New York: New York University Press, 1973).

James M. Mellard, 'The Novel as Lyric Elegy: The Mode of Updike's *The Centaur*', *Texas Studies in Language and Literature* 21 (1979) pp. 112–27.

Larry E. Taylor, *Pastoral and Anti-Pastoral Patterns in John Updike's Fiction* (Carbondale: Southern Illinois University Press, 1971).

Suzanne Henning Uphaus, *John Updike* (New York: Frederick Ungar Publishing Co., 1980).

Edward P. Vargo, 'The Necessity of Myth in Updike's *The Centaur*', *PMLA* 85 (1973) pp. 452–60. Reprinted in *Rainstorms and Fire: Ritual in John Updike* (Kennikat Press, 1973), pp. 77–105.

1

The Nine Lives of Literary Realism

Keith Opdahl

Saul Bellow's heir in American fiction is undoubtedly John Updike. This fact would not please either writer, necessarily, since each has expressed reservations about the other's work. And yet Updike writes as though (in Bellow's words in *The Paris Review*) 'the development of realism in the nineteenth century is still the major event of modern literature.'[1] Updike also, as he said of Bellow in *The New Yorker*, carries mimesis to levels 'deeper than it has gone before.'[2] Updike, like Bellow, catches the texture of American life, whether it be the litter of a kitchen counter or the tremor of an elderly woman. Updike is even more of a realist than Bellow, in fact, since Bellow seeks to shape American culture, giving in to a 'professor-elf', as Updike says; while Updike seems content to record it. To Updike the experience of the American middle class after World War II is infinitely precious, and worthy of literary preservation.

Updike developed this attitude during a new flowering of American realism, moreover. The decade of the 1950s may not have equalled the American Renaissance a century earlier, but it certainly produced a large amount of accomplished fiction. Dominated by Saul Bellow and Bernard Malamud, the period saw work by Robert Penn Warren, Ralph Ellison, Eudora Welty, Vladimir Nabokov, Phillip Roth, Norman Mailer, John Cheever, William Styron, Flannery O'Connor and John Barth – not to mention a large number of writers who did not receive the recognition they deserved, such as Evan S. Connell (*Mrs Bridge*), George P. Eliott (*Among the Dangs*) or J.F. Powers (*Prince of Darkness*). These writers looked at the private lives of their characters with a new intensity, creating a highly poetic prose formed of precise observations – the kind of sharp detail to be found in *Madame Bovary* and *The Adventures of Huckleberry Finn* – and subjective insight. Like Robert Penn Warren, whose *All The King's Men* (1944) set the tone, these writers used their heightened prose to examine social issues through the prism of personal experience. Never before, it

[1] Saul Bellow, *Writers at Work* Third Series (New York: Viking Press, 1968), pp. 175–96.
[2] John Updike, 'Toppling Towers Seen by A Whirling Soul', reprinted from *The New Yorker* in *Hugging the Shore* (New York: Alfred A. Knopf, 1983), p. 263.

seemed, had such a large number of writers rendered with such exact insight the daily experience of ordinary citizens.

And yet signs of strain quickly appeared. By 1967 John Barth could declare that the straight realistic novel had become (as he entitled his essay) 'The Literature of Exhaustion'.[3] Barth noted that the modern novelists of some 45 years earlier had already shown that the realistic mode was used up. How could anyone write realistically after Kafka and Joyce? 'It's dismaying to see so many of our writers following Dostoevsky. . . ,' Barth wrote in *The Atlantic*, 'when the real technical question seems to be how to succeed not even Joyce and Kafka, but those who've *succeeded* Joyce and Kafka.' A host of other critics agreed, proclaiming, like Gabriel Josipovici in *The World and the Book*, that 'it is from literary realism that modern fiction has freed us.'[4] How could it be that writers such as Saul Bellow and John Updike chose to remain in their chains? Others like Phillip Roth, John Barth and Robert Coover moved from an early realism to the experimental, giving up linear plot, consistent reader identification, and cause and effect. If the writers who succeeded Joyce and Kafka were the postmoderns, Barth wrote, those who clung to an earlier realistic convention were the premoderns: the future clearly lay with those who experimented with new techniques.

When the realist looked around him, moreover, he found many cultural reasons to change his style. Sociology and psychology had developed methods for probing those subtle human relations that the realists had heretofore explored. America had developed a mass society in which all citizens (like their mass-produced possessions) appeared alike: to Irving Howe, American life had become diffuse and meaningless, without the cultural distinctions and rigid tradition useful to the realistic writer. And then technology had made the actual world itself excessive and fantastic: what writer could compete with a man on the moon – as Bellow recognized in *Mr Sammler's Planet*? What writer could imagine or explain a society that permitted its cities to rot while it built new ones on the perimeter? 'The American writer in the middle of the twentieth century,' Phillip Roth wrote in *Reading Myself and Others*, 'has his hands full in trying to understand, describe, and then make credible much of American reality.'[5] The writer also had to compete with the technology of film and TV, much as painters earlier had to compete with the photograph. If one could reproduce the world by an inexpensive mechanical means, what use was there for the hand-wrought version? And then who believed that reality could be represented, anyway? The 60s saw a growing conviction that the world could not be known with any certitude, and in any case could not be reproduced by language. Every reader is locked within his self, many believed, and every word slips and crumbles on the page. How could anyone profess to represent reality?

[3]John Barth, 'The Literature of Exhaustion', *The Atlantic*, 220 (August, 1967), pp. 29–34.
[4]Gabriel Josipovici, *The World and The Book* (Stanford, Calif: Standford UP, 1971), p. 65.
[5]Phillip Roth, *Reading Myself and Others* (New York: Bantam, 1977), p. 110.

But this is to pay too much attention to literary fashion. For in spite of these factors, a large number of writers continued to write in some version of a realistic mode. If Saul Bellow reached his peak in *Herzog* (1964), a novel that, significantly enough, defends realism, his subsequent fiction still comprised a highly respectable body of work. John Updike continued to publish with the kind of consistency and quality that marks a major American writer. Phillip Roth returned to the realistic mode, and so did Joseph Heller. Many of the finest younger writers, such as Anne Beatty, Anne Tyler, Frederick Barthelme and William Kennedy, have written realistically as well. Clearly something has been wrong with the generally accepted literary map: for all of the appeal of John Barth's view, America has too many realistic novelists writing too good a fiction to substantiate postmodernist claims. Writers have continued to write realism into the 80s. For realism in American literature had – and still has, it appears – many other forces to sustain it. The tradition is extraordinarily strong, for one thing, and is not nearly as old as it seems. Ernest Hemingway published his classic realistic stories only 39 years after Twain published *The Adventures of Huckleberry Finn*, and Saul Bellow published his first novel (*Dangling Man*, 1944) only 59 years after Twain's masterpiece – a chronology we tend to forget. At the same time, the realistic novel has remained our single major literary mode for over 125 years, habitually springing back to outlast those movements that have ostensibly buried it.

Realism has lasted because it is adaptable, borrowing all kinds of techniques from the movements that would supplant it. Postwar American realism in fact is distinguished by what it gained from the two movements that immediately preceded it. After the war realistic writers enjoyed the freedom of subject matter won by the naturalists – an immense source of vitality to writers who would capture the texture of human experience. The realists also learned from the primary poetic movement of the 30s and 40s, adopting the close attention to language advocated by the New Critics. The realists developed the intensity of such poetry, stressing private consciousness, and learned the value of tension or of a calculated ambiguity in creating that intensity within the reader's experience.

The desire for verisimilitude is a strong one, moreover, reflecting as it does the individual's connection to the world. Realism satisfies many human needs, whether it be a celebration of nature or a perpetuation of our own likeness or an attempt to solve human problems by means of a model. Although most readers are a little embarrassed to admit it, they thrill at the recognition of their own experience, particularly when that experience is private, subjective or intangible. Especially in a positivistic age, realism furnishes an important element of community, permitting large bodies of forbidden or unarticulated experience to be shared publicly. In many ways the realism after World War II enlarged the human community by representing those ever larger areas of private life which prove to be common to all.

Of course realistic writers borrowed from the postmodernists, too, so that it was often difficult to distinguish between a premodernist writer who read his contemporaries and a postmodernist writer who used realistic techniques. Magic requires a real world to be magic, after all: many of the postmodernist writers revelled in realistic detail and wrote to portray their society, harnessing experimental technique to the old-fashioned mimetic sleigh. 'There's not a single line in any of my books that doesn't have its origin in actual fact,' wrote Gabriel Garcia Marquez in 'Fantasy and Artistic Creation in Latin America'.[6] Realism for its part had always wrapped its verisimilitude around a human fantasy: realists found it easy to loosen up their plots and attempt new feats with language, cheerfully adding a touch of the fantastic. Within a short period of time old distinctions seemed to blur and a new hybrid seemed to have arisen, a new synthesis of the real and the irreal, such as John Barth had requested.

And yet true as this synthesis may be in this period, particularly with such writers as Ralph Ellison, Flannery O'Connor, Robert Coover and Donald Barthelme, important differences remain. For while all writers confront the same problem of heightening their style to capture the reader's attention – of forging a fiction that can compete with an increasingly powerful actuality – they divide sharply on the means they use. Some writers meet the challenge of their era by shocking the reader, and breaking expectation; others move even closer to the reader, learning to match not only his world but the very process by which he experiences and imagines.

Those who would shock the reader seek to 'defamiliarize' their content, to use the word coined by the Russian Formalist Shklovsky, aiming to violate the shape of conventional perception, making the reader see what is familiar with new eyes. The conventions of realism are deeply established in the novel tradition, and have become habitual, just as a great deal of our daily experience must become habit. Again and again, whether by violence or dislocation of form or self-conscious language or outright mystification, the writer can shock the reader into focusing on his subject, and so create a powerful fiction. Such techniques make realism seem tame or bland or – what is very much to the point, in terms of the political agenda – hopelessly middle-class. Yet the realistic writers have their own means of winning the reader, and these are far from insignificant. Rather than violate natural perception, the realist can move even closer to it: benefiting from 100 years of realistic prose, the habits of journalism and history-writing as well as of fiction, the writer can pull the reader even more deeply into the fiction, creating a verisimilitude not just of content but of process. The realist can match his style so closely to the structure and sequence of the imagination that the reader imagines with very little resistance, feeling the familiar patterns of actual experience. The realist can move from the surface of his text, in other words, to the effect of his language on the reader's imagination. He can create the illusion of reality

---

[6]Gabriel Garcia Marquez, 'Fantasy and the Artistic Creation in Latin America and the Caribbean', trans Elena Brunet, *Harper's* 270 (January, 1985), p. 15.

not just by literal detail and the conventions of realism, but by any other means that approximate the effect of reality.

I wish to examine this definition of realism in the novel John Updike has confessed to be his favourite ('my gayest and truest book'), *The Centaur*. The novel deviates from realism in its use of myth – a favourite note of the postmodernists – and that deviation will illustrate my point: in *The Centaur* Updike uses myth for the purposes of verisimilitude, creating a more subjective and certainly more powerful mimesis. Updike's use of myth in a novel that is also conventionally realistic has become the source of considerable controversy, as some critics complain that the novel is a muddle, and others claim that the technique creates what amounts to a major American novel. I agree with such critics as Edward Vargo, who argues that myth in *The Centaur* is justified thematically, but I would add that the important point is the aesthetic one. Like many realists, Updike shapes his novel not so much by an idea as by the experience he would create in the reader, and his use of myth shapes that experience. That that experience is finally a realistic one, representing a significant point of actual experience, exemplifies the new and less literal realism that emerges in the 60s and the 70s; a realism that edges away from the literal texture of the world, perhaps, and yet strives even more than ever to catch and express actual and felt human experience.

I

Because it is essentially a portrait of a central character, somewhat in the manner of Henry James's *Portrait of a Lady* or Saul Bellow's *Herzog*, the quality of *The Centaur* (1963) depends greatly upon the quality of its characterization. George Caldwell is at once a remarkable person – a man who is memorably and convincingly good – and a brilliant piece of characterization. Updike makes him live, moreover, without the benefit of a great deal of plot. The novel is a reminiscence by George's son, Peter, as he lies next to his mistress in a New York artist's loft. Peter recounts three winter days in which he and his father (a science teacher) attend Olinger High School, find themselves marooned in town for two nights, and finally return to their farm home. Within this framework, Peter describes the quiet events of their day: the drive to school (they pick up a hitchhiker), the classes, a basketball game, a swimteam practice. George has developed a pain in his stomach which he fears is cancer: his father had died young, he reasons, and he is 50 years old. George sees a doctor and awaits the lab report. He also suffers from his job, since the students are indifferent and the principal is a bully. George would love to quit, if even for a year, but he can't abandon his obligations to his family. By the time Peter and George have returned at last to their farm home, George knows he is not mortally ill and has resigned himself to his role as provider.

From this easy flow of experience emerges a character Updike makes interesting in himself. Updike achieves a certain power – a characteristically realistic power – by his fusion of opposites, or his recognition that George (like most of us) is a tissue of contradictions, mix of qualities which we recognize as probable and which make us believe in his reality. He is a husband who supports a wife and child, as we might expect, and then his father-in-law and a farm, too, so that his wife Cassie can live in the house of her childhood. As he goes through his day, George is kind in many other ways. He praises people; he accepts their image of themselves; he expresses an interest in their specialities; he is not only sacrificing but nice. Yet he is no saint, for he wears his generosity on his sleeve, and Peter even tells us that he is a joke between his son and wife. He talks too much; he flatters too abjectly; he needs approval too deeply. What is more, George shares his troubles with everyone. While it is true that he is generous, it is also true that his complaining makes those around him pay for it.

Just when we begin to feel that George is a bumbler or a fool, however, Updike makes it clear he is a significant man. Peter loves him and so does his wife Cassie. Others love him too, including his students and most significantly, the Hummels, who take care of him. George poormouths himself, but Peter describes him as able. The Caldwell living room was full of magazines, Peter tells us: 'my father would disconsolately plough through the whole pile.' Though he 'claimed never to learn or remember anything', he 'could read at a terrific speed.' George is in fact full of energy, alert to the world and deeply (if noisily) fascinated by it. Peter in his New York loft tells his mistress 'I miss only . . . the sudden white laughter that like heat lightning bursts in an atmosphere where souls are trying to serve the impossible. My father for all his mourning moved in the atmosphere of such laughter.'

We don't analyse George in this manner as we read the novel, however. We experience him, which is to say that we imagine his presence. And what we imagine first of all, as we read the words that comprise this text, is George's voice, which is so distinct that we could recognize it anywhere. 'He worried about the kid, when he had the time.' George uses a slang that is breezy and energetic, self-dramatizing and self-deprecating. He is rigid, and responds automatically, so that what involves real enthusiasm often seems hollow. 'The kid' is a term of endearment ('gotta guard the family silver,' George says of the boy) and yet impersonal or redolent of the days when George was free of responsiblity. Such language shows George to be hurried and hassled and yet full of optimism. George's voice is a brash response to a certain sadness, and we soon sense that George in his patter tells the subjective truth. He negotiates his marriage out in the open, in a comic and biting banter. He negotiates his value, his status, his health, everything in public view, transparently cloaked in slang. George's voice like his character is thus shaped by contradictory elements. He banters with Cassie because he cannot speak in private. He is reticent. And yet his feelings are remarkably accessible, spilling over into the public. He is deeply enmeshed in community, speaking with warmth, and yet alienated too, and so uses his voice to create distance, this outsider among the 'Olinger aristocrats'.

And how exactly do we experience this voice? Because a character's speech consists of words, we clearly reproduce the actual speech. And yet we don't hear that voice, any more than we literally see the speaker. We feel it, absorbing the emotion it embodies. We feel the presence of the speaker too, feeling the person behind the words. This is an automatic process, which we don't necessarily will, and a complex one, since we obtain from George's words an impression of the complex person, sensing a great deal that we do not articulate. And yet it is central to our vicarious experience. We know George because we say his words to ourselves, feeling for an instant the emotions that lie behind them. We may hear them from the outside as well, identifying with Peter, say, and so absorb their emotional content just as we do in real life. And then – even as we imagine the scene, identifying with the characters – we react to the revealed George with emotions of our own. We feel all these emotions in a flow of feeling that defines our vicarious experience, just as it defines our actual experience.

Thus the character of George Caldwell is a feeling. We can think about him abstractly, as an idea – he is a high school teacher in Pennsylvania in the 1940s – and we can represent him without much thought as a name, 'George Caldwell'. We can see George in our mind's eye, in a limited way, as a vague figure, perhaps, or as a bit of image. But just as a great deal of our actual experience is a flow of feeling, so our experience of the imaginary George Caldwell is a feeling too. And it is because of this central fact about our vicarious experience that Updike can add a remarkable element to his characterization, which is the fact that George Caldwell is also (literally) a centaur. He is Chiron, the most gentle and refined of the centaurs, who taught the children of the gods. Whenever George is with Peter, he is a high school teacher in Olinger, Pennsylvania, but when he is alone he is a centaur, walking down the high school hall or even teaching a class.

All of the other characters in the novel are mythic too, and most notably Peter himself, who is – though he doesn't know it – Prometheus, the Titan to whom Chiron gives his immortality. George's wife Cassie is Ceres and the high school principal Zimmerman is Zeus. Updike actually has a great deal of fun with this material, since Peter, who is ignorant of these double identities, gets a special feeling or a peculiar impression he doesn't understand. His father walks quickly and restlessly, like a stallion who is full of balked energy. When Peter enters Doc Appleton's office, he overhears the phrase 'hydra-venom' – the doctor is actually Apollo, treating Chiron, though he immediately reverts to Appleton. Medusa is a schoolteacher with pencils in her hair and Dionysos is a drunken bum. The novel, Updike says, was 'a kind of a gag', permitting him to play with language.

The mythic also permitted Updike to express a special feeling. The novel is, Updike says in the *Paris Review*, 'a serious expression that the people we meet are *guises*, do conceal something mythic, perhaps prototypes or longings in our mind.'[7] George feels himself to be mysterious, and is

[7]John Updike, *Writers at Work* Fourth Series (New York: Penguin Books, 1976), pp. 431–54.

surrounded by mysteriously powerful beings – Cassie and the town fathers belong to a higher social class than he does. But Updike refers most specifically to Peter's peculiar feeling that his father has an identity unknown to him, or that he exists on a level even his son cannot understand, as indeed George does. Updike uses myth to express a feeling we can take as quite common in teenagers who regard their parents. The feeling is part of real life, and the creation of that feeling in the reader amounts to verisimilitude – really a wonderful sense of the division between the private and public selves – even though the means are anything but realistic.

The most important way Updike uses emotion, however, is as a medium or as the very means by which he conveys his subject to the reader. He makes us feel the presence of George, and represents Peter's experience of his father by a feeling as well. And then he represents much of Peter's other experience in the same way. When the mother 'kept her eyes on my cup as . . . she filled it without spilling,' Peter uses a described physical gesture to give the feeling. So Updike employs the detail to create the feeling that represents George, and then uses the feeling to represent the man. How is it that we move so easily from imagining a man to imagining a centaur? Updike has great fun playing the two off one another, and such a double identity does indeed 'defamiliarize' the character, placing him in a new context. But Updike is able to create such a double identity because both of them translate into feelings in the imagination. We experience George the man as a feeling and we experience Chiron the centaur as a feeling too – this in spite of the highly visual quality of the centaur. Our feeling for George the man is coloured by our feeling of his other identity; our feeling for Chiron is coloured by our feeling of the contemporary man; and we feel both identities simultaneously. While visual images are rigid in outline and slow to transform themselves, emotion is definitively liquid, flowing and blending with ease. It is Updike's skilful use of the imaginative process that enables him to portray the fabulous.

II

I want to turn next to an area which does not constitute a process, exactly, but it greatly bears on Updike's use of an aesthetic dependent on realism. This is the way in which Updike uses the techniques of the painter to create the illusion of three dimensions. We know that writing differs from painting, and yet an analysis of the sources of vitality in prose narrative leads us back to what we must suppose is the visual image evoked by the text. Certainly the novelist describes the same literal scene as the painter. If we do not literally see a complete image in our mind, we have the illusion that we do – we have the feeling of seeing an image. The novelist reproduces the patterns and conditions of vision, awakening a dim but familiar sense of sight. The view is partially blocked; we must extrapolate the unseen from the seen, just as in actual life. We take in the overall impression (what we might call the novelist's topic sentence) and then move on to specifics, as the logic of the paragraph duplicates the natural sequence of perception.

Thus the structure of the writer's presentation parallels the structure of vision, creating the illusion of visual space. By arranging his subject in certain ways the novelist may make us feel we imagine in three dimensions, as we can see in Peter's final glimpse of his father at the end of the novel:

> I turned my face away and looked through the window. In time my father appeared in this window, an erect figure dark against the snow. His posture made no concession to the pull underfoot; upright he waded out through our yard and past the mailbox and up the hill until he.was lost to my sight behind the trees of our orchard. The trees took white on their sun side. Two telephone wires diagonally cut the blank blue of the sky. The stone bare wall was a scumble of umber; my father's footsteps thumbs of white in white.

We have a starkly visual scene, self-consciously described in painterly terms, as Peter catches the play of light and colour and the effect of line and form – he sees the wires and the wall less as meaning than as shape, lines across blue and a 'scumble' (an artist's term meaning a thin overlay) of opaque colour. Like a good painter, Updike is aware of composition. The scene is framed in the window – a device that in itself dramatizes space – and describes a figure passing through space until he passes out of sight. The window and our knowledge of Peter serve to anchor the scene. Updike describes George's movements as a diagonal ('out through our yard and past the mailbox and up the hill') and dramatizes the existence of space by blocking: George comes into our vision from outside the window-frame and disappears behind trees. Our eye follows him traversing space, and then the wires are diagonal too, moving *into* the physical scene. Updike uses contrast ('figure dark against the snow') and even chiaroscuro, denoting the way 'trees took white on their sun side', to draw the play of light on spatial forms.

Like Vermeer, whom Peter admires, Updike paints with planes of colour: the figure is dark and the snow is white; the trees consist of two planes, one white in the sun, the other dark in the shade. The sky is a blank blue cut by the black wires. What Updike does in effect is offer a stark scene, barren and powerful in contrasts, and then a hint of more delicate colour. Having described the bolder blocks of light, he offers two subtle colours – the 'thumbs of white in white' and the 'scumble of umber', the brownish-coloured rock washed lightly across the scene.

The starkness has an important thematic point, moreover, for this walk of George's contrasts with the walk which opens the novel, and which Updike had described in terms that are lush, busy and complex. George (as Chiron) had been wounded in the ankle by an arrow, suffering a pain with 'wet wings'. He had walked down the school hallway in a 'bluish bubble of light'. He had felt the arrow as 'a metallic scratch and a stiff rustle', as 'the shaft worked in his wound' and the feathers brushed the floor. 'How strange he had grown', Updike had written, giving a key pattern in the novel. 'His top half felt all afloat in a starry firmament of ideals and young voices singing; the rest of his self was heavily sunk in a swamp where it must, eventually, drown.' Much of the novel has portrayed George sinking into his swamp, as responsibility, low rank, personal hurt and no prospects pull him down. But in this last passage he passes into a clear, cold environment, the purity of which Updike dramatizes as purely visual, since Peter hears nothing through the window. George is now on his way to the stars, to becoming Sagittarius, freed of his pain and his responsibility and the awful ambiguities of his position. Having suffered as a half beast, George is now freed of his early shape, entering a pure form which Updike makes the reader feel by the silence and light and emphasis on pure line and colour.

III

Because we do not visualize photographically, we do not literally imagine in three dimensions. We feel space, rather, experiencing an illusion of dimensionality. And we feel other kinds of dimensionality as well, as the novelist uses the structures of actual sensation to portray the abstract world of human character and consciousness. It is here that we can acknowledge the importance and the difficulty of Updike's use of mythology: at least a dozen critics have complained that the mythology is superfluous to the story and thus distracting. Part of this objection is by way of complaining that Updike 'has nothing to say', as John Aldridge puts it, and part of it too is the shock of critics who prefer their fabulism neat.

Such complaints have led to spirited defences of the novel's mythology as important to its theme. Edward P. Vargo argues that the myth involves a ritual search for meaning on the part of the narrator, Peter, and that it offers a statement of the unity of heaven and earth, or a world in which the mundane is infused with the divine. I believe Vargo is basically correct, but it is not the idea that is important so much as the experience: what counts is not the theme of interpenetration but the aesthetic effect its dramatization produces.

The myth embodies a great deal of content, certainly, representing the hidden and extreme desire of the characters, and yet it is most important in its influence on the reader's imagination. For the myth makes us imagine the characters in a certain way and ultimately to experience a certain feeling. It makes us imagine George's world as a double one, which is the key to Updike's power, as several critics have noted.[8] George is a teacher and a centaur; he is part horse and part man; his experience belongs to Olinger High School in eastern Pennsylvania and Mt Olympus in ancient Greece. Again and again Updike creates a double reference which makes us imagine dimensionally, obtaining a special wholeness and depth in our vicarious experience. In any given scene Updike creates several perspectives which blend or fuse to provide a particularly vivid illusion. To hear a character speak is one thing, but to see his motives analysed is another. To

[8]See George Hunt, *John Updike and the Three Great Secret Things* (Grand Rapids, Michigan: Wm. B. Eerdman's Publishing Co., 1980), p. 50.

see a concrete object is one kind of experience and to learn its history is another. Updike actually expands or intensifies the process that belongs to both reading and our experience in general. On the page the reader absorbs the linear sequence of words as a unified whole, for example, combining them in a non-linear way. In the world the human mind fuses two distinct visual images (one from each eye) and two audio ones. It also fuses the 'data' outside with its meaning, even in the act of seeing, so that the very simplest perception blends two elements of perception.

We have many terms to describe this phenomenon – ambiguity, tension, twinning, dialectic, chiaroscuro. To Samuel Coleridge the fusion of disparate elements defines the basic function of the imagination. But in all of these theories, the point is the quality of the reader's experience, and most specifically the vitality or intensity which such duality creates. Updike creates a memorable novel in *The Centaur* by making good use of this process. George the man is memorable, as we have seen, but George the centaur is more than memorable, since the principle of dimensionality gives him the power and scope of a great fictional character. The myth gives George a second identity, and one that is grand, but the effect is more than arithmetic, for the literal reality and the mythic one tell the same story. They are not merely complements, or ironic contrasts, as we might assume, but duplicates, as the myth gives the psychological reality buried deep in the literal. In this way George the man and George the centaur represent the same story from two perspectives, and our combination of the two offers a psychological version of binocular vision.

Thus George in Part One is wounded by the mythic arrow, on the one hand, and his student's contempt for him on the other. The bizarre behaviour of Zimmerman, the Davis girl, Iris Osgood, and Deifendorf actually involves the hidden or unconscious motives or desires of such characters in real life. Here the similarity between Venus in the locker-room in Part One and Vera in the kitchen in Part Eight is particularly instructive, for the two stories are essentially the same: the goddess proposes sodomic sex while Vera Hummel, laughing at George's comments, rises on her toes to take his kiss. What is broad or violent to the goddess is quietly actual to the PE instructor – and may even be more moving in the realistic version.

Updike achieves a vital character and a living novel because of the way these two levels of story converge. And the principle of fused levels works in a more general way, too: in Part One George is a lecturer, after he has returned to the classroom, giving the well known 'clock' of creation, and a private consciousness, noticing and thinking and feeling. Updike shifts in quick succession from Caldwell's talk to his private awareness and then to activity in the room, as the school bell rings and monitors slip out – and the literal reality slides into the dimension of myth. George continues his lecture on the history of the universe, which would be the ultimate perspective, perhaps, and makes the scene almost as dimensional as Flaubert's famous market window in *Madame Bovary*, in which outside and inside, sound and sight, agriculture and seduction blend ironically. In the classroom knowledge is punctuated by sexuality, and George's attempt to provide the perspective of all time is frustrated by fornication. George's description of the arrival of man, 'a flint-chopping, fire-kindling, death-foreseeing, a tragic animal' – the climax of creation – contrasts with the chaotic (and comically robust) behaviour of his audience.

Updike uses his skill as a realist to create a realistic high school class, in other words, and then uses the lecture to place the class in historic perspective, giving it a special meaning. And he uses myth to give yet another dimension, that of the ancients, clearly, but also that of our extreme and amoral desires, as people on the mythic level repress nothing. But Updike doesn't rely on myth alone to achieve his dimensional effect. We get a clearer picture of his skill in the paragraph we have already begun to quote, as Peter looks through a window at his father slogging through the snow. Having described George, Updike returns in the same paragraph to Peter inside the room:

> I knew what this scene was – a patch of Pennsylvania in 1947 – and yet I did not know, was in my softly fevered state mindlessly soaked in a rectangle of colored light. I burned to paint it, just like that, in its puzzle of glory; it came upon me that I must go to Nature disarmed of perspective and stretch myself like a large transparent canvas upon her in the hope that, my submission being perfect, the imprint of a beautiful and useful truth would be taken.

If Updike writes like a painter, he also 'paints' like a novelist, providing the interaction of several perspectives. Peter's position in his bed offers a different perspective from that of George in the snow, of course, but it also provides Peter's immediate sensations as well as his sense of the future. Outside we see a mute figure and a purely visual world; inside the room we find a self and a meaning and a future and in fact receive a suggestion that Peter will adapt the vision of formal or abstract art ('mindlessly soaked in a rectangle of colored light') to the purposes of representation, obtaining 'the imprint of a beautiful and useful truth' of the world.

But Updike uses an even more important dimension. For just before he looks outside his window, Peter tells his father, 'If you want to quit or take a sabbatical or something, don't not do it on my account.' And George Caldwell – true to himself to the end – answers with a barrage of words: 'Don't you worry about that. Don't you worry about your old man, you got enough on your mind. I never made a decision in my life that wasn't one hundred percent selfish.' It is with such words echoing in our ears – with such a feeling for George, as we sense the man behind the words – that we see this scene, the echo itself making for dimension. To the rich evocation of George's voice, in other words, which by now has the weight of the whole novel behind it, we add the stark figure in the snow, the man as the universe sees him, perhaps, featureless and small. Though now bleak, George has just been offered the love of his son and has himself insisted upon sacrifice, in his characteristic gush of words.

Thus Updike winds down his narrative by referring once again, elegiacally and conclusively, to the themes which are now worn, comforting talismans: the father in the cold while the boy is warm and safe; the camouflaged spirit of the man – as George for all his humility is unbowed, even now; the walk, which is the central image of the book, leading out of Peter's realistic world and into the coda of the centaur, Chiron, where we will once again shift perspective to experience Chiron's personal sensation. And then over it all, adding a note of nostalgic sadness, is Peter's own knowledge, now that he is narrator, that he will be 'an authentic, second-rate impressionist painter', raising the question 'Was it for this my father gave up his life?'

George throughout the novel has presented himself dimensionally in that he combines self-sacrifice and complaining; masculine strength and a fussy weakness; his real self (in glimpses) and a kind of garrulous burlesque of himself. We have seen his obituary, as it will someday appear, and have read the classroom scene as both George's experience, in Updike's third-person account, and the teaching report of principal Zimmerman. The George we see in Peter's window walks in tacit contrast to his weaker self, and in contrast to the way Peter heretofore has seen him. Peter a few pages earlier had imagined his father 'running up and down raggedly heaped mounds in his too-small overcoat like an overgrown urchin.' But Peter here sees a figure erect and undaunted, 'making no concession to the pull underfoot'.

For George is on his way in this final passage to yet another dimension, if we can call it that, his life among the stars. As a centaur his sacrifice has pleased Zeus, who gives him release from pain and an eternal position as Sagittarius, where he continues to play a role in human experience. As a man George finds 'that in giving his life to others he entered a total freedom.' Both stories free George from the swamp and project him into an atmosphere of purity. The snow in which George walks is death, but it is also a purer form of life, and it is the fusion of the two stories that creates the power.

IV

The Centaur is not a perfectly balanced book: Updike is inconsistent in his use of myth, turning to it only when it suits him. We don't know how much Peter the narrator really knows about his father's identity, for example, or whether – since Peter seems not to know he is Prometheus – George Caldwell knows that he himself is Chiron. Updike requires a certain amount of patience on the part of the reader, too, since he opens the novel with the Centaur teaching in an American high school – a startling mix of the real and the mythic. On a more general level, we could argue that Updike as a realist exhibits a certain decadence, since he tends to sacrifice plot to the texture of his prose. Like Bellow before him, he must struggle with the very richness of his detail: when he needs to invigorate his text, he is likely to turn to description, adding colour and vitality at the expense of the plot.

Although *The Centaur* has its defects, however, it works with the kind of finality we associate with a major novel. And it tells us a great deal about realistic American fiction as well. For we have in truth a great many different definitions of realism in our criticism today. To Harold Kolb, realism is defined by the rejection of the ideal. The realist looks to *this* world, to the physical and social texture of our experience. Realism is pragmatic, relativistic, materialistic. To Donald Pizer, conversely, realism represents the ideal smuggled into the real; the realist works off a base of pragmatism or empiricism, recognizing the physical but then acknowledging the ideal too. In the moral assumptions of the protagonist or narrator, in the need for religious meaning or the love of beauty, in the sacrifice for others or the celebration of human community, the realist represents a world tinged by the ideal.

To still other critics, realism is a defence of the middle class, a lack of ideology (as in Robert Frost's 'temporary stays against confusion') or a celebration of the human in a technological age. From our point of view today, realism is an exploration of the limits of human perception. For if realism is a literary convention that has little to do with what is real, as many claim, it is also a sensitive portrayal of just such limiting factors. How accurate is human perception when the individual self contributes so much to what it sees? Writers such as John Updike explore the difficulty of knowing what is true – in Peter Caldwell's feeling of his father's mysterious identity Updike is very much in the tradition of Henry James, portraying a subtle and unverified but accurate perception.

Of all of these definitions, however, the most useful one views realism as a process embodied in the writer's style. Realism involves fidelity to not just the world but the sequence and structure and medium in which we perceive, store, remember and imagine that experience. Such realistic writers as John Updike and Saul Bellow and Bernard Malamud and Eudora Welty offer in their fiction a model of the perceiving and imagining mind. They define a world in which perception and representation of that perception play a crucial role in a character's fate. But most of all, such realistic novelists seek to enrich or heighten their fiction – which inevitably involves the quotidian – by means of vivid representation. They create this special intensity by mimicking or echoing the processes by which we actually experience, so that as we read we feel some of the tugs and intensities of real experience.

Such process is important because realism and experimentalism are in actuality interdependent, each defining itself in terms of the other. Each actually includes the other: with its myth and formal experimentation and love of sound for its own sake, *The Centaur* is as much a post-modern novel as *Metamorphosis* – with its representation of common human feeling – is a realistic one. What matters is the use to which the writer puts his technique. In postmodern hands, realistic detail can be so intense, so compulsively focused, that it defamiliarizes the world. In realistic hands, on the other hand, fabulistic devices can express a feeling or experience the reader recognizes immediately as his own.

The imaginative process is also important to our definition of realism because of the qualities which distinguish the literature of this period. Just as Updike expresses a specific and delicate feeling in *The Centaur* – one that we are pleased to recognize as real – so the realists of this period articulate a deep layer of shared, subjective experience, moving even closer to the centre of middle-class experience than before. This is the great strength of these many realistic novelists, as Saul Bellow defines the grieving desperation of a mediocre man, say, or John Updike defines the loving sorrow of a sacrificing husband. As one surveys such realistic writing, he becomes convinced that realism as a style has continued to grow and deepen with time.

If these writers represent a real world, moreover, they also shape their words to fit the real imagination, gaining in immediacy and vitality. They are ultimately distinguished by their ability to heighten their prose narrative by means of their style – as they had to do in order to survive. A significant amount of prose in this period is extraordinarily fresh or immediate, springing from the page like a stereoscopic image. Benefiting from the example of their predecessors, these realists have learned how to make their imaginary worlds especially vivid. They understand the power of a dual vision, skilfully utilizing ambiguity, contrast and tension. They match in their style the structures of the mind, fusing the general and the specific. And they understand that a great deal of experience consists of feeling, which serves not only as reaction but representation. Much of their finest fiction articulates special and telling human emotions, and portrays their era vividly by catching the special feeling that defines it. Many of their fine descriptions of ordinary experience – ostensibly banal or dull – spring to life because of their use of feeling to represent their subject. They create not those emotions of shock and mystification that make people pay attention – although they don't exclude defamiliarization – but those emotions that in themselves contain and express the subject, and do it vividly. Their skill is much more quiet than that of the postmoderns, and on the surface less dramatic. But it is none the less powerful, creating a convincing and vital experience within the reader.

Appendix

Updike: A Brief Biography

John Updike was born in 1932 in Shillington, Pennsylvania. His father was a high-school mathematics teacher and his mother a writer. He graduated *summa cum laude* from Harvard in 1954, and spent a year in England on the Knox Fellowship, at the Ruskin School of Drawing and Fine Art in Oxford. From 1955 to 1957 he was a member of the staff of *The New Yorker*, to which he has contributed short stories, poems, humour, and, since 1960, book reviews. His own books include 12 novels, eight short-story collections, four volumes of poetry, and a play. In 1964 his novel *The Centaur* won the National Book Award for Fiction, and in 1982 *Rabbit Is Rich* was awarded the Pulitzer Prize. The father of two sons and two daughters, he has lived since 1957 in Massachusetts.

The Principle Publications
The Carpentered Hen and Other Tame Creatures. New York: Harper & Brothers, 1958.
The Poorhouse Fair. New York: Alfred A. Knopf, 1959.
The Same Door. New York: Alfred A. Knopf, 1959.
Rabbit, Run. New York: Alfred A. Knopf, 1960.
Pigeon Feathers and Other Stories. New York: Alfred A. Knopf, 1962.
The Centaur. New York: Alfred A. Knopf, 1963.
Telephone Poles and Other Poems. New York: Alfred A. Knopf, 1963.
Olinger Stories. New York: Vintage Books, 1964.
Of the Farm. New York: Alfred A. Knopf, 1965.
Assorted Prose. New York: Alfred A. Knopf, 1965.
The Music School. New York: Alfred A. Knopf, 1966.
Couples. New York: Alfred A. Knopf, 1968.
Midpoint and Other Poems. New York: Alfred A. Knopf, 1969.
Bech: A Book. New York: Alfred A. Knopf, 1970.
Rabbit Redux. New York: Alfred A. Knopf, 1971.
Museums and Women and Other Stories. New York: Alfred A. Knopf, 1972.
Buchanan Dying. New York: Alfred A. Knopf, 1974.
Picked-up Pieces. New York: Alfred A. Knopf, 1975.
A Month of Sundays. New York: Alfred A. Knopf, 1975.
Marry Me. New York: Alfred A. Knopf, 1976.
Tossing and Turning: Poems. New York: Alfred A. Knopf, 1977.
The Coup. New York: Alfred A. Knopf, 1978.
Too Far To Go: The Maples Stories. New York: Fawcett Crest Books, 1979.
Problems. New York: Alfred A. Knopf, 1979.
Rabbit is Rich. New York: Alfred A. Knopf, 1981.
Bech is Back. New York: Alfred A. Knopf, 1982.
Hugging the Shore. New York: Alfred A. Knopf, 1983.
The Witches of Eastwick. New York: Alfred A. Knopf, 1984.
Roger's Version. New York: Alfred A. Knopf, 1986.

Note

Principal works
Walter Abish, 'The Fall of Summer', *Conjunctions* 7 (Spring 1985), pp. 110–41. 'Family', *Antaeus* 52 (Spring 1982), pp. 149–69. 'Self-Portrait', *Individuals: Post-Movement Art in America*, edited by Alan Sondheim (New York: Dutton, 1977), pp. 1–25. 'The Writer-to-Be, *Sub-Stance* 27 (1980), pp. 101–14.

Stephen Dixon, *Too Late* (New York: Harper & Row, 1978). *Fall & Rise* (San Francisco: North Point Press, 1985).*Work* (Ann Arbor: Street Fiction Press, 1977).

William H. Gass, *Habitations of the Word* (New York: Simon & Schuster, 1985).

Steve Katz, *Cheyenne River Wildtrack* (Ithaca: Ithaca House, 1973). *The Exagggerations of Peter Prince* (New York: Holt, Rinehart & Winston, 1968). *Guest Editor* I (Winter 1984). *Moving Parts* (New York: Fiction Collective, 1977). *Stolen Stories* (New York: Fiction collective, 1984). *Wier & Pouce* (Washington, DC: Sun & Moon Press, 1984).

Charles Newman, *The Postmodern Aura: The Act of Fiction in an Age of Inflation*. (Evanston: Northwestern University Press, 1985).

Ishmael Reed, *God Made Alaska for the Indians* (New York: Garland Press, 1982).

Michael Stephens, *The Dramaturgy of Style: Some Ideas About Voice in Short Fiction* (Carbondale: Southern Illinois University Press, 1985).

Gilbert Sorrentino, *Aberration of Starlight* (New York: Random House, 1980). *Blue Pastoral* (San Francisco: North Point Press, 1983). *Crystal Vision* (San Francisco: North Point Press, 1981). *Imaginative Qualities of Actual Things* (New York: Pantheon, 1971). *Mulligan Stew* (New York: Grove Press, 1979). *Something Said* (San Francisco: North Point Press, 1984). *Splendide-Hotel* (New York: New Directions, 1973; reprinted in 1984 by the Dalkey Archive Press, Elmwood Park Illinois).

Ronald Sukenick, *The Death of the Novel and Other Stories* (New York: Dial Press, 1969). *The Endless Short Story* (New York: Fiction Collective, 1986). *In Form: Digressions on the Act of Fiction* (Carbondale: Southern Illinois University Press, 1985). *Out* (Chicago: Swallow Press, 1973). *Up* (New York: Dial Press, 1968; reprinted by Dell (New York), 1970, in a Delta edition). *Wallace Stevens: Musing the Obscure* (New York: New York University Press, 1967).

Selected critical bibliography
Good introductions to postmodernism can be found in Ihab Hassan's *The Dismemberment of Orpheus* (New York: Oxford University Press, 1971; expanded second edition published in Madison by the University Press of Wisconsin, 1982) and in his *The Postmodern Turn* (Columbus: Ohio State University Press, 1986); Robert Scholes was the first to describe the new innovative fiction in *The Fabulators* (New York: Oxford University Press, 1967), since expanded and revised as *Fabulation and Metafiction* (Urbana: University Press of Illinois, 1979). Among my own books are a literary history of the period, *Literary Disruptions* (Urbana: University of Illinois Press, 1975; revised and expanded, 1980); a cultural study of the same years, *The American 1960s* (Ames: Iowa State University Press 1980); and a theory for these works, *The Self-Apparent Word: Fiction as Language/Language as Fiction* (Carbondale: Southern Illinois University Press, 1984). Literary politics have been explained by Richard Kostelanetz in *The End of Intelligent Writing* (New York: Sheed & Ward, 1974).

2

The Extra-Literary in Contemporary American Fiction

Jerome Klinkowitz

The first truly contemporary American novel I read was in 1970, the Delta paperback of Ron Sukenick's *Up*. A year later I would begin to learn why Sukenick's book seemed so much more from my own times than did the other works of serious fiction published during the years of my undergraduate and graduate education, which had just concluded with a doctorate in American Lit from Wisconsin. Sukenick, I read in Ihab Hassan's *The Dismemberment of Orpheus*, was not 'contemporary' (which is, after all, a hopelessly fluid term) but was instead *postmodern*.[1] Why was Ron's work postmodern? This I had to figure out for myself, and only later did I learn that a critical vocabulary had been developing abroad to articulate achievements such as *Up*: a combination of authorial intention and narrative action known as self-reflexive, an interweaving of source materials and artistic creation known as intertextuality, and a brash challenge to monological authority referred to as dialogical. Yet even today these terms are beyond me, since the forces which shaped Sukenick's *Up* and the works by many of his colleagues seemed extra-literary then and even more so now.

Back in the early 1970s Ron's fiction impressed me as a struggle against certain inhibiting conditions of living, loving, teaching, writing and even publishing itself. Here was the postmodern transformation, right at hand in a life I was experiencing myself:

> What a godawful thing, to be an emerging novelist when the novel has just died. Worse still, to write books which nobody buys, when book companies' stock falls two hundred points in eighteen months, when the returns keep flooding in, when your publisher remainders your first printing. In more ways than one the times are bad, and here is Ronald Sukenick, a good novelist for our times. His own life is an index to modern anti-heroics: a bright boy from Brooklyn who is the only one in

[1]Ihab Hassan, *The Dismemberment of Orpheus: Toward a Postmodern Literature* (New York: Oxford University Press, 1971), p. 254; reprinted as a hardcover and paperback with a new 'Postface 1982: Toward a Concept of Postmodernism' by the University of Wisconsin Press, Madison).

his crowd to miss a ticket to Princeton, Columbia, or Yale; a Brandeis Ph.D. who scuffles from job to job, whose scholarly *magnum opus, Wallace Stevens: Musing the Obscure* (New York: New York University Press, 1967), is sneered away by *American Literature* as having 'almost nothing to commend it to anyone in the least acquainted with Stevens.' And who, if his fictions are as autobiographical as he claims, has one hell of a time even making it with girls. How, in such circumstances, does one survive? That is the question central to all of Sukenick's work, which makes him a significant novelist; as he asks on the first page of his Stevens book, 'with what tenable attitude may one confront the difficult circumstances of contemporary American secular life and avail oneself of the good possible in it? How, in short, does one get along?'[2]

Sukenick's answer to my questions had been to write *Up* and then *The Death of the Novel and Other Stories*. As the latter title implies, Ron was finding that even the most compelling critical theory of the day was just 'another story' and therefore ready to be incorporated in his fiction just like any other material of his life. The institutional aspects of American writing, which range from the commercial pressures of authorship through professional reviewing, university teaching and academic canon-formation, had produced a novel and short story collection, with Ronald Sukenick as their cleverly willing amanuensis.

An entire generation of American fiction writers accompanied Sukenick in his response to these institutional pressures. Although in the end they established a firmly postmodernist theory to support their work, these innovationists of the 1960s began their literary careers by identifying the extra-literary concerns which had determined establishment fiction before them; then, like slaves seizing the weapons of oppression to turn upon their masters, they used these formerly inhibiting factors to liberate fiction in their time. Historically, the American 1970s were the period during which this initially revolutionary theory was given its full practice and was absorbed by the mainstream, so that by the mid-1980s Sukenick & Company could look back at their footprints in the sand and learn that their cumulative efforts had produced a coherent body of trans-fictional theory. By 1985 Sukenick had published his *In Form: Digressions on the Act of Fiction* (subsequently *IF*), joining Gilbert Sorrentino's *Something Said* (subsequently *SS*), Charles Newman's *The Postmodern Aura: The Act of Fiction in an Age of Inflation*, Ishmael Reed's *God Made Alaska for the Indians*, Walter Abish's *The Writer-to-Be*, and William H. Gass's *Habitations of the Word*.[3] Surveying the extra-literary forces which these writers recall as influencing their work will reveal that the great revolution

---

[2]Jerome Klinkowitz, 'Getting Real: Making It (Up) With Ronald Sukenick', *Chicago Review*, 23 (Winter 1972), 73–4.

[3]Many other writers of the innovative fiction generation and after have also collected their essays recently, including John Barth in *The Friday Book* (New York: Putnam's, 1984) and Michael Stephens in *The Dramaturgy of Style* (Carbondale: Southern Illinois University Press, 1985).

in American fiction, coinciding with the post-structuralist debate in literary theory which reached North American shores during these same mid-1960s, was in many respects an attempt to enlarge the literary text so that the full conditions of its production could become part of the fiction itself.

The first extra-literary concern was the lack of theory for contemporary fiction. In America, the modernist novel had been written by amateurs. Eliot, Cummings, and Pound were of an entirely different set than Hemingway, Fitzgerald, and Faulkner – intellectualization of achievement had departed from American fiction with the deaths of James and Wharton. By the 1950s many critics believed the novel as art form had run its course, and was now able to respond to the changes in American social and cultural life only on the level of theme – hence the 'death of the novel' commentaries promulgated as the decade ended and the 1960s began. To find a theory for their postmodern novels, Sukenick and Sorrentino looked back to modernist poets – Wallace Stevens for the former, William Carlos Williams for the latter. From the distance of nearly a half-century, the differences between a symbol-based and an image-conscious poetry faded in favour of a bright enthusiasm for that previously plastic term, 'the imagination'. In Sukenick's and Sorrentino's hands the imagination was tempered to a revolutionary hardness as they used it to alternately slice and bludgeon away at the overwhelmingly institutional conventions which had made the writing of fiction no longer a thinking person's task. 'The imagination, only the imagination, Williams says, will free us from the waste and despair that America has hidden under its continual smile,' Sorrentino insists. 'It is the flight, or the heartbreaking attempt at flight, of the imagination that he seeks to pin down and isolate in all his work' (*SS*, p. 24). Turning to Sukenick, we see him enlisting the aesthetic of Wallace Stevens so that the task becomes epistemological: 'The imagination for Stevens is not a way of creating, but of knowing. The imagination creates nothing' (*IF*, p. 176). For both Sorrentino and Sukenick, there is a form of knowledge which can be called poetic truth. But Sukenick is careful to distinguish it from any possible sense of absolute truth. *Conventional truth* is closer to what he has in mind, since the poetic is only true in the sense that it says something about reality that we can comfortably believe: 'When, through the imagination, the ego manages to reconcile reality with its own needs, the formerly insipid landscape is infused with the ego's emotion and reality, since it now seems intensely relevant to the ego, suddenly seems more real' (*IF*, p. 174).

To index Sukenick's and Sorrentino's essays would be to arrange a catalogue of institutional forces which, by their very obstructiveness, helped shape innovative fiction through the quarter century since 1960. Alternately inhibiting and stimulating to the epistemological power of the imagination as these two writers saw it, these extra-literary problems soon became part of the fictive text. Sukenick's main target was the critical academy, whether established in universities or among professional reviewers. Sorrentino's complaints were more often about the limitations of commercial publishing, though he shared Sukenick's distaste for the canonization of certain poets (Eliot, Lowell, Jarrell) over others (Williams, Olson, O'Hara, Spicer), since from poets would come the poetics which often determined how fiction could be written and read. Together their commentaries form a bridge between the aesthetics of late modernism and emergent postmodernism.

'It seems strange to have to talk about innovation in fiction,' Sukenick complains, 'but the American novel until the end of the sixties was so static that we have not yet fully understood how parochial and narrow the accepted literary norm for fiction had become' (*IF*, p. 241). *Literary* is his key term, because in contemporary American culture that hallmark signals the death of any medium in terms of getting at the truths of peoples' lives. Significantly, these arguments were first written up as a press release for his 1973 novel, *Out*, and later refashioned as a polemic for the journal *fiction international* (1974). Looking over the accepted styles of fiction and the manner of their success, Sukenick notes that 'The form of fiction that comes down to us through Jane Austen, George Eliot and Hemingway is no longer adequate to capture our experience. Either the novel will change, or it will die. Today's money-making novels are those that sell to the movies – in other words, they are essentially written for another medium' (*IF*, pp. 241–2). With the conventions of the traditional novel institutionalized, the only recourse for the truly innovative fictionist is to deconstruct his medium: 'not plot, but ongoing incident; not characterization, but consciousness struggling with circumstance; not social realism, but a sense of situation; and so on' (*IF*, p. 243).

'The form of the traditional novel is a metaphor for a society that no longer exists' (*IF*, p. 3), Sukenick explains. Yet forces of nostalgia and repression keep the old forms in place, creating an artificial standard against which Sukenick and Sorrentino can struggle with productive results. 'Literary values serve the interests of classes, groups, professions, industries, and this is neither bad nor avoidable' (*IF*, p. 49) as long as one understands those interests and can control their force. In *Up* Sukenick engages these interests directly, making them part of his novel. Fiction is not *about* experience; it is simply *more* experience, and thus the novel becomes the record of its own making. Not as parody (Pynchon), nor as the imitation of an imitation of an action (Barth), but as a valid action in itself (along the lines of an action painting by Pollock or de Kooning). Reading *Up* is, in turn, like participating in an account of the world of American publishing, from its academic base, through the mechanics of its production, to the physical existence of the book itself.[4]

Ron Sukenick's experience with publishing derives from his position as an academic: Ph.D.'d from Brandeis (with a dissertation on Stevens), teaching at Hofstra, CCNY, Sarah Lawrence, California-Irvine, and

---

[4] A full analysis of *Up* is found in my *Literary Disruptions: The Making of a Post-Contemporary American Fiction* (Urbana, Chicago, and London: University of Illinois Press, 1975; revised and enlarged second edition, 1980), pp. 120–4.

presently at Colorado, he shares the background which has become so necessary for American writers to survive (and which in the cases of lesser, second-generation academics such as Ann Beattie and Raymond Carver has led to a diminished style of fiction I will describe as 'MFA-modern').[5] Gil Sorrentino is only recently an academic, having been appointed to the prestigious Wallace Stegner chair in creative writing at Stanford University only after a full career of commercial editing (for the original Grove Press when it was publishing Henry Miller and Samuel Beckett) and then subsistence-level writing in New York (living in the subsidized-for-artists Westbeth apartments and teaching only occasional, informal courses at The New School). Yet as academic gripes help form Sukenick's fiction, so do concerns with New York's publishing and artistic worlds help shape Sorrentino's texts. The classic examples are his novels *Imaginative Qualities of Actual Things*, which transcends the *roman à clef* form to become a self-consciously metafictional record of writing a book amid the social jumble of Greenwich Village and uptown New York, and *Mulligan Stew*, a deliberate deconstruction and eventual destruction of virtually every innovative technique 60s and 70s fiction produced.[6] But as with Sukenick, a look at Sorrentino's collected commentary in *Something Said* reveals the theory behind this methodical textualization of writing and publishing experience.

Hubert Selby was one of Sorrentino's authors at Grove, and was also a childhood friend. Most importantly for Gil's own art, Selby was an example of what in publishing had to be overcome: a commercial reliance on outmoded forms, a readerly disposition toward predictable styles, and the artistic temptation to surrender to such pandering. That Selby resisted all of this helped guarantee him both an original art and a career of frustration and rejection. In reviewing LeRoi Jones's *The Moderns* Sorrentino had chided *New Yorker* writers, editors and readers for ignoring 'an entire land, the United States, to be precise' (*SS*, p. 227), but in his longer piece on Selby he defines the particulars of *New Yorker* upper-middle-class style which complements its thematic vacuity:

> Some writers, the best, let's say, of the 'popular' writers, use clothing and 'taste' as an indication of what to expect from the character. . . . [John] O'Hara will use a description of a vulgar character's tasteless clothes as an indication of that character's inherent vulgarity: the reader is clued as to what to think. Occasionally, as if to show you that it's nothing but a gimmick, he'll write a story like 'Exactly Eight Thousand Dollars Exactly': one character is held against another; the reader is given over to the movement of the story in terms of these characters' appurtenances and acts; and at the end, he turns the tables on you, a writer's joke. Which certainly indicates that he knows that these tricks are simply that, no more. (*SS*, pp. 123–4).

[5] Rust Hills, 'How Writers Live Today', *Esquire*, 102 (August 1984), 37–9.
[6] See the Special issue of *The Review of Contemporary Fiction*, 1 (Spring 1981) devoted to an analysis of Sorrentino's work.

It is a loss for fictive art that O'Hara's method can work just as well when its ear for speech and eye for detail is wrong, so long as readers are given what they expect to hear and to see – in other words, comfortable stereotypes. 'Readers are so passive before this assault of the conventional that they often look for these signals: when they are not there, they feel abandoned, they feel the work is difficult, or gauche – they feel, perhaps, betrayed' (*SS*, p. 25). When fiction writers yield to these demands of thoughtless, passive readership, the loss is their own, because 'signals are gimmicks, elements of craftsmanship, or the lack of it. They allow the writer to slip out from under the problems that only confrontation with materials can solve. Novels are made of words. The difficulty in writing fiction is that the words must be composed so that they reveal the absolute reality of their prey, their subject – and at the same time, they must be in themselves real; i.e., they don't have to stand for a specific meaning' (*SS*, p. 26). Selby's words have this power, while O'Hara's don't, Sorrentino insists, because Selby is relying on sharp observation and a genuine talent for writing while O'Hara has surrendered to a manipulation of inert signs. And those signs remain practically effective only because of the institutional weight slick journals like *The New Yorker* give them.

Institutional pressures kill the imaginative spirt of fiction. But when the extra-literary can be incorporated within the writer's creative act and also within the reader's active participation, its formerly inhibiting power can be turned to productive purpose. In *Imaginative Qualities of Actual Things*, Sorrentino will use a gimmicky sign as required by the rules of successful, popular or 'accessible' fiction, but will also footnote the absurdity of this technique as a nod to the knowing reader. He will heed the obsolete but still-encouraged dictum of writing about what he knows, and will even adopt *roman à clef* methods and exploit his own rage at certain people by turning them into characters – yet he will also add a few lines admitting how much he hates this character, and how he is hoping the next paragraph will lead to things even worse. In this way the extra-literary is made to be literary, and hence under Sorrentino's control instead of controlling him.

Thoughout the 1960s and 1970s Sorrentino, like Sukenick, exploited the processes of exploitation and fashioned not so much an anti-novel as a novel redeemed and reborn via its incorporation and transformation of the extra-literary. As opposed to European experiments in textuality which kept the process of creation quite narrow, Sukenick and Sorrentino ranged widely, with great exuberance, into the world around them, textualizing at will. No editor, no publishing house, no English department chairman was safe; nor were the forms of commercial fiction and 'art novels' themselves, as in works like *Out* and *Splendide-Hotel* these two authors exploited every style of organization, from page-length to the alphabet, as a way of showing how anti-systematics was less effective than a demonstration of how utterly conventional (and delightfully useful) any structure whatsoever could be.

The climax of such development has been not surprisingly the deconstruction of textuality itself. Once everything becomes part of the novel, the novel becomes nothing – all that remains is the artist's process of writing. Sukenick's device in this case has been *The Endless Short Story*, originally a tactic by which he wrote seamless fiction, saleable to publications by the foot. It is, as we shall see, a more productive conclusion than is Sorrentino's *Mulligan Stew*, which by running each extra-textual option into the ground successfully closes the book on 60s and 70s innovation. *Mulligan Stew* is written much in the manner of Flann O'Brien's classic *At Swim-Two-Birds* (1939), itself a Beckettian I-can't-go-on-I'll-go-on style of reaction against the supposedly devastated landscape left after the marauding armies of Joycean technique. O'Brien managed to say something after the last word had been spoken, just as did Beckett; but his method, like Sorrentino's would be in *Mulligan Stew*, was to systematically destroy the oppressor's tools which had just recently turned to revolutionary purpose. Hence in Sorrentino's work the nemesis becomes not a conservative English department head but rather a hot-shot young professor of postmodern lit, and the exuberances of style degrade themselves into silly pornography. Throughout the early 70s Sorrentino had published much of *Mulligan Stew* as fragments of a work in progress called *Synthetic Ink*; in the mid 70s he'd tried to publish the novel itself, and only slightly exaggerated versions of its file of rejection letters begin the full work as finally accepted by Grove Press (yet ultimately rejected for distribution by Random House, showing that extra-literary forces can outlive even the novel which purports to kill them after they've been conquered and converted to the cause).

Sorrentino himself used the ground cleared by *Mulligan Stew* to write *Aberration of Starlight*, in which the range of fictional opportunities is opened up for pure delight in language, for the enjoyment of vision as song. Four people experience a summer vacation; and just as in Faulkner's *The Sound and the Fury*, the reader experiences four different summer vacations, even though they are ostensibly the same. But Sorrentino needs no modernist grounding in psychology or myth, for language now can say it all. With the battle against inhibiting conventions of commercial publishing won – in other words, with no more need for social realism – he can respond to what in *Something Said* he calls his 'Genetic Coding': from his father, an Italian joy in 'the art of layering' ('one adds and adds and then adds some more, until the initial impetus, the base upon which the work rests, is almost unrecognizable'), and from his mother, an Irish style 'so far removed from nature that the latter is grotesquely distorted in it: in the Book of Kells, Swift, Sterne, Shaw, Wilde, Joyce, Synge, Yeats, O'Brien, we see a withdrawal from the representative'). Concluding both his book of essays and the combatively experimentalist phase of his writing career, Gil Sorrentino can observe that 'The Italians and the Irish hold reality cheap, and the brilliance of the art produced by these peoples is, by and large, the brilliance of formal invention used to break to pieces that which is recognizable to the quotidian eye' (*SS*, p. 264). From the comfort of his Stegner Professorship at Stanford, far from the smoky battlefield of commercially literary New York, Sorrentino can refract his *Crystal Vision* (a Brooklyn street-corner lyric, 289 pages of candy-store talk) and colour his *Blue Pastoral* (an even longer paean to comically bad writing, so deliberately bad so as to eclipse entirely commercial fears of 'experimental fiction').

Sukenick's *The Endless Short Story* almost exactly parallels his *In Form* as a demonstration of fiction's open form, much as his novel *Up* sits nicely next to the radical re-readings of *Wallace Stevens: Musing the Obscure*. Indeed, part of the theory is that there isn't any theory, or at least shouldn't be. 'Theory is a sign of ignorance', Sukenick argues in *In Form*. 'It becomes important when we are no longer sure what we are doing' (*IF*, p. 4). Turn to *The Endless Short Story* and you'll find him starting out where he left off in the previous book: 'As I was saying, perhaps ignorance is the key. We all of course know what's going to happen next. Only artists don't know what's going to happen next a quirk of ignorance they share with history and the weather' (pp. 2–3). *In Form* had included part of the endless short story as 'The Finnegan Digression', and in this more purely fictional work there is a great deal of critical discussion, largely centred about role models for the extra-formally deconstructive process: Simon Rodia (whose Watts Towers reveal the inadequacies of documentation – the more you know, the less you know), Aziff (a character whose energy transcends the normal drives for food and for sex), and any number of memories from the author's Brooklyn childhood, where in Wordsworthian fashion he suspects 'There is always the possibility that children are little geniuses and it's all down hill from there' (p. 7). As in life, sexual preoccupations recur on schedule, 'grunting gutgrinding orgiastic gritty fleshgrabbing groundfloor jungles of sex' (p. 16), but they are immediately textualized and turned into language: 'the letter g was the magic letter of sex enormous erotic reverberations he once knew a girl named Gugi she drove him gaga his favorite french dish was gigot listening to jug bands threw his whole body into a kind of sexual jig jerking and jumping I like the palsy he loved jam also jelly' (pp. 16–17). As in conventional narrative, things happen. But they are events of life, not of text, until Sukenick textualizes them: 'As usual my imagination had seized on the murky data of experience and had made of it a continuation of my writing' (p. 26). And always the effect is in language. 'As in Paris when your interior monologue imperceptibly switches to French, out here [in Colorado] I was beginning to catch myself thinking in Cowboy: "A short ways up the trail here an ah kin see the tall buildings in Dinver" ' (p. 27).

Like *In Form, The Endless Short Story* proceeds by digression. Experience is textualized, but not formalized – Sukenick's art preserves the random energy of existence without stuffing it and putting it behind glass. For Sorrentino, the inhibiting conventions of traditional fiction could be sprung free, but only to snap back and become traps once again. That was his progress from *Imaginative Qualities of Actual Things* through *Splendide-Hotel* to *Mulligan Stew*. How ironic that Sukenick's poetic-aesthetic model is the closely argued Stevens, while Sorrentino espoused the looser attitude toward form apparent in Williams, only to have form close upon him in the end. Sukenick's endless short story is, by the very contradiction of its title, a subversion of genre and an invitation to grow beyond the limits of form.

The Endless Short Story therefore not only closes two decades of innovation, but opens the field to more than the virtuoso enjoyment of personal lyric. Yet current American fiction continues with its fixation on the extra-literary, which in various forms can still stimulate creation. No less than four distinct styles of reaction dominate the 1980s to date: the prank-sterism of Steve Katz, the generative display of Stephen Dixon, the textual celebrity of Walter Abish, and the egotistical polemic which finds its negative side in Charles Newman and its positive side with Michael Stephens. None of this work is a fiction bred in the hothouse of academia – what is written by students and taught by instructors in MFA workshops is as mechanical as the products of any academy, as Pico Iyer explains in her analysis of Ann Beattie's work:

> *The New Yorker* has long seemed to be written for, by, and about those who lead lives of quiet desperation. In its discreet, fearfully subdued stories the usual milieu is peripheral suburbia, the usual mood penumbral regret. . . . Beattie is perhaps the first and the finest laureate of that generation of Americans born to a society built on quicksand doomed to a life in the long, ambiguous shadow of the sixties. The characters in her stories are left over from that abandoned decade, hung over with its legacy, saddled with hand-me-down customs that have gone out of style. . . . Beattie's tales seem almost mass-produced. . . . Collect some characters and name them Jason, say, or Hilary, or Barrett (not Tom, Dick or Harry – Beattie people invariably wear slightly upper-middle class, faintly original names midway between Zowie Bowie and John Smith. Give them trendy occupations and engaging idiosyncracies. Place their homes in the woods, and supply them with shaggy dogs, coffee, and conversations around the kitchen table. Make it a grey day in winter. Let there be a phone call from a former lover, a child from a sometime marriage. Ensure that someone takes Valium and someone refers to a gynecological operation. Write in a withered present tense and end before the conclusion.[7]

This style of workshop-modern is death-oriented, whereas Steve Katz has used the post-60s phenomena to write beyond the gimmicks and signals so acceptable to commercial publishing's presumed readership (I say 'presumed' because American magazine editors are renowned for the contempt in which they hold their readers).

At the forefront of 60s experimentation with his novel *The Exagggerations of Peter Prince* (the three *g*'s are intentional, the first of the book's exaggerations and a nuisance to typesetters ever since), Katz has sustained his writing and even found areas for growth through the later

[7]Pico Iyer, 'The World According to Ann Beattie', *Partisan Review*, 50 (No. 4, 1983), 548–53.

1970s and into the 80s by feasting on the extra-literary. His *Cheyenne River Wildtrack* transcends literary notions of genre, choosing a cinematic 'wild-track' (a soundtrack produced by leaving a microphone open during filming, which is then used as the outline for the finished soundtrack later on). This same event also becomes one of the moving parts of Katz's next collection, *Moving Parts*, in which the most extravagant fantasies of the creative imagination are tested against a narrowest sense of documentary reality. In the mid 1980s, however, Katz finds it best to be a prankster – a creative anarchist, a constructive deconstructionist, or most aptly a shaman of alternative publishing realities. The key to his pranksterish, shamanistic method is to maintain reverence for the creative act but not to take its consequences seriously. His is the art of performance, not a museum piece, and his special talent is to perform around the wooden conventions of genre-based writing and industry-controlled publishing and subvert them so that original fiction can once again be possible.

Two works published in 1984, his *Stolen Stories* and the novel *Wier & Pouce*, explore a style of comparative realism which eclipses the conventions of both experimental fiction and the traditional novel. In the former, Katz anticipates Michael Stephens and refines fiction down to its most essential component: voice. 'Two Seaside Yarns' is a short diptych which exploits narratology and verbal texture, while pieces like 'Made of Wax' and 'Friendship' take improbable attitudes toward impossible situations and spin out utterly conventional stories based on narrative force alone. *Wier & Pouce* takes a literary factor which has become an extra-literary inhibition – in this case the weight of The Great Tradition in the novel, notably that of *War and Peace* – by running a tsardom of characters through an imperial field of action to a climax of soulful morality, absolutely nothing of which allows itself to be taken seriously except as a send-up of superannuated literary form. Yet Katz has achieved his purpose of writing a nineteenth-century novel in postmodern America, a novel which is creative according to contemporary terms at the same time as it uses every otherwise useless convention from the literary past.

Katz's supreme prank, a send-up which pulls the rug from beneath the pretensions of small press/avant-garde publishing, has been his participation in the single-issue serial publication, *Guest Editor*. Its form is a contradiction in terms, yet corresponds to the reality of many enthusiastically launched little magazines which never live beyond their first issue. And as a performance artist, doing his work within the conventions of such a project tested his abilities to create fiction under conditions even more inhibiting than those of hackneyed commercial publishing.

If *The New Yorker*'s world is limiting, the moment and milieu of so-called 'alternative publishing' can be even more claustrophobic. Within the MFA mafia, such publications exist for the *vita* padding which assures an endless series of academic appointments and arts council gigs for work-shoppers. For the most part, Steve Katz has done without them, but when given the chance to be the first guest editor of this new publication he seized the opportunity with relish, for the very stupidities of its existence gave him a context for some of his best performance art. *Guest Editor* is a 40-page, quarto size magazine printed on heavy, slick paper – about the size and weight of a major league baseball programme or team yearbook. The first and only issue was offered by subscription in the Fall of 1983; in a mailing to a sure-buy readership (subscribers to the Fiction Collective titles, *The American Book Review*, and so forth), founder Laura Stafford and her administrative staff requested substantial donations so that a unique magazine 'created, staffed and edited by writers with the objective of discovering good stories by other writers could be launched.' A different 'well known' author would guest-edit each issue – hence its title. The guest editor would select material by 'underpublished writers' he or she might know, the term 'underpublished writer' being a linguistic invention from the same age and mind-set which referred to handicapped people not as 'disabled' but as 'differently-abled'. With sufficient funds to produce an expensive-looking issue, the founder and staff of *Guest Editor* took advantage of the situation for some unashamed and previously unparalled self-aggrandizement. With the exception of two page-long stories by Katz and and a short piece by Steve's University of Colorado colleague, Michael Brownstein, the *Guest Editor* folks published themselves. From this great class of underpublished writers came an overpriced magazine's worth of generally meritless fiction, beginning with with photographs of the motley crew: Michael Brownstein (the friend) in conventionally thoughtful face, fingertip at lower lip; Normandi Ellis (photo staff), in a village-idiot's photo-booth pose with head cocked and tongue wagging at full extension; John Enck (administrative staff) in arty high-contrast/scratched-negative shadows; Marilyn Krysl (editorial staff) in standard literary pose, chin resting lightly on knuckles; Mark Leyner (editorial), grinning like a possum eating candy; Paula Longendyke (administrative), full length in a nun's habit, flashing some well-turned calf and thigh; and finally Laura Stafford, founder, in the nude.

Katz himself was pictured in a cheery, Grape Nuts studio portrait, completely innocent and unassuming – a photo no one but an insurance salesman or candidate for city council would select. And beneath Steve's winning smile was published his 'Guest Commentary' for this issue, 'Post Hoc Maximalism', which puts the whole affair into devastatingly honest perspective:

> I was pleased to have the opportunity to edit the first issue of Ghost Editor [*sic*]. I had hoped this could be the occasion to present the work of Istvan Kottki, once known as the Charlie Parker of maximalist writing. The visual maximalism of his sister, Muriel, is better known than his verbal contribution; particularly her piece from the mid-sixties called Broadway and Houston, which was composed of that busy intersection and all its traffic. It was removed because of pressure on the Mayor's office and after the departure of John Lindsay, but we recollected her pioneering work each time we pass that intersection in 1984. Little known is that in '72 she transferred her piece to the center of the Verrazano Narrows bridge, causing its collapse. Who let this go

unnoticed? Minimum recognition is one of the salient qualities of maximalist art.

Isvtan Kottki was not an easy artist to find. He seemed to have disappeared, as had most of his works. Do you remember the coy ravelling and unravelling of fact and opinion and propaganda around the date of May 5, 1970, the Kent State tragedy, that brought to a miserable focus all the various rhetorics surrounding the war in Southeast Asia? That verbal display was one of the most spontaneous and ambitious works, a uniquely political work, by Istvan Kottki, Maximalist.

My funds were limited, but my search for the Maximalist did lead me to Inuvik, in the Northwest Territories, where I'd learned his mistress, Isabel Soulever, had gone when she left Istvan to live with an eskimo guitarist of dubious sanity whom she had met at a Christo yacht-wrapping project off Key West. Now she lives alone, twelve miles north of Inuvik, where I found her in the igloo she built for herself, watching a small color TV. She invited me in to sit next to her on the stack of furs that served as her bed. We watched a special from Danish television covering rebel operations in EL Salvador. An hour passed before I felt I could broach the subject of her former lover. I saw she was on the verge of tears. She lifted her hand, shaking in its mitten, to point at the screen. There he was, in camouflage fatigues, sitting at the briefing of a rebel cadre in the Salvadorean jungle.

'That's really Istvan?' I asked. His beard had exploded.

She nodded.

It should have been obvious all along. The verbal stuff buffeting out of that conflict surely shows the touch of Istvan Kottki. Maximalist. It is both reassuring and disconcerting to find him still at work.

I had neither money nor courage to visit him myself, so I asked Isabel if she kept in touch. When she said she did, I asked her to mention in her next letter my interest in placing some of his work in this new magazine. She agreed.

As soon as I got home I began to receive in the mail all the works that follow, attributed to various young authors, and two short pieces actually signed with my own name. I am very pleased to have the opportunity to present all these works, surely a representative sampling of the art of Istvan Kottki, Maximalist.[8]

'Post Hoc Maximalism' is thus as perfect a fiction as any piece in Katz's *Stolen Stories*, and by virtue of its success within the strict limits of the magazine's fleeting occasion it qualifies as pure performance art, formed by the extra-literary forces of its circumstance. From its linguistically transposed title through its odd names and exotic locations to its habitual return to the topics of budgets and funding, 'Post Hoc Maximalist' uses the institutional facts of its creation to provide the rhythms of performance. It does not so much parody those conditions as feed on them for its energy and propulsion, explaining the goofy photos which surround it and the mostly

[8]Steve Katz, 'Post Hoc Maximalism', *Guest Editor*, 1 (Winter 1984), p. 3.

bad stories which follow. By giving the imaginary Istvan Kottki a photo credit for Steve's own mug shot, the story turns full circle within the magazine's extra-literary existence.

Not surprisingly, and perhaps by design, *Guest Editor* existed for only one issue. A year later, contributors and subscribers were sent an unsigned letter from 'The staff of GUEST EDITOR' announcing that 'GUEST EDITOR is now dead editor'; they'd tried their best, but the journal 'did not attract major foundations and corporations for the financial support necessary to continue' (the vision of IBM and the Ford Foundation contributing cash for such shenanigans is hard to comprehend!). People who had been duped into sending money were paid off with a fulfilment subscription to a hopelessly mediocre Canadian poetry journal; my own copies included several back issues from 1967 with egregiously bad poems about Commonwealth citizens mooning over the barefoot girls of Greenwich Village. Mark Leyner graduated from the *Guest Editor* send-up to assume the directorship of another similar project, The Fiction Collective, while Laura Stafford disappeared, at least temporarily, from the arts scene. Katz has continued his career as a performance artist unscathed.

Stephen Dixon is another writer equally beyond *The New Yorker*'s appreciation, yet able to perform as a literary artist. His own genius has been to devise stories which generate their own action: rather than depending upon a *New Yorker* style of conventional references, he allows the conventions to propel themselves through story and situation until a self-supporting work is achieved. His novels *Work* and *Too Late* use the thematic conventions of finding and working at a job (the former) and searching for a missing loved one (the latter) to structure each book and to provide a vehicle for the on-going narrative strategy. One convention leads to another – not just in life, but in the texture of the literary work itself. His story collections[9] do the same within the limits of five to 25 pages (Dixon's most typical length is 10 printed pages or about 3,500 to 4,000 words). His latest novel, *Fall & Rise*, uses the process of writing itself for structure and energy: the alternating fall and rise of action, of interest, and of narrative compulsion itself, just as in the rhythms of the writer's life. The plot is disarmingly simple: at Diane's party, Daniel meets Helene; he is taken with her and pursues her relentlessly, even though she doesn't notice. Daniel's compulsion to pursue matches the writer's compulsion to write, thereby textualizing the conventions of name – place – date and manners which in the hands of a lesser writer – a *New Yorker* writer, Gil Sorrentino might say – would escape the story to become extra-literary.

As Steve Dixon generates, Walter Abish celebrates. Abish's approach to the extra-literary is to surround it and encompass it within his own identity, which as 'a writer' is completely textual. Whereas others would shun the autobiographical as outside the work (Barthes, Derrida), Abish turns this

[9]Stephen Dixon, *No Relief* (Ann Arbor: Street Fiction Press, 1976); *Quite Contrary* (New York: Harper & Row, 1979); *14 Stories* (Baltimore: Johns Hopkins University Press, 1980); *Movies* (San Francisco: North Point Press, 1983) *Time to Go* (San Francisco: North Point Press, 1984).

strategy inside out in order to textualize each event which has led to his present situation of putting pen to paper. In this way entire nations and epochs of history, from the *Anschluss* in Austria through the wartime and postwar transformation of China to the first years of the State of Israel, are no longer determining factors; instead, Abish as the writer-to-be makes them serve his own cause of literary creation. 'From the start', Abish asks, 'does the writer-to-be understand that his enterprise is in the nature of a quest, really a romantic quest for a number of interrelated things: (1) his text-to-be (2) the idea as well as the material for the text (3) his resolve to emulate and follow in the footsteps of the legendary heroes of writing: Hemingway, Miller, Thomas Wolfe, Mailer, Kerouac, etc. (4) and finally the quest for meaning. I mean by that the ontological search for an answer to the question: Why am I *I*, here, writing, thinking?'[10] Moreover, 'The writer-to-be lives under the impression that everything, literally everything he experiences can be accurately transferred onto paper' (the allusion to photography is intentional), and that 'for everything under the sun there is a corresponding sign or word, and that the intensity of his ardor, his passion for life, will impress upon the pages the determination of his new commitment' (p. 105). Creation is possession, and ultimately the writer possesses his or her world, a process which the text celebrates as self: author, world and writing as one. As with Dostoevsky's famous moment, everything at once becomes possible. 'I was crossing the parade ground in Ramle during my second year in the [Israeli] Tank Corps,' Abish recalls, 'when quite suddenly the idea of becoming a writer flashed through my mind. A moment of pure exhilaration' (p. 112).

Before the practice of exhilaration, however, come the moments of test. In his 'Self-Portrait', the first-published example of his 'writer-to-be' work following our 1974 interview,[11] Walter emphasizes how certain life experiences can inhibit the text. 'An individual will use language to give shape to his *I*,' he begins,[12] almost immediately adding that for even dead language, such as the cliché *sink or swim*, there can be a challenge: 'Having once almost drowned in a Shanghai swimming pool I cannot hear the word *or* mentioned without feeling a vague trepidation that is only somewhat assuaged when the speaker in question, out of compassion, says: Or else you can leave it the way it is' (pp. 5–6). Notice how it is the linguistic structure and not the word's referential qualities that tests Walter's command of his art: it is the coordinating conjunction and not the art of swimming that he must master.

That mastery comes not by recounting experience in the conventional mode of autobiography but rather by textualizing the extra-literary, by

[10]Walter Abish, 'The Writer-To-Be: An Impression of Living', *Sub-Stance* No. 27 (1980), pp. 101–2.

[11]Jerome Klinkowitz, 'Walter Abish: An Interview', *Fiction International* Nos. 4/5 (1975), pp. 93–100; reprinted in part in Klinkowitz, *The Life of Fiction* (Urbana, Chicago, and London: University of Illinois Press, 1977), pp. 59–71.

[12]Walter Abish, 'Self-Portrait', in *Individuals: Post-Movement Art in America*, ed. Alan Sondheim (New York: Dutton, 1977), p. 1.

making one's life a life of fiction. The pivotal piece here is 'Family', which examines 'why things happened the way they did'[13] by successively handling his parents' and his uncle's texts until, by the writer's act with language, they become his own – i.e., they become not fact but fiction. And fiction, of course, is much easier to control, for here the writer is master of his language rather than letting language (through the events which have shaped it) master him. Looking back through his past, Abish sees how his parents' style of living yielded freedom of choice for them but determination for him: 'I was their product' (p. 15), he notes, and everything he did, mapped out in painstaking order, was simply to legitimize their role as the father and mother of a child. Yet this function could be reversed, for 'I was the only child. I was put there to observe them', and from this posture little Walter would become the writer-to-be, observing everything:

> How could I have possibly known that I was being trained to be a writer? And that, in turn, my continuous attempts to break my mother's resistance were a preparation on my part to break down the resistance of the blank page I was to face years later. To break down the impediments of the text. Did they not see it? How could they have missed it? It was so obvious. My writerly concerns were, after all, printed all over my hideously distorted face. Deceit. Liar. A prig to boot. The price one pays if one is developing into a writer. (p. 152)

Growing up, Abish learns that his family's routines are rituals devised for understanding the outside world – for understanding history, in other words. As a child, he stands outside of history; but now, as an adult, he is faced with the challenge of making family history fit his own text (his own life) lest it swallow him entirely. Therefore he takes control, escaping the habits of 'a world in which language served the supreme purpose of daily defining and interpreting conduct and planning the next day and the day after' (p. 153) and instead using language to textualize his extra-literary experience, thereby making it literary (and hence controllable). The first step is to close off his free-running memories of his family and stick to photographs, since they can be sorted, studied, arranged, and eventually shaped into a useable form. Then to find a manageable text: not just his memories of Uncle Phoebus, for example, which are prone to quandary and contradiction, but Phoebus's diary, where the 'black-sheep' uncle himself had textualized experience. 'Each event is a self-contained drama, a stage setting in which Phoebus . . . remains, despite his passionate language, the distanced observer of himself' (p. 161). Within these carefully framed tableaux there is 'an almost painterly concern with the presentation of the event' (p. 162), anticipating Abish's writerly fascination with the otherwise historical detail of his own immediate family. The first passage from Phoebus's diary is the uncle's sorrowful account of his brother Fritz's death, a problematic task which Phoebus handles textually:

[13]Walter Abish, 'Family', *Antaeus* 52 (Spring 1984), p. 149.

describing the brother's own diary. There are now three texts, successively within each other like Chinese boxes: Abish's which contains Uncle Phoebus's which contains Fritz's. Yet for the writer-to-be to become the writer-in-fact, Abish must learn to edit. And so we see him putting one photo aside, 'never show[ing] anyone,' because it 'seems to negate the role of black sheep I have applied to him' (p. 163), and concluding that he must equally discard another photograph catching his parents in a casual, affectionate mood because 'It invalidates everything I have described' (p. 169). What triumphs in the end is Abish's art of the text, since it transcends his uneasy memory of his parents' presumed art of their lives, in which everything which succeeded had to be deliberate – or so it seemed to little Walter. Where Abish had been able to textualize, life exists as fiction. Where he hasn't, there is 'no trace' (p. 164), and therefore effectively nothing at all.

Abish's ultimate textualization of the extra-literary is found in his sequel, 'The Fall of Summer'. Here the first person of 'Family' yields to third person narration, as Abish assumes the form of a character so that he may more easily inhabit his text. Autobiographically, Abish travels to West Germany for the very first time (after having imagined it in his novel *How German Is It*)[14] and returns to Austria – in particular, to the apartment building in Vienna where he lived for the first several years of his life – for the first time since 1938. But textually, he is better equipped to transpose the extra-literary into a literary form, for he has with him two guides: Thomas Bernhard's novel *Beton*, which he is savouring page-by-page and using as a kind of *Baedeker* so that 'taste and not the "story"' (p. 139) will determine his response, and the memory of a day 10 years ago in the New York Public Library when he pored over the pages of 'a profusely illustrated book by G.A. Jellicoe, an English landscape architect' (p. 136), by which he came to know the Belevedere's baroque gardens. Even though Abish was born in the gardens' proximity, he hadn't *known* them until experiencing them through a readable text; hence his 'one true moment of elation' on his first return visit comes when he can walk into not a memory but into a text which he can now vitalize by his own participation in it. How anticipatory imagination (the literary) corresponds or fails to correspond to the actual subsequent experience (the extra-literary) was Steve Katz's successful experiment in the sections of *Moving Parts*,[15] but in 'The Fall of Summer' Abish finds that his own goals demand that he invert the structure, using the present experience to recapture a past moment of textuality. We now have a three-part process: a memory of the mid 1930s which has been textualized successfully by a reading experience of the mid 1970s which is vitalized by the writer's own physical participation in an event of the mid 1980s. True, as Dostoevsky says, 'the world seemed to be

14Walter Abish, *How German Is It* (New York: New Directions, 1984), analysed by Jerome Klinkowitz in *The Self-Apparent Word: Fiction as Language/Language as Fiction* (Carbondale: Southern Illinois University Press, 1984), pp. 129–31, and in 'Walter Abish and the Surfaces of Life', *Georgia Review*, 35 (Summer 1980), 416–20.
15As discussed in *The Self-Apparent Word*, pp. 6, 9–15.

created for me alone,' and that 'the whole world would dissolve as soon as my consciousness became extinct'; all would vanish 'without leaving a trace behind' (p. 110). But Abish prefers to celebrate his conquest of the previously untextual by *creating* traces, an inversion of Thomas Bernhard's celebration of suicide as 'the energizer and guide in the text in which the ridiculous 'is the sum of all human intercourse' (p. 111).

In a nutshell, here is how Abish becomes an American writer while Bernhard, by staying within easy reach of home, remains the Austrian writer which Abish so firmly isn't. Outside of history as a child ('Family'), his textualization process in 'The Fall of Summer' lets him skip back over 40 years of history to stand outside of history again: not because it hasn't happened, but because its happening has now been transformed into a text, a life of fiction where he's not just the writer-to-be but the writer-as-being. 'Death is food for Bernhard', Abish notes. 'He chews it thoroughly and comments on it. Death is the food that binds his characters together. It is the food that replaces all need for sex' (pp. 111–12). Walter Abish, on the other hand, chooses life, with all its troublesome extra-literary dimensions, because he has learned how to make them a successful part of his text. 'Survival requires overcoming this resistance/opposition intrinsic to all things in everyday life' (p. 115) he has learned, from the resistance put up by his mother's fetishes of regimentation and expectation ('Family') to the resistance of the smothering, encompassing 'familiarity' of a comfortable world (which is what Abish rediscovers in Vienna – its constant temptation to take a short nap and dream away one's life in neat little pleasures). And above all, there is the resistance of the page – as Ronald Sukenick sums it up in the twelfth of his first 12 digressions toward a study of composition: 'The blank page, the void where everything is called into question' (*IF*, p. 15).

The conditions of writing in the United States today, in the last analysis, can lead to two extremes: to polemic, or to lyric. The inhibitions of a commercial literary establishment pandering to an entertainment-oriented audience are unfavourably balanced by an academic community which too often makes the same easy sales to moralistic teachability. In each case a product is packaged and distributed for results which undermine its creative purpose. Metaphors from commerce and industry abound: fiction is *manufactured*, its received value is *inflationary*, its effect on the market is, as bad fiction, *to drive out the good* – such allegorization through analogy controls the entire argument of Charles Newman's *The Postmodern Aura: The Act of Fiction in an Age of Inflation*, which concludes that the fatalism of anticipated inflation degrades the present product and that such circumstances buy out the avant-garde before it can even have a chance to set its sell-out price. Newman's argument succeeds only to the extent that he redefines the wide range of innovative fiction into the unfairly narrow category of 'metafiction' (fiction which explores its own making). For a writer such as William H. Gass and for the very first works of Sukenick and Katz (1968), Newman's argument would be sound; but he has failed to read their succeeding works with an open mind, his perception of their art having been so traumatized by the shock of their experiments two decades ago that nothing else they write can make it through the defensive screen he's erected (Newman is himself a novelist whose career has been frustrated by the extra-literary pressures of commercial publishing, in turn made worse by the failure of innovative academicians to embrace his cause as they have Sukenick's and Katz's).

A more successful appraisal of the writer's lot in present-day America is Michael Stephens's *The Dramaturgy of Style: Some Ideas About Voice in Short Fiction*. To write in America, Stephens admits, is to write with much of Europe behind one: what Harold Bloom would call the anxiety of influence. In Stephens's case, as both a third-generation Irish American and as a postmodernist succeeding the modernists (among whom were such transpositional Irish styles as those of Yeats, Joyce and Beckett), the question of such once-literary forces becoming extra-literary obstacles is solved by turning full circle: not just back East across the Atlantic, but all the way West to the Orient where much of America's recent past and present is found (notably the Vietnam War and its domestic aftermath) and where Michael has looked for the future (to the situation of Korean literary culture). 'Writing is a product of the physical world,' he insists, 'not a by-product of a mental process' (p. 83), yet a 'range of intelligence' (p. 57) can never be a substitute for 'voice', which he defines as an idealization of speech's voice patterns, the energy of which is concentrated in a given textual space (hence the term 'dramaturgy'). A seeing voice results in an image, and that image is 'charged by the rhythm of experience' (p. 3). Beckett offers a combination of objects with a manner of concision: in Beckett's case a way to go on after one can't go on (after Joyce), but for Stephens a model of the ultimate open end. And likewise for other writers past and present, who when viewed in terms of their voices present less of an anxiety of influence (or even less of a tradition against which to strain one's individual talent) and more of a dialogue to which one can listen and critically participate, all the while clearing the vocal tubes for one's own expression (as Stephens has remarked elsewhere, 'even the tenor John McCormick . . . had to clear his voice before he sang'[16]). As for Vietnam, the enormity of which effected great change in the world and at home, but which most Americans did not experience at all and which even the relatively small percentage of Americans who worked or fought there find it hard to articulate today, one must trust to the dramaturgy of fictional style in the hopes of having literary form make extra-literary experience understandable. So too for America understanding another culture – not the familiar mother-country or father-land of Europe, but the ultimate Western horizon of its experience: the Far East:

> Fiction is representational, and fiction which is created out of a seeing voice is also presentational. It is an imaginary world. You cannot, I am told by these writers [who have written successfully of the war], capture the experience; i.e., the terrors of combat are *sui generis*. But the

---

[16]Klinkowitz, *The Life of Fiction*, p. 47, citing a letter from Stephens.

rhythm of that experience works itself into you, not the reasoning mind but that part of the mind with its seeing voice. (p. 144)

Of all the metaphors for writing, Michael Stephens's is the most lyrically comprehensive. Beyond text, he finds not experience but *breath*: 'By making fiction voice-centered, the stress goes away from representational art toward the presentational' (p. 190), or as Katz might say, toward the performative. When fiction draws upon breath, upon 'the unique way each person enunciated the syllable, whether spoken in the mind or from the mouth' (p. 189), it is allowing for universal diversity, an endless field of action in which no forces, whether literally influential or institutionally restrictive, can limit the writer's expression. Like the Bastille's stones on 14 July, the prison house of language yields its formerly inhibiting materials to pave a grounds for free expression. As Stephens is fond of recalling from Beckett, as long as there are words and voices to speak them 'All is not then yet quite irrevocably lost.'

Note

Criticism

John Aldridge, *The American Novel and the Way we Live Now* (Oxford: Oxford University Press, 1983).

Joe David Bellamy, *The New Fiction: Interviews with Innovative American Writers* (Urbana: University of Illinois Press, 1974).

Italo Calvino, 'Notes towards a definition of the Narrative Form as a Combinative Process', *20th Century Studies* (Kent) 2 (1970).

Raymond Federman, *SurFiction: Fiction Now and Tomorrow* (Chicago: Black Swallow Press, 1975).

Leslie Fiedler, 'Cross that Border – Close that Gap: Postmodernism', *Sphere History of Literature in the English Language, vol.9: American Literature Since 1900* (London: Sphere, 1975) ed. M. Cunliffe.

John Gardner, *On Moral Fiction* (New York: Basic Books, 1978).

William H. Gass, *Fiction and the Figures of Life* (Boston: Nonpareil Books, 1971).

Gerald Graff, *Literature against Itself* (Chicago: University of Chicago Press, 1979).

Ihab Hassan, 'The Literature of Silence', *Encounter* xxviii (Jan. 1967).

Ihab Hassan, *Paracriticisms* (Urbana: University of Illinois Press, 1975).

Jerome Klinkowitz, *Literary Disruptions: The Making of a Post-Contemporary American Fiction* (Urbana: University of Illinois Press, 1977).

Tom LeClair and Larry McCaffery, *Anything Can Happen: Interviews with Contemporary American Novelists* (Urbana: University of Illinois Press, 1983).

Larry McCaffery, *The Metafictional Muse: The Works of Robert Coover, Donald Barthelme and William H. Gass* (Pittsburgh: University of Pittsburgh Press, 1982).

Robert Scholes, *Fabulation and Metafiction* (Urbana: University of Illinois Press, 1979).

Ronald Sukenick, *Wallace Stevens: Musing the Obscure* (New York: New York University Press, 1967).

Ronald Sukenick, '12 Digressions Toward a Study of Composition', *New Literary History*, 6 (1974–5).

Texts

Walter Abish, *How German Is It, Wie Deutsch Ist Es* (New York: New Directions, 1980).

Walter Abish, *In the Future Perfect* (New York: New Directions, 1975; this edn. London: Faber & Faber, 1984).

Donald Barthelme, 'See the Moon', in *Unspeakable Practices, Unnatural Acts* (New York: Farrar, Straus & Giroux, 1968).

Donald Barthelme, 'Brain Damage', in *City Life* (New York: Farrar, Straus & Giroux, 1970).

Raymond Carver, *The Stories of Raymond Carver* (London: Pan/Picador, 1985).

Raymond Carver, *Fires* (London: Collins Harvill, 1985).

Ronald Sukenick, *98.6: A Novel* (New York: Fiction Collective, 1975).

Ronald Sukenick, *Long Talking Bad Conditions Blues* (New York: Fiction Collective, 1979).

3

Brain Damage: The Word and the World in Postmodernist Writing

Allan Lloyd Smith

I

Over recent years American writers have debated whether and to what extent fiction should bare the device, that is, draw attention to the techniques of writing itself; or whether it should be transparent and permit its readers the illusion of access to the real. In *Anything Can Happen* (1983) Tom LeClair and Larry McCaffery use the terms invisible and visible art to describe fiction that conceals its illusionary methods as against fiction that calls attention to its creator. An interview shows John Gardner as a proponent of invisible art, calling for writing that is a 'vivid and continuous dream' (p. 24), or ' a beautiful and powerful apparition' (p. 30), whereas William Gass provides an example of the visible artist, claiming that the work 'is filled with only one thing – words and how they work and how they connect, (p. 28). These terms (which hold an echo of Roland Barthes's distinction between the *lisible* and the *scriptible*, loosely, readerly or writerly texts), have the advantage over such categories as metafiction in that the one does not implicitly denigrate the other, as metafiction implies that it transcends and supersedes mere naive fiction.

It is tempting to argue that these are the only poles of debate in contemporary fiction: between those writers who practise techniques of invisibility, or realism, and the visible writers who prefer the realms of self-conscious *écriture*, fantasy or fabulation. In the 70s this seemed to be the case, as the interviews in Joe David Bellamy's *The New Fiction* (1974) demonstrate, and for several years the titles of books on American fiction indicated the dominance of the second of these alternatives: Raymond Federman's *SurFiction* (1975), Ihab Hassan's *Paracriticisms* (1975), Jerome Klinkowitz's *Literary Disruptions: the Making of a Post Contemporary American Fiction* (1975), Robert Scholes's *Fabulation and Metafiction* (1979), and finally Larry McCaffery's *The Metafictional Muse* (1982). But such an argument would be misinformed, because most contemporary writers work in both forms, mixing transparent with opaque modes in their writing. A further complication is that the label of metafiction or surfiction imposes an assumption of ahistoricism and non-significance that has recently met with censure in John Gardner's *On Moral Fiction* (1978), John Aldridge's *The American Novel And The Way We Live Now* (1983), and Gerald Graff's *Literature Against Itself* (1979). However, this stricture does not in fact accord with many writers' practices. Even Robert Coover now says 'Maybe I think that all my fiction is realistic and that so far it has simply been misunderstood as otherwise.'[1] To find a better understanding we can reconsider some of the positions taken up in the development of visible fiction and draw attention to the various possibilities they encode.

The views of Ronald Sukenick may provide a starting place:

> When, through the imagination, the ego manages to reconcile reality with its own needs, the formerly insipid landscape is infused with the ego's emotion, and reality, since it now seems more intensely relevant to the ego, suddenly seems more real.[2]

The psychologism evidenced in these lines is a model for the involvement of the author in the reading process, his concern for how the interactions operate. The author is not, in Italo Calvino's words, 'in charge of the machine without knowing how it works,' the 'spoilt child of the subconscious,' but he is instead a salvager of that domain who 'annexes it to the language of the conscious waking self.'[3] Sukenick's playful name for this is psychosynthesis, the opposite of psychoanalysis. Psychosynthesis is based on the Mosaic Law. 'The Mosaic Law the law of mosaics or how to deal with parts in the absence of wholes.'[4] The writer is not off paring his fingernails but down there scuffling with the typewriter and the paper in the mutuality of meaning creation:

> Interruption. Discontinuity. Imperfection. It can't be helped. This very instant as I write as you read a hundred things. A hundred things to tangle with resolve ignore before you are together. Together for an instant then smash its all gone still its worth it. I feel. This composure grown out of ongoing decomposition.[5]

This seems partly a return to the techniques of romantic writing, an ironic recognition of the conspiracy between writer and reader in the service of an illusion that is itself a higher, or at least a more intense, reality. Even the interest in fragments and the transience of moments of integration can be recognized as an essential aspect of romantic aesthetics. But a difference is apparent too: instead of organicist completeness is only on-going decomposition, and behind the veil lies not some transcendent ordering of chaos but rather '. . . odd gaps in consciousness concerning the new conditions and the curious lacunae in the conditions themselves . . .'[6]

---

[1]Coover, interview in LeClair, *Anything Can Happen* p. 67.
[2]Ronald Sukenick, *Wallace Stevens: Musing the Obscure* pp. 14, 15.
[3]Italo Calvino, 'Notes Towards a definition of the Narrative Form as a Combinative Process, pp. 97, 98.
[4]Ronald Sukenick, *98.6* p. 167.
[5]Sukenick, *98.6* p. 167.
[6]Sukenick, *Long Talking Bad Conditions Blues* p. 22.

The literature of Silence and the Absurd is sidestepped by such writing, and the ennui produced by oppressive freedom from the conventions of realism is shrugged off. Writers like Sukenick do not affect the tired dignity of negativity, like Beckett, Sartre or Robbe-Grillet; or strive for Silence by accepting chance and improvisation (see Ihab Hassan, 'The Literature of Silence'); they are not indifferent to meaning; but neither are they, for that matter, 'apocalyptic, anti-rational, blatantly joyous and sentimental' products of 'an age dedicated to joyous misology and prophetic irresponsibility . . .' as Leslie Fiedler once enthused (in 'Cross that Border – Close that Gap: Postmodernism'.) Instead the arsenal of what are generally called postmodernist literary techniques is trained upon the creation of significant points through epistemic dislocations, in excess of the real, where new recognitions can be made: 'The mind orders reality,' says Sukenick, 'not by imposing ideas on it but by discovering significant relations within it.'[7]

II

Before Modernism there was a period of linguistic innocence when it was believed that language could conform to reality or nature like a second skin, following exactly the contours of experience. This was the period of romanticism and of realism (with differing emphases on the degree of interiority accomplished by language but a shared faith in its powers). The snake in this Eden was the discovery of the arbitrary nature of the sign; in Saussure's fatal vision of separation the worlds of discourse and things split apart, a process already imaginatively anticipated by the novels of James, Proust, Woolf and Joyce as a necessary consequence of the elaboration of realism within the novel form, so that even in late James we have the detached signifier, emptied of referential, and increasingly, of symbolic freight. Contemporary writers have to reckon with the fissure between words and things as a matter of course. Thus, for example, William Gass speaks of 'the arbitrary relationship between symbol sounds and their meanings', but, he adds, 'no real writer wants it that way.'[8]

An early response to the popularization of this idea was playfulness, a gratifying literary freedom; delight in story telling and fabulation; or self-referentiality, metafiction. John Barth, Robert Coover, even Saul Bellow and Bernard Malamud found a gleeful challenge in this openness. But also, a despair. The openness came to look like closedness, as reality balefully (and joyfully) persisted in the face of fiction's dismissal of it. Barth's 'used-upness' of certain forms came to look like an apt description of his own prose experiments, sailing off in amphorae on mythical waters. The challenge then became the *re*-attachment of words to things: in the certain knowledge of arbitrariness of signification a new kind of adequation is called for; making the shock of connection across the prised-apart worlds.

[7]Sukenick, *Musing The Obscure*, p. 12.
[8]Gass, interview in LeClair, *Anything Can Happen* p. 160.

As Ronald Sukenick puts it, the desire is to 'bang' the readers with reality,[9] and to close the gap between words and things, a fiction must be 'not an ideological formulation of belief but a statement of a favorable rapport with reality.'[10]

Behind Sukenick's remarks is a desire to reclose the broken circle and make a fuller unity, in which the creative is not set off from the critical, nor are these simply mirrors of one another:

> When consciousness of its own form is incorporated in the dynamic structure of the text – its composition, as painters say – theory can once again become part of the story rather than about it. . . . one of the tasks of modern fiction, then, is to displace, energize, and re-embody its criticism – to literally reunite it with our experience of the text.[11]

This is an idea resembling romantic irony: including an awareness of the work's own form within itself in the service of a larger unity. But for the romantics symbolism offered a bridge between realms, either philosophically, as for Emerson and his followers; or aesthetically, as for those who refused epistemological idealism but, like Hawthorne and Melville, saw the possibilities of romantic philosophy in engendering meaning in fiction. No such resource is available for contemporary writers whose faith in the referential possibilities of language has come unstuck and whose view of symbolism is entirely distrustful. The acerbic recognition in Joseph Heller's *Catch-22* of the language manipulations of war-time power structures, or the demoralizing inquiries of Thomas Pynchon among the corridors and lumber rooms of history and the linguistic deformations of the technocracy in *Gravity's Rainbow* and *The Crying of Lot 49*, insist upon a refusal of even the possibility of real communication, unless it might be a desire for the one 'epileptic' word that would begin and end communication in a fatal fusing of the realms. Instead we are shown the demons of information science, and the success of linguistic shifters like Major Major.

Many of the theoretical pronouncements from these writers seem initially to promote an active anti-historicism: 'a novel conveys information about itself,'[12] 'a novel is a flow of energy and feeling as in a piece of music not a subject matter as in a newspaper. I mean if all you want to do is convey information why not write journalism.'[13] So, in a shift similar to that made decades ago by poets and abstract painters, and heralded but never quite achieved in fiction even by Gertrude Stein, the irrealists attempt to produce a writing that is its own justification, saying that fiction like poetry, 'will not only mean, but it will be,'[14] and that:

The obligation of fiction is to rescue experience from history, from

[9]Sukenick, interview in Bellamy, *The New Fiction*, p. 71.
[10]Sukenick, *Musing The Obscure*, p. 3.
[11]Sukenick, '12 Digressions Toward a Study of Composition,' p. 430.
[12]'12 Digressions,' p. 433.
[13]Sukenick, in *Partisan Review* 40, 1973.
[14]Raymond Federman, *SurFiction*, pp. 13, 14.

politics, from commerce, from theory, even from language itself – from any system, in fact, that threatens to distort, devitalize, or manipulate experience.[15]

But words are different from paint; they carry a whole constellation of meanings along with them. As Raymond Federman now says:

> For a while we had something like *self*-consciousness, and now we have more of a self-*consciousness*. The two terms are not yet separated, but they have achieved a different kind of balance, so that we are going to have much more *consciousness*, much more *reflexiveness* (in the sense of thinking), much more awareness in the novel, with a lesser emphasis on the self. In this sense the novel will reconnect with the outer world, not necessarily with reality, but with history – history which is, of course, also a form of fiction, 'a dream already dreamt and destroyed,' as John Hawkes once put it.[16]

An awareness of fictionality does not necessarily deny history its weight; it merely refuses its manipulative effect as system. Behind the play of these language games is a registered historical presence and the event of irrealism (to adapt John Barth's term: not 'antirealism or unrealism, but irrealism'[17]), is an engagement across the separated poles. But how can history be said to be actually engaged in these texts?

The possibility is perhaps best demonstrated by an example from Walter Abish's *In the Future Perfect* (1975). In 'The English Garden' an academic visitor to a town in Germany called Brumholdstein discusses his sexual adventure with Ingeborg Platt, the local librarian, and his purchase of a colouring book for his child. It soon becomes evident that a larger interest lies in his awareness that Brumholdstein is actually a new town created on the site of the Durst concentration camp. This knowledge profoundly alters even such apparently trivial matters as the drawings in his colouring book, filled with contented and good-humoured Germans: 'The country, according to the coloring book, is once again bursting with activity, a deep compressed energy that on every page displays a space for the color that will become its driving force.' The reader is thus required to speculate on the nature of that energy that is waiting only to take on colouration. Ingeborg Platt, too, develops a new significance and historical presence when we learn that her father '. . . had been a colonel in the Waffen SS. I showed her my coloring book,' continues the narrator 'and the crayons, surprised by her response. "It is a gift for my little boy," I said, forcibly having to restrain her from coloring the pages. "Is your father alive," I asked her cautiously.'[18]

This narrative is a force-field, a 'field of action, a context that will modify whatever enters it.' Although there is not necessarily plot or a story

[15]Sukenick, '12 Digressions,' p. 434.
[16]Federman, interview in LeClair, *Anything Can Happen*, p. 141.
[17]Barth, interview in Bellamy, *The New Fiction* p. 3.
[18]Walter Abish, *In The Future Perfect* (1984) p. 12.

in a narrative, 'there is always a field of action, and in a field of action the way energy moves should be the most obvious element.[19] The force-field, although it is first and most importantly the product of the interactions of words and language structures may also be seen to be composed of elements which pre-exist in the consciousness of the reader, who no longer needs to be told in detail of the underlying assumptions behind fiction but will instantly 'fill in' from the cultural superstore created and serviced by the media and by homogeneous educational resources. As E.L. Doctorow, author of *Ragtime* and *The Book of Daniel*, puts it, the rhythms of perception in most people who read today, have been transformed by films and television.[20] And by history, one is compelled to add, a history so over-powering and omnipresent that it may be most powerfully suggested through elision, as in Abish's story here, or in his fuller exploration of Brumholdstein in *How German Is It (Wie Deutsch Ist Es)*.

In another of Abish's short pieces, 'In So Many Words' we find italicized an apparently meaningless collage of terms:

34
also America American are as brains but city come etc. every imprinted in institutions like live major mapped not of one only other outlines parks people streets the this to visit well who work.

But the next section rearranges the scrambled message:

43
Like every other American city in America, the outlines of this one, as well as the major streets, institutions, parks, etc., are not only mapped but also imprinted on the brains of the people who live, work, or come to visit the city.[21]

In this instance, what seems at first a merely formal investigation of the different properties of language when disposed as list or as sentence becomes on closer examination exemplary of its own proposition: that the language, like the city, is imprinted on the mind, so that in the words of the next section, 'Looking at a map of the city [or the sentence] is like peering deep into the brain.'[22] And conversely, to alphabeticize language is to 'retake the reality studio' as William Burroughs suggested, is to offer suggestive liberations of the obsessive patternings encoded in culture and language. It seems reasonable to argue that the predilection of recent fiction for narcissistic experience, and especially its use of sexual description as a come-on refers back to the fundamental psychic realities of the culture. And of course, to be inside a force-field is to be unable to adopt a position of externality and objective indifference. As Donald Barthelme says in *City Life* there is also '. . . the brain damage caused by art. I could describe it better if I weren't afflicted with it.'[23]

[19]Sukenick, '12 Digressions', pp. 434, 435.
[20]Doctorow, interview in LeClair *Anything Can Happen*, p. 99.
[21]*In The Future Perfect* p. 74.
[22]*How German Is It*, p. 75.
[23]Donald Barthelme, 'Brain Damage'.

Abish's and Barthelme's work provides an effective instance of the way in which irrealists may be engaging indirectly with the assumed realities of the culture, using techniques such as collage 'to modify the world by adding to its store of objects the literary object', at which point the question becomes: 'what is the nature of the new object?'[24] The object does not actually mean something, but it is not necessarily thereby out of all relation with the world. The narrator of Barthelme's 'See the Moon' hopes that one day the elements of his collage of views will 'merge, blur – cohere is the word maybe – into something meaningful.' This hope may be less forlorn than it appears, given Sukenick's perceptive note on collage in '12 Digressions':

> The idea of collage linkage implies discontinuity and the value of the collage fragment in itself, beyond any system. Causal narrative implies continuity and wholeness, but with the constant threat of discontinuity and fragmentation. Non-causal narrative implies discontinuity and fragmentation *reaching towards continuity and wholeness*, which seems more appropriate to a time when mystiques and their processes are laid bare.[25]

Another metafictionist, Raymond Federman, says that his interest in destroying illusions (of verisimilitude) is not simply for the sake of destroying illusions, but 'in order that we may face up to reality, and now what passes for reality.' Federman's *The Voice in the Closet* is, although fictional, a version of his own experience at the age of 13 in 1942 when he was hidden in a closet while his parents and sisters were deported to Auschwitz, where they died.[26] Federman and Abish then, would agree with John Hawkes that 'history and the inner psychic history must dance their creepy minuet together if we are to save ourselves from total oblivion.'[27] In fact such traumatic realities are frequently presented as a backdrop to the inner life of the voices (one can hardly call them characters) of irrealist fictions. So Sukenick, in *98.6*, registers the oppressive undismissable phantoms of modern consciousness:

> 1/7 the blond comes in two parts here comes the second part she falls in love with him. It happens during a party of the first part the two of them drinking wine in the sun the wine is the color of her hair her hair is the color of the light this precious light he thinks insipidly but that's okay gloating over the fact that he's not dead. That's what he does when he's in a good mood he gloats over not being dead especially not dead by suffocation under a pile of shit in the camp latrine say or beaten to death by guards after having been forced to copulate with his daughter or watch

[24]Barthelme, 'After Joyce', in *Location 1*, quoted by Larry McCaffery in *The Metafictional Muse*, p. 118.
[25]Sukenick, '12 Digressions' (italics added), p. 437.
[26]Federman, interview in LeClair, *Anything Can Happen*, pp. 142, 144.
[27]Hawkes, conversation with Robert Scholes on *The Blood Oranges*, in *Novel* (Spring, 1972), p. 205.

his wife being gangraped or being thrown out of a helicopter after torture interrogation or having his skin toasted off in a napalm attack or any of a number of grotesqueries he carries in his memory of the vast culture failures of recent generations.[28]

Jay Martin, writing in 1979 in the *Partisan Review*, had some harsh words to describe the work of the Fiction Collective, of which Sukenick has been a founder. He saw the group as the product of the 50s and 60s, a historical period characterized by 'personal affluence, social abundance, behavioural permissiveness and political indifference.'[29] Even passing over the inadequacy of this summation of the period of McCarthyism and Korea, the Cold War, Freedom Marches, Vietnam protests and the extraordinary politicization of youth in the 60s, we can still see that political indifference is not an accurate description of fiction like 98.6, a satire of the USA, 'Frankenstein', and the attempts of the 'children of Frankenstein' to build an alternative culture 'the monster'. The monster, of course, as an alternative ideology, is equally inescapable: 'After all that's why you create a monster to do things you can't do. Isn't it? And then it does them to you.'[30] Rather than assume that such writers are indifferent to the politics of their time it seems preferable to acknowledge their different way of approaching the issues, from the inside out, as it were. Thus Sukenick, also in *Partisan Review*: 'Our particular moment and place is located in our heads and our bodies and at the risk of solipsism we must start there and push outwards.'[31] Jay Martin attacks such ideas as idealist-existentialist aesthetics[32] but the implication that exterior reality is denied by Sukenick's stance is contradicted in a recent interview in which Sukenick says his feeling is that 'you always have to move in the direction of the data of experience in reality, whatever the chances that you can't do this', and argues that although language does not make any direct relation with reality it does make a changing metaphorical contact with the world through breaking down the old constructs.[33]

We must ask what happens to language when it becomes literature. Words have meanings, but their meanings in the literary object are not the same as their meanings in ordinary discourse. William Gass offers the entertaining example of the word 'Gents':

> Words mean things. Thus we use them every day: make love, buy bread, and blow up bridges. But the use of language in fiction only mimics its use in life. A sign like GENTS, for instance, tells me where to pee. It conveys information; it produces feelings of glad relief. I use the sign but I dare not dawdle under it. It might have read MEN or borne a moustache. This kind of sign passes out of consciousness, is extin-

[28]Sukenick, 98.6, p. 32.
[29]Jay Martin, in *Partisan Review* 46, 1979, on the Fiction Collective, p. 287.
[30]Sukenick, 98.6, p. 95.
[31]Sukenick, in *Partisan Review* 39 (1972), p. 450.
[32]Martin, in *Partisan Review* 46, p. 281.
[33]Interview in LeClair, *Anything Can Happen* pp. 282, 283.

guished by its use. In literature, however, the sign remains; it sings, and we return to it again and again.[34]

Gass thinks that the relation of literature to life can be compared to the two parts of a metaphor, tenor and vehicle: literature has a metaphorical relation to the real, rather than a directly descriptive function. This provides a route by which even this most famous proponent of the dissociation between art and reality can be perceived as working in relation to the real: his 'there are no descriptions in fiction, only constructions,'[35] therefore not a rallying cry for irrelevance but a recognition of the facts, like his suggestion that '. . . a word is like a schoolgirl's room, a complete mess – so the great thing is to make out a way of seeing it all as ordered, as right, as inferred and following.'[36]

Although Sukenick says that he never agreed with Gass's position (of pure formalism, presumably,)[37] his identification of a metaphoric relation between literature and reality echoes Gass's opinion that the two can be compared to the tenor and vehicle of metaphor and indicates that there is (now at least) common ground between these writers.

More common ground, and more unexpected perhaps, can be found in the comments of Tom Wolfe, doyen of the world of things:

> The best thing is to have *both* – to have someone who will bring you bigger and more exciting chunks of the outside world *plus* a unique sensibility, or rather a unique way of looking at the world, a unique fantasy life even, to use the way Freud explains it, a unique emotional reality of his own that somehow echoes or vibrates with the emotional states of the reader. So that you get both the external reality and the subjective reality. I'm not denying the existence of a subjective reality. Far from it. I'm just saying that there is also an objective reality that everyone in the world has to deal with.[38]

The problem remains, of course, how to achieve any such integration, given the acknowledged difficulty of conforming the worlds of language and of things in a period of almost universal scepticism about their interrelatedness. To say that the contact between the fiction and the world is metaphorical may be as precise a statement as we can manage at this point; but it hardly establishes why some constructions of literary metaphor function more powerfully than others and possibly just substitutes the larger mystery for the lesser.

All writers are of course engaged in the negotiation of meaning. The other answer to the riddle of reconnection between words and things, language and experience, is the route of invisible fiction, and this has been increasingly significant in recent American writing. The articulation of

---

[34]William H. Gass, *Fiction and the Figures of Life*, pp. 30, 31.
[35]Interview in LeClair, *Anything Can Happen*, pp. 172, 173 and *Fiction and the Figures of Life*, p. 17
[36]Interview in LeClair, *Anything Can Happen*, p. 160.
[37]LeClair, *Anything Can Happen* p. 282.
[38]Tom Wolfe, interview in Bellamy, *The New Fiction*, p. 90.

alternative language and ethnic experience is perhaps the most obvious example, in the work of writers like Alice Walker, or Toni Morrison. The urgency of the historical messages of these writers, and their sense that language and experience must be won away from the 'cruel fallout of racism' inherent in Standard English and its non-recognition of the other language of black people, to use Toni Morrison's terms,[39] disallows too much fictive self-consciousness. We must, however, avoid any reductive assumption that such works simply reproduce experience in its authentic voice as autobiography. Fiction is still fiction, even when it uses the cloak of autobiography.

A similar emphasis emerges in the work of the Dirty Realists, as Bill Buford calls writers like Raymond Carver, Richard Ford, Elizabeth Tallent and Jayne Anne Phillips in a recent issue of *Granta*.[40] Dirty Realism is a catchy but perhaps inaccurate name for the new vernacular writing, in the same way that the American realists and naturalists of the late nineteenth century were assumed to find a fascination in all the sordid aspects of life; in fact much of the work of these writers is impossible to group under this term. But it does offer an intimation of the unwavering, unabashed gaze brought to bear on the details of working-class – or perhaps in America we should say redneck – experience: of hunting, shooting, and fishing, unemployment, divorce and inarticulacy. Of these the last is the most significant, for this writing focuses itself through the problematic expression of vernacular voices, and the silences that surround them. Thus it evades the question with which this essay begins, of the relation of language to the world, by restricting itself to the language of people in the world, not simply in dialogue but in the narrative and descriptive sequences also.

Raymond Carver, the best known of these vernacularists, whose *Will You Please Be Quiet, Please* (1976), *What We Talk About When We Talk About Love* (1974), and *Cathedral* (1983) have recently arrived in an accessible collected edition (*The Stories of Raymond Carver*), provides differing voices in his stories, echoing the expression of the characters portrayed. 'After the Denim' offers a typical idiom in describing the actions of a retired accountant and his wife after an ambiguous encounter with pushy young people at their regular Bingo evening:

> He shut the door and spit the last of the juice into the sink. Then he rinsed his mouth and made himself a cup of instant coffee. He carried it into the living room. He sat down in front of the TV and lit a cigarette. He understood that it only took one lunatic and a torch to bring everything to ruin.

Carver was much affected by the teachings of John Gardner, when he himself was an unpublished novelist teaching creative writing in Chico State College, California. It was known that John Gardner carried his

[39]Toni Morrison, interview in *Anything Can Happen*, pp. 256, 257.
[40]'Dirty Realism: New Writing From America.' *Granta 8* (Harmondsworth: Penguin Books, 1983).

unpublished work around with him in boxes, as Carver became acutely aware when trying to write his first serious fictions in Gardner's borrowed office. These handings on of influence are always appealing to critics, who like to notice that Thoreau built his cabin on Emerson's land, or that Hawthorne bought Thoreau's boat. But in this case the power of connection is attested to by Carver's own account of 'John Gardner: The Writer as Teacher' in his collection of essays and poetry, *Fires* (1985). It was Gardner's conviction, says Carver, that 'if the words in the story were blurred because of the author's insensitivity, carelessness, or sentimentality, then the story suffered from a tremendous handicap. But there was something even worse and something that must be avoided at all costs: if the words and sentiments were dishonest, the author was faking it, writing about things he didn't care about or believe in, then nobody could ever care anything about it.' This, says Carver, 'is what I've kept by me in the years since that brief but all-important time.'[41]

It is Carver's view, and borne out in his stories, that it is possible to write about commonplace objects and things using 'commonplace but precise language' and thereby to endow those things, which may be as simple as a chair, a fork, a woman's earrings, 'with immense, even startling power'. The essay in which these notes appear, 'On Writing', concludes: 'The words can be so precise they may even sound flat, but they can still carry; if used right, they can hit all the notes.'[42]

Other critics have noticed that in this writing, it isn't so much the words used as those not used, the silences that surround them, that strike home.[43] At its best, the writing seems as hard, spare and finished as a stone; or as limited, inconclusive, and total as an ordinary conversation that is, nevertheless, all there is. Their titles, if we may borrow a favourite form of the irrealists, the list, will give a sense of his work:

They're not your husband
Are you a doctor?
Nobody said anything
What's in Alaska?
What do you do in San Fransisco
The student's wife
Put yourself in my shoes
Bicycles, muscles, cigarets
Will you please be quiet, please

In most of Carver's characters there is a sort of lucid madness, enabling us to glimpse the parameters of an experience that appears so ordinary, so everyday, that it creates a kind of awe, and which, when we stop to think about it, is not ordinary at all. A man lays out the furniture of his living

[41]Raymond Carver, *Fires*, p. 45.
[42]*Fires*. pp. 24, 27.
[43]Buford, for example, in *Granta 8*, p. 5.

room on the front lawn; this would not be so striking except that he lays it out in order, and connects up the electrical equipment. When a young couple stop to make him an offer for some of the pieces he invites them to drink whisky, and they dance to his record player. The story concludes with a note of the effect of this on the girl:

> Weeks later, she said: 'The guy was about middle-aged. All his things right there in the yard. No lie. We got real pissed and danced. In the driveway. Oh, my God. Don't laugh. He played us these records. Look at this record-player. The old guy gave it to us. And all these crappy records. Will you look at this shit?'
>
> She kept talking. She told everyone. There was more to it, and she was trying to get it talked out. After a time, she quit trying.[44]

Carver's people resemble Hemingway's damaged heroes, the walking wounded of stories like 'Big Two-Hearted River'; but Carver's people suffer not from the ravages of war but the atrophy of their culture: they have the brain-damage caused by TV, bowling alleys and trailer parks, the lack of money and the lack of words to cope with their experiences. But just as Henry James elevated cliché into sublime expression, so Carver manages to imbue his characters' voices with a desperate fluency: 'There was this funny thing of anything could happen now that we realized everything had.'[45] Brain damage may be, finally, the best way to describe these 'odd gaps in consciousness concerning the new conditions, and the curious lacunae in the conditions themselves . . .,'[46] perceived by both the irrealists and the new realists.

---

[44]'Why don't you dance?' in *What We Talk About When We Talk About Love, Stories*, p. 191.
[45]'Gazebo', in *What We Talk About, Stories*, p. 202.
[46]Sukenick, *Long Talking Bad Conditions Blues*, p. 22.

Note
Below, I list a number of books and periodicals relating to the three main areas addressed in the paper: critical theory of postmodernism, theory of the subject and the concept of character. Obviously there is some overlapping between these categories.

Postmodernism
Jean-François Lyotard, *The Postmodern Condition: A Report on Knowledge* (1979; Manchester, 1984); Richard Rorty, 'Habermas and Lyotard on Postmodernity', *Praxis International*, 1984; Fredric Jameson, 'Postmodernism or the Cultural Logic of Late Capital', *New Left Review*, 146, July 1984; Hal Foster (ed.), *Postmodern Culture* (London, 1985); Michael Benamou and Charles Caramello (eds.), *Performance in Postmodern Culture* (Wisconsin, 1977); Charles Caramello, *Silverless Mirrors: Book, Self and Postmodern American Fiction* (Florida, 1983); Robert Kroes (ed.), *The American Identity: Fusion and Fragmentation* (Amsterdam, 1982); Christopher Butler, *After the Wake: An Essay on the Contemporary Avant-Garde* (Oxford, 1980); Christopher Butler, 'The Pleasures of the Experimental Text', Jeremy Hawthorn (ed.), *Criticism and Critical Theory* (London, 1984); Ihab and Sally Hassan, *Innovations/Renovations* (Wisconsin, 1983); Manfred Pütz, *The Story of Identity: American Fiction of the Sixties* (Stuttgart, 1979); Harry R. Garvin (ed.), *Romanticism, Modernism, Postmodernism* (London, 1980); Alan Wilde, *Horizons of Assent: Modernism, Postmodernism and the Ironic Imagination* (Baltimore, 1981).

The Subject
Amélie Rorty (ed.), *The Identities of Persons* (Berkeley, 1976); Michel Foucault and Richard Sennett, 'Sexuality and Solitude', *London Review of Books*, May 21, 1981; Editorial Collective, 'Psychology, Ideology and the Human Subject', *Ideology and Consciousness*, I, May 1977; see also Stuart Hall's response, 'Some Problems with the Ideology/Subject Couplet', followed by the authors' reply, in the third issue of the same journal, Spring 1978; Julian Henriques (*et al.*), *Changing the Subject: Psychology, Social Regulation and Subjectivity* (London, 1984); Peter Leonard, *Personality and Ideology: Towards a Materialist Understanding of the Subject* (London, 1984); Joel Whitebook, 'Saving the Subject: Modernity and the Problem of the Autonomous Individual' *Telos*, 50, Winter, 1981–2; David Carroll, *The Subject in Question: The Language of Theory and the Strategies of Fiction* (Chicago, 1982); Centre for Contemporary Cultural Studies, *Culture, Media, Language* (London, 1980); Rosalind Coward and John Ellis, *Language and Materialism: Developments in Semiology and the Theory of the Subject* (London, 1977); Fred Dallmayr, *Twilight of Subjectivity: Contributions to a Post-Individualistic Theory of Politics* (Amherst, 1981); Charles Lamore, 'The Concept of a Constitutive Subject', Colin McCabe (ed.), *The Talking Cure: Essays in Psychoanalysis and Language* (London, 1981).

Character
Leo Bersani, *A Future for Astyanax: Character and Desire in Literature* (New York, 1976); Rawdon Wilson, 'The Bright Chimera: Character as a Literary Term', *Critical Inquiry*, Summer 1979; Roberta Satow, 'Narcissism or Individualism?', *Partisan Review*, 2, 1981; Jacquelyn Kegley, 'The End of the Road: The Death of Individualism', A. Phillips Griffiths (ed.), *Philosophy and Literature* (Cambridge, 1984); Robert Adams, 'Rags, Garbage, Fantasy', *Bad Mouth: Fugitive Papers on the Dark Side* (California, 1977); Thomas Docherty, *Reading Absent Character* (Oxford, 1984); Martin Price, 'The Other Self: Thoughts About Character in the Novel', Maynard Mack (ed.), *Imagined Worlds* (London, 1968); Hélène Cixous, 'The Character of "Character" ', *New Literary History*, 5, 2, Winter 1974; 'Character as a Lost Cause' (symposium), *Novel*, II, 3, 1978; Malcolm Bradbury, 'Putting in the Person: Character and Abstraction in Current Writing and Painting', *The Contemporary English Novel* (London, 1980); Anne Jefferson, *The Nouveau Roman and the Poetics of Fiction* (Cambridge, 1980).

4

The Eccentric Self: Anti-Characterization and the Problem of the Subject in American Postmodernist Fiction

Peter Currie

> The one thing which we seek with insatiable desire is to forget ourselves, to be surprised out of our propriety. . . . Emerson, *Circles*

I

'It doesn't exist, America,' a character in Henry Miller's *Tropic of Cancer* (1934) remarks, 'it's a name you give to an abstract idea.' The 'postmodern' American novel has a similarly equivocal status. Many writers and critics justifiably contest the introduction of yet another vague concept – the postmodern – into a critical lexicon overstocked with amorphous and unwieldy categories, and insist upon the diverse and unique qualities, the specific characteristics of particular works subsumed under that undiscriminating heading. At the risk of appearing to sanction that lack of critical rigour and precision, the postmodern rubric has been retained here in order to aid the task of provisionally grouping together and determining the significant interactions between a collection of relatively autonomous American novels, from the mid-60s onwards, which in some ways represent a shift in literary direction – a departure from, if not an advance on, the premises of Modernist practice.

My method throughout, in keeping with the fiction discussed, is less syncretic – intent, that is, on resolving discordant contradictions into a harmonious closure – than openly pluralistic: a speculative interdisciplinary approach rather than a modish eclecticism, the analysis moving inwards yet working outwards from the novels into larger, ideological concerns, observing the correspondences between contemporary literary activity, cultural, social and economic practices. The aim is to provide a conspectus of recent 'experimental' fiction, focusing primarily on the marginalization of character, rather than to attempt a comprehensive account of a remarkably productive period. To recognize certain regularities is not, I stress, to argue for a unanimity of effect. My purpose is to demonstrate equivalences and affinities between the novels without eliminating their alterity or otherness. For however we choose to define or circumscribe the American version of postmodernism – 'version' since it is an on-going international movement of relatively recent date, a historically specific phenomenon rather than a categorical hypostatization – it should not be regarded as a homogeneous aesthetic creed, individual writers merely aspects of the one corporate identity.

Perhaps it is a solecism after all. Can we have a post-Modern style when there never was a uniform Modernist style to begin with? How are the post-modernists to be differentiated from the modernists? Have we witnessed a periodic mutation, holistic shift or rapid change of consensus? Is there, to adapt Foucault's concept, a distinctively postmodern *épistème* or dis-cursive formation which breaks decisively with the tenets of what we now agree to call Modernism? Or is Frank Kermode correct in distinguishing a postwar neo-Modernism which continues to exploit – at less exalted level but without abrupt epistemological cleavage – the stylistic conventions characteristic of the 'high Modernism' of the early twentieth century? I am here less interested in tracing uninterrupted continuities, a unilinear development or teleological progression, than noting the ways in which postmodern fiction is discontinuous with, or runs counter to, the poetics of the 'modern' tradition; in demonstrating differences and transformations without thereby positing a seismic rift in the cultural sensibility, still less proposing a theory of a unitary Spirit of the Age, something like a mono-lithic postmodern *Zeitgeist* (Pound's term *paideuma*, borrowed from the anthropologist Frobenius, is preferred; a disentangling of the 'inrooted ideas of the period . . . the gristly roots of ideas that are in action').

If postmodern fiction presupposes a familiarity with the literature and art of the modern period, it further presumes at least an acquaintance with the critical scaffolding which now surrounds that imposing edifice, Modernism. For postmodernism contests not Modernism as such so much as that view of Modernism – domesticated, contained and rendered harmless – refracted to us through the mythopoeic lenses of the old New Criticism. In much recent fiction, for example, no particular order or 'point of view' is privileged, with the narrative voice as moral arbiter or the comfortable camaraderie of an irony assuming shared values: 'irony', Barthes once remarked, 'always proceeds from a *sure* site'. The constituent elements of the postmodern text seldom integrate thematically nor do the characters cohere psychologically; discontinuities of narrative and disjunc-tions of personality cannot be overcome – as they often can with canonical Modernism, however scrambled or unstructured character or text may first appear – by an appeal to the logic of a unifying 'symbolic' metalanguage, a dominant stable discourse, settled hierarchy or the consistency of a core self. Obviously indebted to the innovations of the major tradition preceding it, postmodernism could also be understood as the revolt of epigone against mentor, actively opposing the techniques of a revered precursor (Nietzsche: 'If something is falling, give it a shove'). Yet there can be no emergent postmodernism without its residual Modernist com-ponent, nor without the shadow of an ill-defined realism, the rough magic of which – the Cratylist tradition with its belief in the intrinsic connection of word and object, 'the Voodoo at the heart of mimetic theory' in Ronald Sukenick's phrase – both Modernist and postmodernist alike abjure. The contemporary postmodern aesthetic gestures towards or openly incorporates Modernist strategies where appropriate – recourse to a mythic and archetypal order, arcane reference, surreptitious allusion – only the more effectively to sunder, by relentless parody or direct inversion, its symbiotic relation to Modernist iconography and style.

This ludic propensity, the general playfulness of much recent American writing, is surely in part a protest against the formality, the standing-on-ceremony of High Modernism in its more solemn, as opposed to serious, moments; an attempt also to renounce the superficial espousal of existential *Angst*, the enfeebled 'meaninglessness of life' routines of absurdist drama and fiction of the early postwar period. 'I tend to think of tragedy as a kind of adolescent response to the universe', the novelist Robert Coover has commented, 'the higher truth is a comic response.' Similarly, in his neglected *A Child's History of America* (1973) – a generically indeterminate book, ostensibly autobiography but more an intellectual peregrination, a Baedeker to the events and ideas of the 60s – Charles Newman queries

> Why is this *nothingness*, so schematic, so transcendental in its force, always described in terms of forlornness, nausea, alienation, etc.? Why does dwelling upon death and neurosis reveal more of existence than concentrating upon life? There is a peculiar brand of American 'nothingness', after all, which has always been profoundly, if just as a-priorily, optimistic. . . . If we do live in a world of signifiers, why describe it as vicious rather than magical, in the terminology of circumscription rather than access?[1]

Thomas Pynchon, Ronald Sukenick, Gilbert Sorrentino, Robert Coover, Raymond Federman, Ishmael Reed ('check out Ishmael Reed' Pynchon urges us midway through *Gravity's Rainbow*) all show a predilection for intellectual clowning and habitual recourse to persiflage – a levity, it need hardly be added, in no way contrary to serious intent. 'If there's one fundamental thing about this fiction', Raymond Federman commented in conversation with Ronald Sukenick, 'it's that it's always amusing, always full of laughter. It's always playful . . . playful for the sake of playfulness.' American culture may have the power to co-opt what threatens to undermine it, Federman acknowledges, 'but playfulness', Sukenick contends, 'is the kind of thing an established and official culture cannot tolerate'. Modernist tragedy, we could say, repeats itself as postmodernist 'farce'. It is this exuberantly ludic quality of the new American fiction – 'it all comes back to that', to recall Henry James's preface to *The Golden Bowl*, 'to my and your "fun", if we but allow the term its full extension' – which most

---

[1]Charles Newman, *A Child's History of America* (Chicago, Swallow Press, 1973), p. 68.

clearly distinguishes it from the work of the 'new' (and 'nouveau nouveau') French novelists.[2]

Many contemporary American novels are conventionally labelled 'metafictional' or 'self-referential'. By way of summary, a metafictional novel or self-referential text refers openly to its own devices and strategies, turns on itself to debate its fictional nature, to exhibit its 'made-upness.' The writer's problems in constructing the novel are prominently displayed, the reader kept constantly aware of the fabricated nature of the enterprise, the authorial voice abruptly disrupting the spectacle, dispelling the illusion, intruding like an uninvited guest into the body of the text. Unlike the novel of social realism which presents itself unproblematically to the reader as a transparent window on the world ('Good prose', Orwell claimed in his essay 'Why I Write', 'is like a window pane'), the postmodern 'metatext' focuses attention on the pane of glass itself, on the lexical surface of the page rather than on a reality divorced from the contrivances of fiction, the figures and practices of discourse. The postmodern novel repeatedly lays bare the conditions of its existence in signifying practice, the mode and process of its production, revealing itself as a factitious got-up assemblage. By so demystifying the activity of composition, writing is liberated from its thralldom to the referent, a reality 'out there' (or 'in here') which it was formerly its duty to transcribe. Foregrounding rather than effacing its status simply as writing, 'value', following Barthes's later hedonistic conception of textual freeplay and *jouissance*, 'is shifted to the sumptuous rank of the signifier': which is the pleasure of the text.

I shall suggest a correlation between the phenomenon of self-reflexive narrative and introspective self-absorption in American culture – a metafictional textual narcissism corresponding to a widespread inward-turningness. Yet the tendency of recent fiction to reflect critically on the nature of its own fictionality is as much worthy of commendation for rejecting once and for all the myth of 'organic form' as it is open to the reproach of idealism, of retreating from an empirical reality (somehow prior to signification) the better to contemplate its own navel. The debate for and against postmodernist self-consciousness can be seen most starkly in the competing yet interrelated claims of the early *Tel Quel* group (arguing for the larger political import of postmodernist innovation, connecting radical signifying practice – the novel at the barricades – with revolutionary praxis) and the embattled anti-modernist position of Lukács (berating modernism for its abstract, ahistorical, metaphysical tendencies). Recent critical approaches to self-referential fiction favour either a broadly 'materialist' interpretation (drawing attention to the active production of meaning) or denigrate metafiction as a sterile and arid 'formalism' (a self-infatuated preening, a hyperconscious textuality).

Reading the postmodern text we have to content ourselves, like Keats's

[2]Federman and Sukenick, 'The New Innovative Fiction', *Antaeus*, 20, Winter 1976, pp. 146, 148.

Chameleon Poet, with remaining in doubts and uncertainties, stalking the work without ány irritable reaching after fact and reason, willing to let go, at every turn of the page, our tentative schemes to accommodate the text as the recalcitrant narrative disarms critical speculation by refusing readily to yield any manageable frame of reference. This suspension of certainty and postponement of premature foreclosure places the critic in an especially invidious position as he or she vaguely discerns, perched behind the narrator, the figure of the fugitive author (grinning gargoyle-like from some remote corner of the text) hugely enjoying the reader's earnest and pathetic attempts at recuperation.

The prominent foregrounding in the postmodern novel of the intimate relation between reader and text directs attention away from the interaction of characters to the imaginative collaboration of implied reader and the fiction-making process; a shift away from the author–text axis, with its hierarchy of active author and passive reader, to writing and reading as undifferentiated, symbiotic activities. That the work of writing implies that of reading as its dialectical correlative is an obvious point to make, perhaps, but one which Sartre insists upon in *What is Literature?* (1948): 'it is the conjoint effort of author and reader which brings upon the scene that concrete and imaginary object which is the work of the mind. There is no art except for and by others.' A statement later endorsed by Robbe-Grillet in *For a New Novel* (1963): 'far from neglecting him the author today proclaims his absolute need of the reader's cooperation, an active, conscious, creative assistance.' Given that a book is an intentional object which requires reference to the act of reading as constitutive of its mode of being, it may be said to exist in itself only in a 'not-yet' condition, a potentiality which is realized, a virtuality produced, brought into being through the activity of reading. The goal of literary work, Barthes claimed in *S/Z* (1970), 'is to make the reader no longer a consumer but a producer of the text'. The reduction of reading to consumption, in Barthes's diagnosis, 'is obviously responsible for the boredom many people feel when confronting the modern ("unreadable") text, or the avant-garde film or painting: to suffer from boredom means that one cannot produce the text, play it, open it out, *make it go*.' Reading the new American fiction – a body of work which demands an especially active form of participation – we are best advised to follow Charles Olson's advice and learn 'how to dance/sitting down'. In his preface to *A Child's History of America* Charles Newman further endorses and encourages this shift in the relative status of sender and receiver by advocating a 'writing without genre' (his own work is a case in point) which

> not only increases the number of voices available to the author, but invites contingencies which do not certify the text as much as they offer access from it. To question one's own means of production is to assist the reader in producing his own text. And it is a marvellous paradox that the recovery of our antecedents requires the reader as collaborator[3]

[3]Newman, *A Child's History*, p. 8.

II

> Maybe the target nowadays is not to discover what we are, but to refuse
> what we are . . . Foucault, 'The Subject and Power'

'In democratic countries', Tocqueville presciently noted, 'each citizen is
habitually engaged in the contemplation of a very puny object, namely,
himself.' David Riesman has similarly characterized the past two decades
in the United States as an era in which 'the cult of what is supposed to be
candour' is widely prevalent, a period of rampant egocentrism and the conspicuous pursuit of self-gratification. Even the briefest sampling of the
comments of the culture pundits – and they are not in short
supply – offers a consensus impression of the American Citizen as
obdurate isolato, marooned like a Crusoe on the reef of self-determining
autonomy. This near pathological individualism, romantic solipsism and
debilitating concern with 'finding yourself' finds expression in the frantic
search for instant salvation in a waste of novel therapies. 'The cosmic', as
Nabokov wryly noted, 'is only one slippery "s" away from the comic.' The
collective social aspect of human mutuality within the community recedes
into the background as the privatized self looms ever larger. In such a
society, as the poet Wendell Berry points out, 'relationships with all other
creatures become competitive and exploitive rather than collaborative and
convivial.' The so-called identity crisis (with the attendant pseudo-rituals
of psychotherapeutic self-discovery) becomes in some quarters a perversely
desirable condition, betokening a finer sensibility, a higher degree of
sensitivity on the sufferer's part. 'It seems likely', Berry continues

> that the identity crisis is a conventional illusion, one of the genres of
> self-indulgence. It can be an excuse for irresponsibility, or a fashionable
> mode of self-dramatization. It is the easiest form of self-flattery – a way
> to construe procrastination as a virtue – based on the romantic assump-
> tion that 'who I really am' is better in some fundamental way than the
> available evidence would suggest.[4]

The conviction that there is a more profound or fundamental self hidden
beneath superficial appearances, a primordial bedrock of identity to be
located by a patient and laborious archaeology of the psyche, is surely
founded on an enduring faith in the existence of some remote yet
accessible Ultima Thule of inwardness, some unimaginable innermost sub-
stratum. (Walter Benjamin noted Brecht's comment that 'depth doesn't
get you anywhere at all. Depth is a separate dimension, it's just
depth – and there's nothing whatever to be seen in it.')[5] The interminable
quest for the chimera of an inviolable identity follows inevitably from the

---

[4]Wendell Berry, *Recollected Essays, 1965–1980* (San Francisco, North Point Press, 1981),
p. 287. David Riesman, 'Egocentrism: Is the American Character Changing?', *Encounter*,
August 1980.
[5]Walter Benjamin, 'Conversations with Brecht', *Understanding Brecht* (London, NLB,
1977), p. 110.

belief that one can never be happy, authentic, genuine, sincere or 'free' until one has finally discovered, through the perilous voyage of self-exploration (an infinite regress to an ever-receding origin), that El Dorado of pure presence and unmediated plenitude of being: The Real Me.

The 'consciousness raising' or 'awareness' movement is probably best understood historically as the secularized variant of a residual Puritan asceticism; for the intense preoccupation with the internal state, the emphasis on introspection and inwardness, the need to account continually for the state of one's inner health (whether spiritual or emotional: witness the voluminous journals and diaries of the early American settlers, the spate of 'candid' autobiographies in the post-war decades) is common to the Protestant Ethic of the Puritan dissenters and the 'narcissistic' personality of our own day. The contemporary discourse of self-awareness and sexuality, the vocabulary of liberation and authenticity, operates as a less overt, ostensibly non-coercive yet equally manipulative mode of social control, addressing the subject in the role of patient-to-be-cured, the passive recipient of freely dispensed 'expert' advice.

'Know Thyself' the Delphic Oracle commands, to which Norman O. Brown in *Love's Body* (1966) replied: 'The solution to the problem of identity is, get lost.' What seems like a facile evasion of the imperative of self-knowledge, a depreciation of the examined life, has an important precedent in Nietzsche, who interpreted Apollo's injunction as meaning exactly the opposite of what one would conclude at first glance: 'What did the god mean who proclaimed to Socrates "Know Thyself"? Did he perhaps mean, "Cease to be concerned about thyself"?' This is in notable contrast to the situation which the social pundits reveal in their commentaries on the condition of contemporary American society: a 'triumph of the therapeutic', an empty exaltation of self in abstraction from other selves, the jargon of authenticity, a 'self-consciousness about the unconscious', in Charles Newman's phrase, quite at odds with the radical 'de-centring' of the subject to be found in the innovative fiction and criticism of the same period. Here the subject is dispersed among the interstices of language, enmeshed within and finally lost among the endless relay of signification, the infinite substitutions in the chain of the signifier (Lacan: 'a signifier is that which represents the subject for another signifier . . . the consequence is that the subject disappears').[6]

On the one side, then, a fetishization of the inmost me, a deification of an original, essential self; on the other, an effective negation and diffraction of the self, a transgression of the identity principle. This explains the pun, of a sort, in my title. For while the 'self' of the title puts itself in quotes – how speak confidently of a self after Hume? – the 'eccentric' which precedes and conceptually qualifies that term should be understood

---

[6]Jacques Lacan, *The Four Fundamental Concepts of Psychoanalysis* (Harmondsworth, Penguin, 1977), p. 207. Norman O. Brown, *Love's Body* (New York, Random House, 1966), p. 161. Nietzsche quoted in Rollo May, *The Courage to Create* (London, Collins, 1976), p. 108.

not in its modern figurative sense, meaning 'a character' ('the individual-ities imported into America', Adorno remarked, 'and divested of their individuality in the process, are called "colourful personalities" ') but in the earlier, literal meaning of the word: 'not centrally placed not refer-able to a fixed centre' (OED). 'The Eccentric Self' – not, in other words, the unity and self-presence of the 'centermentalized' subject; it is a de-centring which is intended, an acknowledgement of the truth disco-vered by Freud as resurrected in Lacan's creative (mis) reading: 'the self's radical ex-centricity to itself'.[7]

Lacan was never slow to denounce, usually in scathing terms, the domestication of psychoanalysis as handmaiden to American ideology. He saw in the 'identity quests' of the ego-psychologists an effort to inoculate the culture against the horrors of the Freudian plague. The American psychoanalytic industry (the school of therapy-as-adjustment and adapta-tion to things as they are) he believed inculcated a socially acceptable pattern of neurosis which effectively reinforced existing social conditions and defused the potentially revolutionary theory he discovered in his return to the 'radical' Freud – hence the fairly recent, if still wary, recon-ciliation of materialist and psychoanalytic discourse. The ubiquitous shrink is given equally short shrift in recent American fiction. There is the paranoid, gun-toting Dr Hilarius in Pynchon's *The Crying of Lot 49* (1966); or there is Utterson, Director of the 'Institute for Deprogramming Potential Human Beings' in Susan Sontag's short-story, 'Dr Jekyll' (*I, etcetera*, 1978); the ridiculous Leonard Levin Fichte Rothenberg, Dallas psychiatrist to D.J.'s mother in Norman Mailer's *Why are we in Vietnam?* (1967); or Jacob Horner's self-styled 'mythotherapist' in John Barth's *The End of the Road* (1962). The professional analyst is probably the most lampooned figure in contemporary American writing and cinema. For such parody to be successful the target of the parody, the butt of the joke, much be clearly conspicuous, instantly recognizable to the audience. Woody Allen, notably, has made a career out of recording the foibles of affluent middle-class New Yorkers 'in analysis', elevating their trivial per-sonality problems to the level of existential crisis.

III

> Generally speaking, it can be said that people wish to escape from them-selves . . . Wyndham Lewis, *The Art of Being Ruled*

In his article 'The New Tradition' the novelist Ronald Sukenick claims that there are 'two ways of going about things: one is to put everything in and the other is to leave everything out.' In the context of recent American prose fiction, *Gravity's Rainbow* and Sukenick's *Out*, both published in 1973, could be juxtaposed as representative examples of these alternative strategies: the encyclopaedic narrative on the one side and the novel

---

[7]Lacan, 'The Agency of the Letter in the Unconscious', *Écrits: A Selection* (London, Tavistock, 1977), pp. 171, 174.

stripped bare on the other. Where Pynchon's work is a 'progressive knotting into' the densely woven tapestry of Plot, Sukenick's novel is an unravelling of the intertwined strands of narrative, a pulling apart rather than a drawing together. In terms of the information overload characteristic of contemporary American narrative, *Out* appears an insubstantial, decidedly ephemeral text. This bare, cloud-like quality of Sukenick's work – light, mercurial, swift – must be the starting point for any subsequent critical reading. For while Gaddis, Pynchon, Barth, McElroy, De Lillo and Sorrentino tend towards the excessive and transgressive, an exhaustive over-articulation – gargantuan, replete, grotesque, exorbitant – Sukenick eschews inundation and over-determination as narrative strategies in favour of a consciously underarticulated, parsimonious style, at once scrupulously mean and laconically flip. 'I want to write a book like a cloud that changes as it goes' we learn in *Out*; an ambition later echoed in Raymond Federman's *Take It Or Leave It* (1976): 'I want to tell a story that cancels itself as it goes.'[8]

The discrete segments of intersticed prose in *Out* suggest a relation of simple elementary components within the context of an open and mobile whole. A first-person, present-tense narration, lacking the relative security of a retrospective account, further accentuates the forward momentum of the book's propulsive prose. Figures merge into one another in a non-stop metamorphosis or conflux of character; age and grammatical person alter with cartoon-like rapidity from one sentence to the next, 'character' becoming little more than a gesture at representation in an essentially abstract composition. Rather than move towards the totalizing coherence and closure of the autotelic or bounded text, attention is shifted from the completed action to the process of composition itself. Although we remain aware of the book's elementary mathematical schema – language is subtracted, pace increases – the effect is oddly aleatoric; the reader experiences not a rule-determined structure but a random concatenation of causally unrelated events. The text-in-process appears to court the flux of the unfolding moment as it haphazardly develops, engaging directly with what one figure calls 'the sowhatness of things'.

Sukenick is careful to resist the allure of integrated personality as the subject-substratum or 'cause' of action. Like the Lacanian subject, in Catherine Belsey's gloss, Sukenick's disintegration of character demonstrates that 'the human being is not a unity, not autonomous, but a process, perpetually in construction, perpetually contradictory, perpetually open to change.' His work calls for the displacement of an authoritative, if imaginary, centre to being, an unsettling of the unitary, monadic subject. A constitutive instability, an 'ontological insecurity' in Laing's phrase, is opposed to the fiction of an empirically unified self (not unlike 'that continual vanishing away, that strange, perpetual weaving

[8]Ronald Sukenick, 'The New Tradition', *Partisan Review* 39, 4, p. 585. Sukenick, *Out* (Chicago, Swallow Press, 1973), p. 136. Federman, *Take It Or Leave It* (New York, Fiction Collective, 1976), p. 19.

and unweaving of ourselves' of which Walter Pater writes). 'My drive is to dissolve character' Sukenick has expressly declared in interview, 'I think that's not only a need on my part, but I presume to think that's also a cultural need for a lot of people, for the culture in general perhaps. And I think that it is happening, that modes of character are breaking down as a matter of fact. They're becoming inadequate.'[9]

Although the self is ostensibly negated in *Out* this negation proves, at the same time, the necessary prelude to an endless re-creation or play of personality. The critic Doris Elder has summarized this apparent paradox in an interesting review of Raymond Federman's *Surfiction* anthology: 'the dissolution of the self and the multiplication of roles', she claims, 'are complementary strategies in postmodern fiction. Multiple identity often turns out to be non-entity.' Elder's operative antithesis (multiplication/dissolution) could be developed still further; for what I have termed 'anti-characterization' in the postmodern novel signifies less a complete negation than a suspension, less the extirpation of character than its sublation. The concept of character, in these broadly Hegelian terms, is superseded while maintained or, in Joyce's *Wake* language, 'abnihilated' (destruction/reconstruction *ab nihilo*), untenable and necessary, legible yet effaced. Think of Pynchon's characters: Slothrop in *Gravity's Rainbow* and 'Mucho' Maas, Disc Jockey husband to Oedipa in *The Crying of Lot 49*. Slothrop progressively loses his status 'as any sort of integral creature' while 'behind Mucho's back', the programme director informs Oedipa, 'they're calling him the Brothers N. He's losing his identity, Edna, how else can I put it? Day by day, Wendell is less himself and more generic. He enters a staff meeting and suddenly the room is full of people, you know? He's a walking assembly of man.'[10]

When Walter Abish confesses that 'I lack the proper enthusiasm for characters that appear in my work. I would be incapable of ever saying *"Madame Bovary, c'est moi"*. Characters are, if anything, points of departure', the now common dissatisfaction with character or identity conceived in the essentialist mode is openly advertised: the repudiation of psychological probity related to an ideological denunciation of individualism, depth or salience of characterization and involvement of reader and author in the characters' suppositious lives as criteria for 'serious' literature.[11]

Like Sukenick, Abish advocates a mobility of the subject rather than the fixity of identity, an indefiniteness or versatility of being which recalls both Robert Lifton's 'protean style of self-process' and Richard Poirier's concept

[9]Joe David Bellamy (ed.), *The New Fiction: Interviews with Innovative American Writers* (Urbana, University of Illinois Press, 1977), p. 64. Catherine Belsey, *Critical Practice* (London, Methuen, 1980) p. 132. Walter Pater, 'Conclusion', *The Renaissance* (1873).
[10]Thomas Pynchon, *Gravity's Rainbow* (1973; London, Picador, 1975) p. 740. *The Crying of Lot 49* (1967; Harmondsworth, Penguin, 1974), p. 106. Doris Elder, 'Surfiction', *Boundary* 2, 5, Fall 1976, p. 156.
[11]Walter Abish quoted in Jerome Klinkowitz/Behrens, *The Life of Fiction* (Urbana, University of Illinois Press, 1977), p. 69.

of a 'performing self' – a claim for the heterogeneity of the subject which takes its place in a long American tradition of theorizing about 'the self'. In his synoptic article 'The Illusion of Personal Individuality' Harry Stack Sullivan claims that 'one of the greatest difficulties encountered in bringing about favourable change is this almost inescapable illusion that there is a perduring, unique, simple existent self variously called "me" or "I", and in some strange fashion, the patient's or subject-person's private property.' Sullivan further claims that it is imperative to jettison 'the deeply ingrained illusion' we have of personal individuality: 'it makes no sense to think of ourselves as "individual", "separate", capable of anything like definitive description in isolation. The notion is just beside the point. For all I know', he further speculates, 'every human being has as many personalities as he has interpersonal relations.' This latter sentiment perhaps intentionally echoes Emerson's earlier contention, 'we have as many personalities as we have friends', and William James's belief that 'properly speaking, a man has as many social selves as there are people who recognize him.' To bring this list of examples closer to the present, the pragmatist heritage is also clearly in evidence in the recent work of Richard Rorty when he protests, for instance, against 'the self-deception of thinking that we possess a deep, hidden, metaphysically significant nature which makes us "irreducibly" different from inkwells or atoms'. Almost all contemporary accounts of the subject accept the broadly 'existentialist' rejection of consciousness as reified entity in favour of consciousness as process, for consciousness, as Sartre reminds us, is always consciousness of something, not an illusory 'in itself'. Existence not only precedes essence, man is the being whose essence is to have no essence: 'There is no character, there is only a project of oneself.'[12]

The problem remains, however, that in seeking to avoid the Scylla of a repressive psychology (an essentialist, transcendent or idealist conception of the self), the protean model of the empirical subject or fictional character – the self in and as process – sails perilously close to the Charybdis of a romantic ontology, what Jonathan Culler has appropriately labelled, 'the myth of the innocence of becoming'. The belief, that is, 'that continual change, as an end in itself, is freedom and that it liberates one from the demands that could be made of any particular state or system'; an activistic philosophy of human malleability as retrograde, in its own way, as any from which it claims to deliver us. Seen from this alternative perspective, the figures in Sukenick's *Out* are simply the victims of a vocabulary of perpetual transformation. Barely delineated, fleetingly individuated, the 'characters' are closer to molecular particles in a state of agitated Brownian movement, equally likely to move in any direction, further motion seeming totally unrelated to past motion, and the motion never stopping. The corollary of their flight from stasis is a corresponding

[12]Sartre quoted in Patrick Gardiner, 'Sartre on Character and Self-Knowledge', *New Literary History* 9, 1, Autumn 1977. Harry Stack Sullivan, 'The Illusion of Personal Individuality', *Psychiatry* 13, 1, 1950, pp. 317–32. Richard Rorty, *Philosophy and the Mirror of Nature* (Oxford, Blackwell, 1980), p. 373.

bondage to movement. Like the 'yo-yo' figures in Pynchon's work, Sukenick's evanescent characters are the slaves of motion, swapping the imperative 'Sit still' for the equally prohibiting, and oddly American, injunction 'Keep moving'.[13]

IV

> Property was thus appalled,
> That the self was not the same . . . Shakespeare, 'The Phoenix and the Turtle'

A 'non-linear' conception of character has so far emerged, constructed on a set of transformations rather than the consistency of an 'evolving' or 'developing' personality. The plausible coherence, pre-existent unity and propriety of the firm and fixed identity has also been called into question. The focus of attention has shifted from the psychology of character (an irreducible essence, something 'human') to the inadequacy of the concept of character; to a recognition of subjectivity as the trace of plural and intersecting discourses, of non-unified, contradictory ideologies, the product of a relational system which is finally that of discourse itself ('discourse' here understood in Foucault's terms as a form of power, never 'innocent' but value-saturated, ideologically motivated). Not the synthesis of the constitutive subject then, but the dispersion of subjectivity, of a 'fundamental' self, among the endless oppositions, the relations-without-terms of language ('Really', Henry James conceded, 'universally, relations stop nowhere . . .').

American postmodernism may be seen to endorse a rhetorical view of life which begins with the primacy of language. Richard Lanham's work on literary rhetoric in the Renaissance indirectly corroborates this distinguishing feature of Franco-American critical theory and postmodernist practice, particularly with regard to the question of character; for personality theory formed on the analogy of rhetorical theory exemplifies a typical Renaissance process, one which closely parallels Lacan on the relationship between figures of speech and the mechanisms of the unconscious: 'The parts of speech and the parts of man can be discussed with the same vocabulary.' The rhetorical view of life, in Lanham's definition, is satirical because the rhetorical stylist can see no central self or irreducible identity to be true to: 'the concept of a central self, true or not, the idea of an unreduced residue rather than a candid acknowledgement of the rhetorical aspects of life, flatters man immensely.' The fictions of Pynchon, Sukenick, Abish, Gass and Federman certainly refer to a reality outside the text, but they privilege language as constitutive of this primary objective reality, not merely superfluous to it. Their work questions the nature of our perception of the real or referent by demonstrating that human consciousness does not experience the 'real' material world directly but only through

---

[13]Jonathan Culler, *Structuralist Poetics* (London, RKP, 1975), p. 251.

discourse, through social convention and context, through the forms of the ideological environment.[14]

'One summer evening Mrs Oedipa Maas came home from a Tupperware party . . .' – in the opening words of *The Crying of Lot 49* (1966) Pynchon foregrounds the brand-name 'Tupperware' and caricatures the proper name of the heroine, Oedipa Maas. By juxtaposing the trivialized proper name and the intrusive brand-name, Pynchon adumbrates the theme of a 'post-scarcity' consumer society, determined by property relations, in which objects – fetishized commodities invoked by brand-names – have usurped the place of the human subject, no longer background to character but proclaiming themselves as 'living' presences. As human qualities and social relations are reified so, in complementary fashion, inanimate goods, mere things, are invested with an enigmatic life of their own. Compare the opening sentence of *V* (1963): 'Christmas Eve, 1955, Benny Profane, wearing black levis, suede jacket, sneakers and big cowboy hat, happened to pass through Norfolk, Virginia.' Benny is here presented as a mere appendage, a cluster of appurtenances – jeans, jacket, plimsolls, hat – in an arbitrary and contingent world ('happened to pass through . . .'). Once again the brand-name, here 'Levis', is pushed to the fore.

Pynchon's comic-book style of cartoon characterization pointedly subverts the status of proper names as expressions of the particular identity of each person (for naming and the question of identity are indissolubly linked). To name your characters Pig Bodine, Diocletian Blobb or Richard M. Zhluub is to make a parodic thrust towards the negation of nomenclature and, by extension, of the personality ('that property which men have in their persons', in Locke's phrase) which the proper name is intended to confirm. *Nomen omen*, a Latin tag has it, indicating that what a person or thing is called is connected, in some mystical way, to its innermost being; but in the new American fiction the name is instead comically and grotesquely parodied. Most readers of modern fiction have, I suspect, a sneaking sympathy for Nasty Roche, the school bully in Joyce's *A Portrait of the Artist as a Young Man* (1916). 'What is your name?' he asks the young 'artist'. 'Stephen Dedalus' comes the reply. 'What kind of a name is that?' Nasty rightly objects. What reader of contemporary American fiction has not echoed Nasty's complaint? An onomasticon (character index) would bear out this contention. In Ishmael Reed's *The Free-Lance Pallbearers* (1967) – 'I'm not a big man on characterization, I deal in types' – the protagonist bears the ludicrous appellation Bukka Doopeyduck; the characters in Rudolph Wurlitzer's *Flats* (1970) are arbitrarily named after American towns; in Sukenick's *Up* (1968) we learn of the adventures of Strop Banally; in her short story 'American Spirits' Susan Sontag presents Miss Flatface and Mr Obscenity; Raymond Carver offers Mr Coffee and Mr Fixit; in *Giles Goat-Boy* (1966) John Barth gives us Billy Bocksfuss. The New Journalist 'Dr Hunter S. Thompson goes so far

---

[14]Richard A. Lanham, *The Motives of Eloquence: Literary Rhetoric in the Renaissance* (New Haven, Yale UP, 1976), Chapter 1, p. 27.

as to make himself into a work of performance art. We are confronted with a purposeful confusion of the symbolic, the trivial and the mythical, with characters that are doodles or sketches, more outlines or stencils of recognizable human traits than they are individuated subjectivities: flat, etiolated figures without any redeeming psychological chiaroscuro.

Proper names, in this context, no longer resonate with symbolic suggestiveness, other than with parodic intent. They are appendages rather, arbitrarily 'stuck on' to be changed at the authors' caprice. Mercifully deprived of the 'tinny click and whirr of toy psychologies' (William Gass praises Nabokov for sparing us the same) we are offered neuter figures in the place of fully rounded, three-dimensional, plausible characters; a depthlessness that erects a barrier between reader and character and which usually makes further inspection unwarranted. Everywhere one is struck by the characters' lack of intrinsic properties, of qualities, their deficiency in that 'precious ipsissimosity' of which Belacqua speaks in Beckett's *More Pricks than Kicks* (1934). While Pynchon, as noted, undermines the epistemological status of the Proper Name as an index of the ontological self, Sukenick's use of multiple, interchangeable names diminishes the individual identity of his characters by denying them the differentiation and singularity which the proper name conventionally confers. In their work we do not find characters as such but ciphers, narrative functions rather than psychological identities, a virtual eradication of the self as constitutive subject; a shift, in a broader sense, from the subject as privileged centre in phenomenology and existentialism to a decentred fiction from which the subject, as focal point and locus of consciousness, has been excluded. Characters are here less presences than indices of absence: traces.

There is perhaps a further homologous correspondence between the problem of personal identity (character, the subject) within the postmodern text and critical uncertainty as to the generic identity or status of the postmodern text itself: the rejection of a single, consistent style or genre related to the liquidation of illusory self-identity. Over the past two decades American fiction has yielded a significant number of novels – James's 'loose baggy monsters' seems an apt description – which purposely blur the demarcations between established generic realms; works which do not strive to attain an 'organic unity' so much as they aim to treat a multiplicity of subjects in a variety of styles. The imperial/apocalyptic version of the American postmodern novel (Gaddis, Pynchon, De Lillo, Barth, McElroy) indiscriminately plunders every type of literary convention to create an extravagant intertextual *bricolage* with roots in the prehistory of novelistic discourse: in the ancient *cento* or patchwork form; in the grotesque; in the *serio ludere* of Menippean satire. A teratological *mélange de genres* (or grab-bag, in other words), a style Emerson lauded as the 'panharmonic'. It could of course be safely argued that the novel in general – and the American novel/romance in particular – has never been anything other than a capacious and accommodating genre, a hybrid or mongrel form with little more than nominal status.

The novel in its contemporary American manifestations, it follows, simply explores the limitless possibilities of the novel's protean formlessness. An important consequence of this extensive stylistic eclecticism has been to challenge the legitimacy of categorial resemblances and to render problematical any approach to the new fiction by way of traditional literary taxonomy or through the use of such novel concepts as that of a putatively 'postmodern' style. Without cravenly recanting my frequent recourse to that rubric at this late stage, what we are left with, finally (as in the beginning, now and ever shall be) is writing.

Recent American fiction could be broadly defined as characteristically 'characterless' (it is difficult, for example, to think of many novels with a proper name either for or in their titles). It is a highly deterministic fiction in which the 'human' subject is paradoxically constrained in the freeplay of the text, constructed in the discursive order rather than 'free' in an existential sense. Identity is suggested by the very structure of language itself, a language logically prior to the subject. A stylistic imperium – reign of rhetoric or monarchy of the signifier – has installed itself in place of the hitherto supreme American fiction of the Imperial Self. The subject, in other words, is subjected, its pre-eminent position usurped; no longer sovereign but dethroned, constructed in and through discourse, a creature at the mercy of the monarchical Signifier.

This insistence, in post-structuralist theory and postmodernist practice, on the discourse-determined nature of the 'real' and the ideological interpellation of the subject, undoubtedly offers an important corrective to the illusion that the individual is somehow *sui generis*, a self-begetting, self-governing entity. But it is one matter to claim that the human subject is constituted in discourse and ideology – how imagine a non-social individual? – quite another to assert that the subject is therefore wholly determined in behaviouristic fashion, servilely obedient to the dictates of the prevailing 'structure in dominance'. We should envisage the subject not submitting passively to its subjection in the economic and discursive realm, but conceive instead of a mutual mediation or reciprocal determination of subject and social structure, a subject both product and agent, at once constituted and constitutive. This is properly to understand the subject as historically contextualized, an active agent for social change, rather than blithely to deconstruct and celebrate the subject's promiscuous textualization, shorn of its effectivity. Nor is there a single, uniform, omnipresent, 'dominant' ideology as such – no more than there is a unitary self-same subject – only the material operation of warring ideologies, discursive formations in a state of disintegration and in process of transformation; ideologies which are, in their turn, riven with contradictions and determinate absences, symptomatic *lacunae* conveniently elided or occluded in the interests of promoting the seeming coherence and consistency, ultimately 'natural' and immutable character of a hegemonic system of social and economic practices.

In keeping with my initial proposal to 'work outwards' into larger ideological concerns, a further issue needs to be addressed: Does the phenomenon of postmodernist anti-characterization and post-structuralist theoretical anti-humanism adumbrate some supra-individual 'collective' stage of human existence? Or is it rather a mirror-image of corporate rationalization, of the subjugation and depersonalization of the individual in a world of reified relations? To take the latter argument first, an obvious way to account for attenuated characterization in the contemporary post-realistic novel would be to draw a symmetrical correspondence between a dehumanized art and its external determinations: anti-characterization, it follows, exemplifies the subordination of the individual to the commercial network, the occultation of the subject at a specific conjuncture in the development of late monopoly capitalism. What we could term the 'dehumanization thesis' signally fails to take account of, however, is the purposive and intentional (rather than merely symptomatic) nature of anti-characterization. The open hostility to the burdensome heritage of untrammelled American individualism, its rise inversely proportional to the individual's demise – 'the fewer the individuals', as Adorno put it, 'the more the individualism'. The serious questioning of the reactionary ideology implicit in American psychoanalysis and its exaggerated distortion in the crude psychologizing and vulgar Freudianism of the media therapists, exacerbating the very anxieties they purport to relieve. The retreat from the vestigial Cartesianism of a shopworn existentialism, now a degenerate parody of its Sartrean version, a fashionable *culte du moi*. The profound affinity between the 'flat', meagrely fleshed-out figures of innovative American fiction and the corrosive anti-essentialism of the Parisian *savants* with their conception of the subject as an effect of language.

Against the dehumanization thesis outlined above, it could be argued that anti-characterization, far from endorsing the dehumanization of the subject, actively reinstates the claims of the concrete individual by opposing the ideology of abstract individualism (attacking as it does the essentialist foundations of the myth of the autonomous individual). Yet it is one matter critically to negate the identity principle; what do post-modern fiction and post-structuralist theory positively affirm in its place? Although one may of course negate a theory without incurring any obligation to affirm an alternative, certainly no emergent 'transindividual collective subject' (Lucien Goldmann's phrase) can be discerned on the horizon ready to replace the negated subject of possessive individualism, the self-possessed self. Understood as a manifestation of contemporary philosophical anti-humanism, anti-characterization should be carefully discriminated from the dehumanization with which it is invariably confused, but the dismantling of that central category of humanist mythology – the subject – does not of necessity herald the imminent collapse of the humanistic paradigm nor augur the emergence of a post-individualistic collective dynamics. But as Fredric Jameson rightly contends, 'it becomes a matter of more than mere intellectual curiosity to interrogate the artistic productions of our own time for signs of some new, so far only dimly conceivable, collective forms which may be expected to replace the older, individualistic ones (those either of conventional realism or of a now conventionalized modernism).'[15]

It becomes a matter of equal importance to recognize the vital process and experience of negation in postmodernism as an essential opposing force to the abstract pseudo-affirmation, the yea-saying of commodity culture as a whole. In the *Concluding Unscientific Postscript* (1846) Kierkegaard claimed that 'negative thinkers always have one advantage, in that they have something positive, being aware of the negative element in existence; the positive have nothing at all, since they are deceived.' Negation, that is, implies a correlative positive belief in the necessity for disbelief. Postmodern fiction and post-structuralist criticism may well have displaced or decentred the concept 'Man', but we can no sooner dispense with the category of the subject than step outside the metaphysical enclosure; the ideological position of the subject can only be unsettled, reconstituted and resituated. This radical decentring does not aim at further dehumanizing an already degraded and threatened race, even if it records that degradation, but rather at freeing the subject from illusory notions of 'the self', 'the individual' and, in terms of fiction, the psychologism of the sovereign subject-character. If, finally, the foregoing account of postmodernism can be said to have argued the case for anti-characterization as functioning negatively to effect a productive dissolution of character, it does so by way of counterpoint to the partially accurate if still unqualified critical reprise of 'dehumanization'.

[15]Fredric Jameson, 'Class and Allegory in Contemporary Mass Culture: *Dog Day Afternoon* as a Political Film,' *Screen Education*, Spring 1979, 30, p. 92.

Note

Every survey requires some principle of selection and mine has been to concentrate on those writers who explore the particular character of Jewish-American experience. In the process, some significant Jewish-American writers have been ignored while others have been treated only in passing. Some readers may regret the absence of Norman Mailer from this survey but he has, for the most part, deliberately avoided questions of Jewish-American experience in his fiction. Others may be surprised at the scant space devoted to the central triumvirate of Saul Bellow, Bernard Malamud and Philip Roth but so much critical attention has been directed towards their work that it seemed unnecessary to add to what is already available. Instead I have chosen to deal with other no less interesting writers whose work over the past quarter of a century comprises another chapter in the development of Jewish-American fiction.

The extensive list of critical books and articles on the subject is daunting and my indebtedness to many of them is indicated in the text. Those seeking a convenient introduction to the literature might consult Mark Schechner's essay on 'Jewish Writers' in the *Harvard Guide to Contemporary American Writing* (Cambridge, Mass., Harvard University Press, 1979). A more ambitious and extensive argument is presented in Sam B. Girgus's recent book, *The New Covenant: Jewish Writers and the American Idea* (Chapel Hill, NC, The University of North Carolina Press, 1984). But the best account of Jewish-American experience is Irving Howe's *World of Our Fathers* (New York, Harcourt Brace Jovanovich, 1976). Howe's monumental history of the migration of East European Jewry to America is indispensable for anyone who wishes to understand the Jewish contribution to American life.

5

Recent Jewish-American Fiction: From Exodus to Genesis

Paul Levine

> The Jewish slice of the American piety – it's what we fed on for years.
> Philip Roth, *Zuckerman Unbound*

The awarding of Nobel Prizes in literature to both Saul Bellow and Isaac Bashevis Singer has given the official stamp of recognition to what has become perhaps the most stimulating and significant development in postwar American fiction: the emergence of a 'school' of Jewish-American writing. When one considers the impact of writers like Joseph Heller, Norman Mailer, Bernard Malamud, Philip Roth, J.D. Salinger, and of course Bellow and Singer, one must recognize the size of the achievement. If one adds the names of perhaps younger and less well known writers like E.L. Doctorow, Stanley Elkin, Leslie Epstein, Herbert Gold, Mark Helprin, Cynthia Ozick, Grace Paley and Chaim Potok, then one can begin to speak of a Jewish-American 'tradition'.

But to call such a disparate group of writers a 'school' is perhaps stretching a point. In fact, to call Bellow and Singer 'American' writers might seem to some an exaggeration since the first was born in Canada and the second was born in Poland. But, for better or worse, both Bellow and Singer share a common experience with the other writers I have mentioned. In a sense, they belong to opposite ends of the spectrum of their generation: Singer the last major writer to write of the Jewish experience in the Old World in Yiddish, and Bellow, the first major writer to write of the Jewish experience in the New World in English. This dual experience is the ground of Jewish-American writing.

The central event in the history of Jewish experience in the New World is certainly the mass migration of East European Jews to America at the end of the nineteenth century and the beginning of the twentieth. We are all aware of the popular folklore concerning the mobility achievements of these people but we sometimes forget the terrible costs that had to be paid as well. Irving Howe has compared the social upheaval created by this mass migration to the trauma caused by the Industrial Revolution nearly a century earlier: 'Masses of people being forced out of, and then choosing to flee, the land; a loss of traditional patterns of pre-industrial culture; the sudden crowding of pauperized and proletarianized human beings into ghastly slums and their subjection to inhumane conditions of work; a cataclysm that leaves people broken, stunned, helpless – these elements of the Industrial Revolution were re-enacted, within a shorter time span, in the mass migration of Jews during the last two decades of the nineteenth century.'[1]

The traumatic effects of mass migration were also felt by other immigrant groups but there was a significant difference. Whereas groups like the Irish, Italians or Scandinavians experienced the feeling of displacement upon coming to the United States, the Jews had already experienced it in Europe. They had never belonged but had been marginal people wherever they had lived. Thus they were both more self-consciously alienated and doubly displaced. As C. Bezalel Sherman observes:

> The need to adjust to conditions of life in a strange country first became a problem for other groups only in America; but for Jews it was a problem they had had to face for many centuries. Others came to their new country with one culture; the Jews came with two, and frequently more than two, cultures. One culture they carried deep *within* themselves, within their spiritual and psychic being. The other they bore *upon* themselves, like an outer garment.[2]

Because of their dual heritage, Jews developed a double vision towards the necessary process of accommodation to conditions in the New World. As they approached the individual problem of making a living and the collective problem of preserving their culture, they found themselves torn between an idealistic Jewish tradition and materialistic American practice. One immigrant described the struggle vividly when he explained: 'I was the victim of a severe conflict. If the American spirit would conquer, it would spur my efforts and energies and I would accomplish a lot. If the Russian spirit would conquer, I would become dependent and go around with a dream of forcefully bringing the Messiah . . . who would free the world from slavery and exploitation. Then my hands would not be lifted to do business and the ambition to work myself up in the world would be stilled.'[3]

This conflict between Jewish ethics and American materialism was central to the Jewish immigrant experience. Indeed, opposition between the Jewish vision and the American dream became the central theme of Jewish-American fiction from Abraham Cahan's *The Rise of David Levinsky* through Henry Roth's *Call It Sleep* to Delmore Schwartz's 'In Dreams Begin Responsibilities'. In *World of Our Fathers*, Irving Howe suggests how the conflict was settled:

> America – of the full significance of which no Jewish thinker could yet take account – imposed its own decision. Once past initial barriers, the Jews were allowed an entry into social and economic life on terms more

[1]Irving Howe, *World of Our Fathers* (New York, Harcourt Brace Jovanovich, 1976), p. 115.
[2]*Ibid.*, p. 71.
[3]*Ibid.*, p. 252.

favorable than any they had dreamed of. But America exacted a price. Not that it 'demanded' that the immigrant Jews repudiate their past, their religion or their culture; nor that it 'insisted' they give up the marks of their spiritual distinctiveness. American society, by its very nature, simply made it all but impossible for the culture of Yiddish to survive. It set for the East European Jews a trap or lure of the most pleasant kind. It allowed the Jews a life far more 'normal' than anything their most visionary programs had foreseen, and all that it asked – it did not even ask, it merely rendered easy and persuasive – was that the Jews surrender their collective self. This surrender did not occur dramatically, at a moment of high tension. It took place gradually, almost imperceptibly, and with benefits so large and tangible that it would long remain a question for legitimate debate whether Jews should have tried to resist the process of absorption. That they could have succeeded, hardly anyone supposed.[4]

Thus the chronicle of Jewish immigrant experience is the American success story *par excellence*. In merely two generations, an astounding number of Jews moved from the urban ghettos to the affluent suburbs. But the price of success in America was often high, as post-war Jewish-American writers took pains to point out. In Philip Roth's *Goodbye, Columbus*, for instance, the hero, Neil Klugman, must decide how much he is willing to sacrifice to catch his princess, Brenda Patimkin. The Patimkins are Jews who have 'made it' in America but at a terrific cost to their identity and character. Even Brenda's nose is not her own after she has had it 'bobbed'. The same conflict occurs in Saul Bellow's *Seize the Day*, where Tommy Wilhelm has changed his name to make it sound less Jewish in his pursuit of the American dream. Similarly, in Bernard Malamud's *The Assistant*, Morris Bober must choose between surviving economically and preserving his ethical values. What is interesting is that in all three works the terms of the dream of success are rejected. Morris Bober is exemplary because he refuses to succumb to the terms of the dream; Neil Klugman is admirable because he finally chooses another standard than that of the Patimkins; and Tommy Wilhelm is pathetic because in the end he recognizes that in his pursuit of success he has lost more than he has gained. In much classic Jewish-American fiction, the Jewish success story takes an ironic twist; as Bellow's hero, Moses Herzog, puts it: 'the story of my life – how I rose from humble origins to complete disaster.'[5]

Herzog's lament, like Portnoy's notorious complaint, suggests how complex the chronicle of Jewish upward mobility had become by the 1960s. Whereas the first generation of Jewish fictional protagonists went into business and contended with failure, a second generation enters the professions and struggles with success. Herzog and Portnoy are not the only Jewish heroes who sweat through identity crises in the swinging decade. Norman Podhoretz's memoir, *Making It*, recounts his rise from a Brooklyn

[4]*Ibid.*, p. 641.
[5]Saul Bellow, *Herzog* (New York, Viking Press, 1964), p. 152.

slum to editorship of *Commentary* Magazine but it is not so much a
'success story' as 'the story of an education'.[6] What Podhoretz learns is that
the journey from Brooklyn to Manhattan is longer than it looks and that it
involves a deep personality change. 'It appalls me to think what an
immense transformation I had to work on myself in order to become what I
have become,' Podhoretz confesses; 'if I had known what I was doing I
would surely not have been able to do it, I would surely not have wanted
to.'[7]

Like Portnoy, Podhoretz discovers that the price of upward mobility
involves family betrayal. 'My mother wanted nothing so much as for me to
be a success, to be respected and admired. But she did not imagine, I
think, that she would only purchase the realization of her ambition at the
price of my progressive estrangement from her and her ways.[8] But, again
like Portnoy, Podhoretz is willing to pay the price to achieve his heart's
desire though *his* 'dirty little secret' has to do with the sweetness of success
not sex. As Mark Schechner has pointed out, the two books are parallel,
each achieving a '*succès de scandale*' for different reasons. For *Making It* is,
according to Schechner, the only book by a Jewish-American writer 'whose
hero is allowed to achieve social success without paying a moral price.'[9]
What both books suggest is that in the 1960s the traditional identification
'between the Jew and conscience, and the Gentile and appetite' was being
questioned.[10]

Podhoretz quotes approvingly Freud's observation that 'A man who has
been the indisputable favorite of his mother keeps for life the feeling of a
conqueror, the confidence of success which frequently induces real
success.'[11] But the obverse of Freud's dictum presents itself in Jewish-
American fiction as 'Portnoy's Complaint'. In either case, the folk wisdom
concerning the dominating Jewish mother, confirmed in novels like
Portnoy's Complaint and Bruce Jay Friedman's *A Mother's Kisses*, is mis-
leading. As Sol Gittelman has observed, Jewish literature is always concerned with 'the rights of the father' and most Jewish-American fiction is,
in fact, taken up with the relationship between fathers and sons, as in
Bellow's *Seize the Day*, Malamud's *The Assistant* and Roth's *Zuckerman
Unbound*.[12]

Herbert Gold's *Fathers*, another personal memoir of the 1960s but in
the form of a novel, uses the father/son relationship to illustrate the costs
of upward mobility. Gold relates his family history over several generations
and describes how his own father 'had abandoned the paths of his fathers'
in journeying from the Old World to the New. 'My twelve-year-old father

[6]Norman Podhoretz, *Making It* (New York, Random House, 1967) p. xii.

[7]*Ibid.*, p. 4

[8]*Ibid.*, p. 25.

[9]Mark Schechner, 'Jewish Writers', *Harvard Guide to Contemporary American Writing*
edited by Daniel Hoffman (Cambridge, Mass., Harvard University Press. 1979), p. 204.

[10]Philip Roth, *Reading Myself and Others* (New York, Farrar, Straus & Giroux, 1975),
p. 229.

[11]*Making It*, p. 57.

[12]Sol Gittelman, *From Shtetl to Suburbia* (Boston, Beacon Press, 1978), p. 176.

clung to the idea that he would go to America to be a man, another man, another sort of man, inventing his own curses and his own fate.'[13] But, like Podhoretz and Portnoy, Gold must reject the world of *his* fathers as well. 'He did not draw the consequences of his ambition for me. If he judged our neighborhood to be better than that of his childhood, then our neighborhood would judge his world.'[14] Similarly, Portnoy says of his father, 'Where he had been imprisoned, I would fly: that was his dream. Mine was its corollary: in my liberation would be his – from ignorance, from exploitation, from anonymity. To this day our destinies remain scrambled together in my imagination.'[15]

For Gold, the son's rejection of the father's path is the key to under-standing his father's journey from Kamenets-Podolsk to Cleveland as well as his own migration from Cleveland to San Francisco. But, unlike Podhoretz and Roth, Gold neither celebrates nor condemns the upward spiral. Instead, he sees continuity in this discontinuity. 'The circle of life is never completed, but the spiral turns round, remembering other turnings.'[16] Yet something *was* lost. When Gold's father abandoned Russia, 'he left family, home, language': to 'leave home' was to 'abandon history'.[17] This living in America 'with no history' is, as we shall see, both a blessing and a curse. Herbert Gold is not the only Jewish-American author to describe his characters as both free and trapped at the same time:

> My father seemed to be freed by his absolute commitment to insecurity and action, to adventuring in his golden America. At the same time, I believed him to be crippled by the loss of his past as if it were an encumbering organ from some previous incarnation or from some step on the ladder of evolution. Sometimes I envied his freedom and calm; sometimes I pitied his isolation, the steady gaze of loneliness in his humorous eyes.[18]

Whatever Herbert Gold's ambivalences, his novel remains a touching tribute to the author's father who, in taking the name of Gold, 'meant to be known as an American and to create himself pure, out of the streets of this country.'[19] Joseph Heller's *Good as Gold* is quite another matter: a frenetic frontal attack on both the American dream and Jewish upward mobility. In *From Shtetl to Suburbia*, Sol Gittelman argued that the existence of the family has provided the essential theme for both Yiddish literature in Europe and Jewish literature in America. 'For the Jew, survival of family means survival of the Jewish tradition.'[20] Both Gold and Podhoretz describe the unravelling of traditional family ties as the price of

[13]Herbert Gold, *Fathers* (New York, Random House, 1966), p. 15.
[14]*Ibid.*, p. 177.
[15]Philip Roth, *Portnoy's Complaint* (Random House, 1969), p. 9.
[16]*Fathers*, p. 299.
[17]*Ibid.*, p. 25.
[18]*Ibid.*, pp. 248–9.
[19]*Ibid.*, p. 122.
[20]*From Shtetl to Suburbia*, p. 176.

assimilation but they ultimately celebrate the possibilities of Jewish life in American society. Not so Joseph Heller who finds very little to cheer about in the loss of traditional values and ethnic identity. Thus *Good as Gold* reads like a modern jeremiad: an assault on the side-effects of Jewish upward mobility launched from the vantage point of the late 1970s.

The anti-hero of Heller's novel is one of those ubiquitous college professors who populate recent Jewish-American fiction. Bruce Gold decides to write a book about 'the Jewish experience in America' to add to his fame and fortune. But, as in all of Heller's fiction, there is a catch. 'How can I write about the Jewish experience,' he asks himself, 'when I don't know what it is?'[21] In the course of the novel he comes to know it by realizing that he is living it. As he reviews his past, he attempts to transcend it by avidly pursuing a government post in Washington. Finally, he must choose between his old life as a Jew in New York and a new career as a Gentile in Washington.

In chronicling Bruce Gold's Jewish experience, Heller spares no one. Gold's family is a loud and quarrelsome mob ruled by a tyrannical and incompetent father whose main pleasure in life is humiliating his son. Gold's friends are opportunistic New York intellectuals without integrity while his younger sister rejects the old family ties for the new assimilated 'life style'. 'If you want to know what my Jewish experience is, I can tell you,' she says to Gold. 'It's trying not to be. We play golf now, get drunk, take tennis lessons, and have divorces, just like normal Christian Americans. We talk dirty. We screw around, commit adultery, and talk out loud a lot about fucking.'[22]

But if New York is bad then Washington is infinitely worse. Filled with spineless careerists and rabid anti-Semites, the nations's capital is certainly no place for a nice Jewish boy. 'People in government don't have friends,' Gold is told, 'just interests and ambitions.'[23] The drive for power is, according to Heller, as unnatural an activity for Jews as drinking or tennis and those who pursue it in Washington become taller, slimmer and more Gentile. No wonder that Gold decides to write a book proving that Henry Kissinger isn't Jewish! With his naked ambition, Kissinger is the man Gold most hates and envies; and as he strives to follow in Kissinger's footsteps, he wonders: 'How much lower would he crawl to rise to the top?'[24]

Heller's detailed assault on Kissinger is as ham-fisted as his earnest broadsides against contemporary American society. There is a whiff of misanthropy in *Good as Gold* (as in Heller's next 'Biblical' novel, *God Knows*) only slightly mitigated by a nostalgia for a distant past when Gentile politicians were less corrupt and Jewish families stayed together. 'Imagine those old people,' Gold says of his parents in a rare moment of affection, 'leaving with children from a small town in Russia more than

[21]Joseph Heller, *Good as Gold* (London, Jonathan Cape, 1979), p. 11.
[22]*Ibid.*, p. 87.
[23]*Ibid.*, p. 427.
[24]*Ibid.*, p. 378.

sixty years ago and coming all the way here. How did they do it? They knew they would never go back. I can't go anywhere without hotel reservations and I can't go out of town two days without losing some laundry or luggage or having a plane connection cancelled.'[25]

Though *Good as Gold* suggests that we may have reached the point of diminishing returns in describing the hazards of Jewish upward mobility, it is certainly not the last word on the subject of 'the Jewish experience in America'. Two recent works prove that the richness of the traditional themes has not been exhausted. In 'Ellis Island', Mark Helprin distills the immigrant experience recounted in countless memoirs into a comic fantasy of New York as the promised city, 'a new world of new dreams' being created by men and women who do not even know they are dreaming. It is as if the imposing bulk of Cahan's *The Rise of David Levinsky* had been whipped into a delicate froth in the space of a novella. Similarly, in *World's Fair*, E.L. Doctorow describes in glowing detail a Jewish boyhood in the Bronx during the Depression. The novel is a kind of memoir also: a portrait of the artist as a young boy in which Doctorow depicts the child's growing consciousness of the wider world, culminating in his visit to the 1939 World's Fair, the model of the adult world he will inherit. In its celebration of the complexity of the child's moral life, *World's Fair* may be compared to Henry Roth's *Call It Sleep*. Clearly, Helprin and Doctorow are working within a Jewish-American literary tradition which they triumphantly renew.

'What does *he* know about being Jewish? asks Bruce Gold's father of his son. 'He wasn't even born in Europe.'[26] In Jewish-American writing, assimilation is described as a process of eliminating the European, the *authentic* Jewish characteristics. To leave Europe, as Herbert Gold observed, was 'to abandon history'. But the typically American desire to escape history here takes on a tragic dimension. 'In this period,' Leslie Fiedler pointed out, 'Jewish self-consciousness in America has endured certain critical readjustments under pressure from world events: the rise and fall of Hitler; the consequent dissolution of virtually the whole European Jewish community; the establishment of the state of Israel, and the need to redefine the allegiance of American Jews as Jews and as Americans.'[27] The success of the Jews in America together with their annihilation in Europe created a complex psychological burden combining elements of the guilt of the survivors, the self-hatred of the victims and the aggressive pride of those who have escaped history. Irving Howe has described contemporary Jewish-American experience as 'inherently schizoid':

At home: improvements in social and economic conditions, a growing

---

[25]*Ibid.*, p. 287.
[26]*Ibid.*, p. 30.
[27]Leslie Fiedler, 'The Jew in the American Novel', *Collected Essays of Leslie Fiedler*, Volume II (New York, Stein & Day, 1971), pp. 97–8.

sense of ease, comfort, security. Abroad: the greatest horror in the history of mankind, the destruction of six million Jews for reasons no mind could fathom, no intuition penetrate. How were these two elements of Jewish experience to be reconciled? The only honest answer was that they could not be: it was a division which anyone who retained even the faintest sense of Jewish identity would have to live with as best he could.[28]

This 'schizoid' tendency is expressed imaginatively in the encounter between the hero and his double. In some cases, for instance, Saul Bellow's *The Victim* and Bernard Malamud's *The Assistant*, these doubles are Jew and Gentile. But often they are the American and European Jew. In Malamud's 'The Lady of the Lake', Cynthia Ozick's 'Bloodshed' and Philip Roth's 'Eli the Fanatic' the encounters are strikingly similar: the European returns the American to the Jewish identity he has attempted to escape. Roth's hero, Eli Peck, is a lawyer called upon to defend the interests of his assimilated neighbours against orthodox refugees of the Holocaust who wish to invade the insular American suburbs. At first, Eli sympathizes with the demands of his neighbours. 'No wonder then they would keep things just as they were,' he thinks.

Here, after all, were peace and safety – what civilization had been working toward for centuries. . . . It is what his parents had asked for in the Bronx, and his grandparents in Poland, and theirs in Russia and Austria, or wherever they'd fled to or from. . . . And now they had it – the world was at last a place for families, even Jewish families. After all these centuries, maybe there just had to be this communal toughness – or numbness – to protect such a blessing.[29]

But in the process of handling the case, Eli finds himself unaccountably drawn to the very people he is trying to expel. The story recounts Eli's transformation into the very image of the Jew he has rejected. Eli's conversion is an acceptance of his *historical* identity. Thus when he insists that Jews must accept that this is the twentieth century, his orthodox teacher, Tsuref, replies: 'For the goyim maybe. For me the fifty-eighth.'[30]

According to Roth, Tsuref is correct. For the Jew it is still the fifty-eighth century. Eli's insistence on the modernity of his own assimilated outlook is undercut by the fact that when he confronts his orthodox European double he is face to face with the situation of the Jew in the twentieth century. This insistence on the historical dimension of Jewish identity is perhaps characteristic. According to Mark Schechner, 'The major Jewish writers of the postwar era have all been acutely attuned to political history and to its characteristic modern themes: war, brutality, depression and unemployment, the implications of money, class and ideology, and, especially, the

[28]*World of Our Fathers*, p. 626.
[29]Philip Roth, *Goodbye, Columbus* (New York, Modern Library, 1966), pp. 279–80.
[30]*Ibid.*, p. 266.

individual sentiments and sensibilities that grow out of such a history.'[31] Several recent novels support the point: E.L. Doctorow's brilliant exploration of the Rosenberg case in *The Book of Daniel* and Chaim Potok's more pedestrian meditation on Jewish involvement in the creation of the atomic bomb in *The Book of Lights*. As Malamud put it in his own historical novel, *The Fixer*: 'We're all in history, that's sure, but some are more than others, Jews more than some. If it snows not everybody is out in it getting wet.'[32]

This situation is not without irony. For if the European Jews may be said to have abandoned history upon coming to America, they had only entered it a short time before. 'For centuries,' observed Jules Chametzky, 'what did Jews have to do with – except to feel, peripherally, the effects of – the rise and fall of princes, the movements of armies and peoples, diplomatic intrigues and embassies, the stuff, in short, of "history"? Their concern has traditionally been with the relationship of man and God, of a people and God. Such a view prevailed basically unchallenged among the mass of Jews until the post-Enlightenment phase of the life of the Jewish people.'[33] As Chametzky pointed out, one of Isaac Bashevis Singer's many virtues is that he has chronicled the Jewish entry into modern history. Beginning with his first novel, *Satan in Goray*, Singer has portrayed the gradual dissolution of European Jewry since the seventeenth century. Yet Singer's depiction is not simply historical but mythic. According to Irving Howe, 'The historical settings of East European Jewish life are richly presented in Singer's stories, often not as orderly sequences in time but as simultaneous perceptions jumbled together in the consciousness of figures for whom Abraham's sacrifice, Chmielnicki's pogroms, the rise and fall of Hassidism and the stirrings of the modern world are all felt with equal force.'[34]

Writing in Yiddish for an ageing audience in America that declines almost daily, Singer is providing a living testament for a European culture that is all but defunct. 'It strikes me as a kind of inspired madness,' argued Howe: 'here is a man living in New York City, a sophisticated and clever writer, who composes stories about places like Frampol, Bilgoray, Kreshev, *as if they were still there*.'[35] But when Singer turns to Jewish experience in America he sometimes writes as if America were not there for his displaced persons, so obsessed are they by the European past. In stories like 'The Cafeteria' and 'The Joke' or a novel like *Enemies, A Love Story*, his characters seem like ghosts possessed by the *dybbuk* of history. 'Everything has already happened,' thinks the narrator of *Enemies*. 'The creation, the flood, Sodom, the giving of the Torah, the Hitler holocaust.'[36] In America,

---

[31]*Harvard Guide to Contemporary American Writing*, p. 196.
[32]Bernard Malamud, *The Fixer* (Farrar, Straus & Giroux, 1966), p. 314.
[33]Jules Chametzky, 'History in I.B. Singer's Novels', *Critical Views of Isaac Bashevis Singer*, edited by Irving Malin (New York, New York University Press, 1969), p. 174
[34]Irving Howe, 'I.B. Singer', *Critical Views of Isaac Bashevis Singer*, p. 110.
[35]*Ibid.*, p. 101.
[36]Isaac Bashevis Singer, *Enemies, A Love Story* (New York, Farrar, Straus & Giroux, 1972), p. 156.

Singer's characters have not so much abandoned history as they have been abandoned by it.

In recent years, Jewish-American writers have frequently turned to European history to provide a metaphor for authentic Jewish experience but with mixed results. In *The Fixer*, Malamud uses the Mendel Beilis case as the basis for another of his instructive parables on the impossibility of eluding one's Jewish identity. In *Mr Sammler's Planet*, Bellow's spokesman is a survivor of both Auschwitz and Bloomsbury. In *The Professor of Desire* and *The Ghost Writer*, Roth confronts his protagonists with imaginative encounters with Franz Kafka and Anne Frank. The controversy surrounding Roth's treatment of Anne Frank points up the interesting fact that Jewish-American writers employ the Holocaust as metaphor rather than as subject. It would seem that only Gentile writers like William Styron have the *chutzpah* to directly address Adorno's famous admonition: 'After Auschwitz, no more poetry.'

One exception to the rule is Leslie Epstein. His early novella, 'The Steinway Quintet', introduced elements of the Final Solution into a fantasy about a bungled New York holdup but his later novel, *The Elder* (called *King of the Jews* in the United States) took the Holocaust as its subject. Based loosely on the history of the Jewish ghetto of Lodz and its notorious leader, Mordecai Chaim Rumkowski, *The Elder* attempts to recreate the tragic experience of a European Jewish community unwilling to believe what is happening to it and therefore willing to cooperate in its own destruction. Though historical in content, the novel is fabulistic in form. Epstein seeks not only to recapitulate the moral debate about Jewish complicity stimulated by Hannah Arendt's *Eichmann in Jerusalem* but to make comprehensible the unfathomable tragedy of the destruction of European Jewry. In his portrait of the Elder, I. C. Trumpelman, he fashions a grotesque and tragic figure, both charismatic and charlatan, who is greedy for power and immortality. Where others see him as a murderous accomplice, Trumpelman sees himself as a death-defying lion tamer:

> In this same cage with us there is a hungry lion! He wants to devour us all! He's ready to spring! And I? Trumpelman? I am the lion tamer. I stuff his mouth with meat! It's the flesh of my own brothers and sisters! The lion eats and eats! He roars! But he does not spring. Thus, with ten Jews, I save a hundred, I save a thousand. With a thousand, ten thousand more. My hands are bloody. My feet are bloody. My eyes are closed with blood. If your hands are clean, it's because mine are dirty! I have no conscience! That's why your conscience is clear! I am covered in blood completely![37]

The Elder has been alternately praised and condemned but there is no denying Epstein's skill and seriousness. In combining history and fable he may remind us of Singer and his magical recreation of European Jewry '*as if they were still there*' but there is this significant difference: whereas

[37]Leslie Epstein, *The Elder* (London, W.H. Allen, 1979), p. 268.

Singer's story-telling creates a sympathetic bond between the writer and his world, Epstein's fabulism achieves an ironic distance between the narrator and his world. 'What the Ghettoites – the children first, and then the older people – had glimpsed, what became clear to them, was the nature of history. A fable. A misunderstanding. A kind of joke.'[38] In transforming history into fable, Epstein has made it more comprehensible but infinitely less moving.

In *The American Scene*, Henry James describes his reactions to the changes taking place in American life at the beginning of the twentieth century. At Ellis Island he is stunned by the massive wave of immigration which threatens to transform the country. As he sits in a café on the lower East Side of New York listening to English being spoken in a myriad of accents, he pauses to reflect not simply on the future of his nation but on the future of his language: 'The accent of the very ultimate future, in the States, may be destined to become the most beautiful on the globe and the very music of humanity (here the "ethnic" synthesis shrouds itself thicker than ever); but whatever we shall know it for, certainly, we shall not know it for English – in any sense for which there is an existing measure.'[39]

In an unintended way, James's observation proved prophetic. For in the two decades after James wrote those words, the American language was to undergo as profound a transformation as American literature itself. Indeed, in revising the language of the Genteel Tradition, writers like Hemingway, Cummings and Dos Passos comprised the first generation of native modernists to shape a new American idiom. But those who spoke in what James called 'the accent of the future' belonged to the same social group as James himself. They were not 'the inconceivable alien' but, almost without exception, members of the dominant white, Anglo-Saxon, Christian culture. And it should be remembered that more than a few of them shared the attitudes and prejudices of the established society against which they were rebelling. Fitzgerald, Hemingway and their contemporaries wrote from inside the culture they were rejecting. For the most part, they were small-town boys from the middle class and often from the Middle West whose field of vision was generally limited to the America they knew. What they left out of their picture of a changing America – the urban, immigrant, ethnic and racial experience – became the subject of the second generation of modern American writers. These younger writers, who were often Jewish or black, were faced with the problem of creating a personal idiom which could shape and order their experience. This new idiom might be 'the very music of humanity' but would Henry James recognize it as English? Saul Bellow described the problem of forging a personal style amid these cultural constraints:

My first two books were well made. I wrote the first quickly but took

[38]*Ibid.*, p. 319.
[39]Henry James, *The American Scene* (Bloomington, Indiana, University of Indiana Press, 1968), p. 139.

great pains with it. I labored with the second and tried to make it letter-perfect. In writing *The Victim* I accepted a Flaubertian standard. Not a bad standard, to be sure, but one which, in the end, I found repressive – repressive because of the circumstances of my life and because of my upbringing in Chicago as the son of immigrants. I could not, with such an instrument as I developed in the first two books, express a variety of things I knew intimately. These books, though useful, did not give me a form in which I felt comfortable. A writer should be able to express himself easily, naturally, copiously in a form which frees his mind, his energies. Why should he hobble himself with formalities? With a borrowed sensibility? With the desire to be "correct"? Why should I force myself to write like an Englishman or a contributor to the *New Yorker*? I soon saw that it was simply not in me to be a mandarin. I should add that for a young man in my position there were social inhibitions too. I had good reason to fear that I would be put down as a foreigner, an interloper. It was made clear to me when I studied literature at the university that as a Jew and the son of Russian Jews I would probably never have the right *feeling* for Anglo-Saxon traditions, for English words. I realized even in college that the people who told me this were not necessarily disinterested friends. But they had an effect on me, nevertheless. This was something from which I had to free myself. I fought free because I had to.[40]

Saul Bellow's struggle to find his own true voice as a writer was typical of many artists and intellectuals of his generation. Yet, for many, choosing a career in what some called 'the Republic of Letters' meant coming to terms with, and even embracing, the literary norms and cultural values from which they felt excluded. With the waning of Socialism at the end of the 1930s, Jewish writers and intellectuals transferred their commitment from society to culture, from Marxist politics to Modernist literature. 'Indeed,' as Sol Gittleman remarked, 'in the academic world, it was the Jewish academician who seemed drawn to those writers whose view of America was one unmarred by mass immigration: Eliot, Henry James, and Ezra Pound.'[41]

As heirs to Modernism, Jewish-American writers have been as concerned with problems of literary form as with questions of ethnic identity. If Bellow adopted a Flaubertian standard for his first two novels then Roth chose a Jamesian model for *Letting Go* and Malamud embraced Eliotic mythomania in *The Natural*. As their careers progressed, their protagonists all became writers who in each successive incarnation were less concerned with ethnic insecurities. The main subject of Malamud's *Dubin's Lives*, Roth's *Zuckerman Bound* and Bellow's *Humboldt's Gift* is the act of writing itself. Finally, in *The Dean's December*, Bellow escapes the ethnic

[40]*Writers at Work*, Third Series, edited by George Plimpton (Harmondsworth, Penguin, 1977), pp. 182–3.
[41]*From Shtetl to Suburbia*, p. 147.

question completely by making his protagonist of French Huguenot descent.

As this second generation of American modernist writers abandoned its concern for Jewish identity and entered the mainstream culture which it had helped to create, a new group of novelists has moved self-consciously into the space so recently vacated. Ruth Wisse explains: 'In much the same way that the financial and social security achieved by the second immigrant generation has permitted its children, when so inclined, to turn back to their "roots", so the commercial and critical success of the second *literary* generation, which has affirmed the legitimate presence of Jews in American literature, now invites the Jewish writer to turn inward if he pleases.'[42] This inward turning is reflected in the work of newer writers who often seem spiritually closer to Isaac Bashevis Singer than to Saul Bellow.

Of this group, which includes writers as different as Arthur A. Cohen, Hugh Nissenson and Chaim Potok, the most talented and audacious is indisputably Cynthia Ozick. Like Bellow, Ozick began by caring 'about high art and its issues' and fashioning 'a style both "mandarin" and "lapidary," every paragraph a poem.'[43] But she soon discovered that this style was in conflict with her own identity as a Jew. Where Bellow could resolve the conflict by forging a new idiom that combined the philosophical with the demotic, Ozick discovered that her problem was not one of idiom but of language itself. 'Since coming from Egypt five millennia ago, mine is the first generation to think and speak and write wholly in English,' she observes. 'To say that I have been thoroughly assimilated into English would of course be the grossest understatement – what is the English language (and its poetry) if not my passion, my blood, my life?'

> Still, though English is my everything, now and then I feel cramped by it. I have come to it with notions it is too parochial to recognize. A language, like a people, has a history of ideas; but not *all* ideas; only those known to its experience. Not surprisingly, English is a Christian language. When I write in English, I live in Christendom.
>
> But if my postulates are not Christian postulates, what then?[44]

In creating her fiction, Ozick faces the seemingly insurmountable problem of writing 'in a language of a civilization that does not understand its thesis.'[45] But this problem – which appears overwhelming enough! – is exacerbated by her understanding of Judaism and its prohibition against the fashioning of false idols. Thus she wonders whether all storytelling isn't a form of idolatry and worries 'whether Jews ought to be storytellers.'[46] Most of Ozick's work reflects an obsession with the struggle between the imperatives of belief and the demands of imagination.

[42] Ruth R. Wisse, 'American Jewish Writing, Act II', *Commentary*, (June 1976), p. 41.
[43] Cynthia Ozick, *Bloodshed and Three Novellas* (New York, Alfred Knopf, 1976), p. 4.
[44] *Ibid.*, p. 9.
[45] *Ibid.*, p. 10.
[46] *Ibid.*

This obsession is revealed in the richest and longest story in her first collection, *The Pagan Rabbi*. 'Envy; or, Yiddish in America' describes the competition between two ageing Yiddish writers. Ostrover is a success because he has found an English translator. Edelshtein is a failure because he is condemned to write in a dead language for a dying public. Thus he is reduced to eking out a living lecturing on his own predicament. 'Synagogues, community centers, labor unions underpaid him to suck on the bones of the dead. Smoke. He traveled from borough to borough, suburb to suburb, mourning in English the death of Yiddish.'[47] The story recounts in hilarious detail Edelshtein's desperate attempt to find a translator. Edelshtein's failure is pathetic but Ostrover's success is also a living death because translation is a form of conversion. 'Naturally the important thing is to stick to what you learned as a slave including language, and not to speak their language, otherwise you will become like them, acquiring their confusion between God and artifact and consequently their taste for making slaves, both of themselves and others.'[48]

Variations on the theme of Jewish exile are explored in many of the stories in *Bloodshed* and *Levitation* as well as in the novel, *The Cannibal Galaxy*. But always she returns to the questions of language and culture. By now it should be apparent that Ozick is a kind of fabulist more at home with abstractions than with characters: in Ruth Wisse's words, 'an intellectual writer whose works are the fictional realization of ideas.'[49] Something similar might be said of Stanley Elkin, a very different writer. Admired by Robert Coover and William Gass for his 'rhetorical intensity'[50] and 'rich wild oratory',[51] Elkin is the closest we have to a major Jewish-American postmodernist. Like Ozick, he is intoxicated with language but, unlike her, he has no religious inhibitions against idolatrous creation. Indeed, Elkin's extravagant love affair with language is both his virtue and vice. A comic monologist who is quite different from Philip Roth, his verbal energy seems best suited to the shorter form like the novella. Here is an example from his first novel, *Boswell*:

> Who knew Schmerler? I told him a million times, 'Schmerler, you're an enigma, Schmerler,' It was a shame he didn't make himself understood better. He could have been the biggest name in the Zionist movement. But no, *he* had to insist upon making the Jewish Homeland in Northern Ireland. He used to argue with Weizman night and day. 'Weizman,' he says, 'your Jew isn't basically a desert-oriented guy.' That was Schmerler for you. If you say you don't know him, that's your clue. He was always correct in principle, in theory. Mao used to call him 'The On-Paper Tiger.'[52]

[47]Cynthia Ozick, *The Pagan Rabbi and Other Stories* (London, Secker & Warburg, 1972), p. 43.
[48]*Ibid.*, p. 86.
[49]Wisse, *Commentary*, p. 46.
[50]Stanley Elkin, *Stanley Elkin's Greatest Hits* (New York, Warner Books, 1981), p. x.
[51]Stanley Elkin, *The Franchiser* (Boston, Nonpareil Books, 1980), p. ix.
[52]Stanley Elkin, *Boswell* (New York, Warner Books, 1980), p. 20.

Evidently, Elkin isn't basically a desert-oriented guy, either. His scene is the city and his work reveals an obsession with ordinary life and, unlike some other Jewish-American writers, with the crass materialism of American society. 'How crowded is the universe,' observes a character in his novel, *The Franchiser*. 'How stuffed to bursting with its cargo of crap.'[53] But Elkin finds spiritual significance in the seedy materialism of our popular culture. As Coover observed, 'Elkin relates rhetorical intensity – what we call "heroic extravagance" – to a vision, a reach for significance, a spiritual connection to mystery.'[54] This religious concern might seem to link him to orthodox Jews like Ozick but the resemblance is tenuous. Her interest is in reconciling imagination with belief, his interest is in confronting belief with imagination. Where her concern is with divinity, his concern is with mortality.

From the first sentence of his first novel, Elkin has been obsessed with the question of death. 'Everybody dies, everybody,' Boswell begins his story. The theme is sustained throughout his fiction. 'Death is an education,' reflects the protagonist of one of his best short stories, 'Criers and Kibbitzers, Kibbitzers and Criers'.[55] In fact, all of Elkin's characters learn while living under a death sentence, from Ben Flesh who suffers from multiple sclerosis in *The Franchiser* to Leo Feldman who is serving a life sentence in prison in *A Bad Man*. As John Irving noted, 'The doomed and the dying are Elkin's loved ones.'[56]

The theme is most vividly explored in *The Living End*, a short and pungent novel in the form of a Bosch-like tryptich depicting life and death, Heaven and Hell, and ending with the Last Judgement. In Elkin's vision, life after death follows the conventional wisdom: the Pearly Gates are actually pearly and Hell is really hellish. But, in fact, death is remarkably like life. 'Hell was the ultimate inner city'[57] while 'Heaven was like nothing so much as one of those swell new cities in the Sun Belt – Phoenix, Tucson.'[58] When Elkin turns to the portrayal of the divine his depiction is wonderfully vulgar. Jesus and Joseph speak in 'vaudeville Yiddish'[59] and God is both narrow-minded and absent-minded: an arbitrary God who wears contact lenses.

But Elkin is not simply playing the Village Atheist. When God is asked to reveal the mystery of Creation, He responds that his motivation was not moral but aesthetic: '*Goodness?* No. It was art! It was always Art. I work by the contrasts and metrics, by beats and the silences. It was all Art. *Because it makes a better story is why.*'[60] Elkin and Ozick may agree on the

[53]*The Franchiser*, p. 21.
[54]*Stanley Elkin's Greatest Hits*, p. x.
[55]Stanley Elkin, *Criers and Kibitzers, Kibitzers and Criers* (New York, New American Library, 1973), p. 9.
[56]*New York Times Book Review*, (June 10, 1979), p. 7.
[57]Stanley Elkin, *The Living End* (London, Virgin Books, 1981), p. 30.
[58]*Ibid.*, p. 119.
[59]*Ibid.*, p. 118.
[60]*Ibid.*, p. 142.

equivalence of creation and divinity but only he would celebrate the correspondence between the Creator and the Artist. Yet his blasphemy is finally reminiscent of another earlier Jewish writer, Nathanael West, as Frank Kermode has pointed out.[61] What Elkin shares with his contemporaries from Bellow to Ozick is a love of language, a reverence for the fallen world, and a belief, in Ozick's works, in 'a literature that interprets and decodes the world.'[62] Or as Bernard Malamud writes in his most recent novel, *God's Grace*: 'God was Torah. He was made of words.'[63]

[61]*New York Review of Books*, (16 August, 1979), p. 45.
[62]Cynthia Ozick, 'Innovation and Redemption: What Literature Means,' *Art and Ardor* (New York, Alfred Knopf, 1983), p. 247.
[63]Bernard Malamud, *God's Grace* (London, Chatto & Windus, 1982), p. 92.

Note

About 20 contemporary writers are cited in this essay; unfortunately there isn't room here for notes on them all. However, nine writers are more central to this discussion than the rest, and the footnotes to this Chapter focus on them and those of their texts which figure prominently in my remarks. Reference is made here to selected critical texts and interviews.

Roseann P. Bell, Bettye J. Parker, and Beverly Guy-Sheftall (eds.) *Sturdy Black Bridges* (New York, Doubleday-Anchor, 1979). See Bell on Gayl Jones, Parker on Toni Morrison, and Mary Helen Washington on Alice Walker.

Susan Blake and James. A. Miller, 'The Business of Writing: An interview with David Bradley', *Callaloo* 7 (Spring-Summer 1984), pp. 19–34.

Jerry H. Bryant, 'John A. Williams: The Political Use of the Novel', *Critique: Studies in Modern Fiction* 16 (1975), pp. 81–100.

John F. Callahan, *In The Afro-American Grain* (Urbana, Ill., University of Illinois Press, 1987). Important discussions of Ernest Gaines and Alice Walker are included.

Barbara Christian, *Black Feminist Criticism* (New York, Pergamon, 1985). Many studies of Walker, Morrison, Marshall, Naylor.

Michael G. Cooke, *Afro-American Literature in the Twentieth Century* (New Haven, Yale University Press, 1984). Illuminating remarks on virtually all of the authors cited in this discussion, but especially on Walker, Bradley, Wideman, Jones, and Reed.

Henry L. Gates, Jr (ed.), *Black Literature and Literary Theory* (New York, Methuen, 1984). See especially Susan Willis's essay on Morrison and Gates's remarks on Reed.

Michael S. Harper, 'Gayl Jones: An Interview', in Michael S. Harper and Robert B. Stepto (eds.), *Chant of Saints* (Urbana, University of Illinois Press, 1979), pp. 352–75.

Jerome Klinkowitz, *Literary Disruptions* (Urbana, University of Illinois Press, 1975). Provides helpful remarks on Reed.

Nellie McKay, 'An interview with Toni Morrison', *Contemporary Literature* 24 (1983), pp. 413–29.

Charles H. Rowell (ed.), 'Ernest J. Gaines: A Special Issue', *Callaloo* 1 (May 1978). Number includes an interview with Gaines by Rowell, a Gaines bibliography by Rowell, essays by Alvin Aubert, John Wideman, Todd Duncan, Barry Beckham, Michel Fabre.

Charles H. Rowell (ed.), 'Gayl Jones: Poet and Fictionist, A Special Section', *Callaloo* 5 (October 1982), pp. 31–111. Section includes an interview with Jones by Rowell, essays by Jerry W. Ward, Jr, and Trudier Harris, fiction by Jones.

Wilfred D. Samuels, 'Going Home: A conversation with John Edgar Wideman', *Callaloo* 6 (1983), pp. 40–59.

Barbara Smith, 'Toward a Black Feminist Criticism', *Conditions* 2 (1977), pp. 25–43. The now-famous essay that argues Morrison's *Sula* is a lesbian novel.

Robert B. Stepto, ' "Intimate Things in Place:" A Conversation with Toni Morrison', in Harper and Stepto, (eds.), *Chant of Saints*, pp. 213–29. Discussion of Morrison's *The Bluest Eye* and *Sula* conducted while *Song of Solomon* was in progress.

Claudia Tate (ed.), *Black Women Writers at Work* (New York, Pergamon, 1983). Offers recent interviews with virtually all of the women writers cited in this discussion.

Alice Walker, *In Search of Our Mothers' Gardens* (New York, Harcourt, 1983). A comprehensive collection of her essays.

Jerry W. Ward, *Ishmael Reed and the Problem Modernity*, CAAS Occasional Paper no. 18 (Atlanta, Center for African and African-American Studies, n.d. [ca. 1976]).

Joe Weixlmann, 'A Gayl Jones Bibiography', *Callaloo* 7 (Winter 1984), pp. 119–31.

Joe Weixlmann and Chester J. Fontenot (eds.), *Studies in Black American Literature, I: Black American Prose Theory* (Greenwood, Penkevill, 1983). The studies of Morrison and Reed are especially pertinent to this discussion.

6

After the 1960s: The Boom in Afro-American Fiction

Robert B. Stepto

One of the curiosities about Afro-American culture is that for some people it doesn't seem to exist unless the newspapers are full of headlines about marches, demonstrations, and such like activities. A result of this view is that the Afro-American writer is only visible to some when he or she helps to lead a march or rally, or when writers are called in by, say, a television station, to help explain why that march or rally is occurring. All such activity leads to the general public 'knowing' some writers above all others – Amiri Baraka and James Baldwin readily come to mind – and unfortunately to assuming in the process, since the same writers are seen and heard over and over again, that there are very few Afro-American writers of note.

During the past decade, there have been relatively few large political events comparable to the huge marches on Washington in the 1960s, and so it is entirely possible that the general public is not as aware as it should be of the many fine Afro-American writers writing today, and of the remarkable ways in which they are sustaining Afro-American culture while producing a solid, inventive literature. This latter point cannot be over-stressed: art-making and culture-bearing have always been concerns for the Afro-American writer, but rarely have we seen so many writers pursuing both concerns at once, and doing that work so well. There has been in short a 'boom' in Afro-American fiction, comparable to that more readily acknowledged in Latin American letters, especially in terms of it being an indigenous or locus-specific literature capable of attracting an international audience.

With numerous writers in view, I have had to make some difficult choices as to which authors are to be discussed in these pages. This is always a tricky business, as it is so easy to leave a good writer out. Let me therefore say that I will be touching upon those writers who have helped Afro-American fiction evolve from where it was in the early 1960s. Put another way, I wish to emphasize those writers who, for the most part, came to their

---

This essay substantially enlarges a short article more simply entitled 'The Boom in Afro-American Fiction' that appeared in *Focus* (a Paris-based USIA journal), Summer, 1984.

craft after the apex of the civil rights activities of that decade, and who now seem to be among the most conspicuous heirs to Zora Neale Hurston and Ann Petry on the one hand, and to Richard Wright, Ralph Ellison and James Baldwin on the other. Let me begin with Toni Morrison.

Morrison is what we might call a perpetual writer. She is always writing, always experimenting, and frequently growing as an artist as a result of these experiments. To date, she has produced four novels – *The Bluest Eye* (1971), *Sula* (1974, Knopf), *Song of Solomon* (1977, Knopf), and *Tar Baby* (1981). (*Dreaming Emmett*, a play that probes the infamous Emmett Till murder case of the 1950s, was completed in 1985 and mounted in 1986.) While this list confirms her productivity in the period under review, it also in great measure defines the period, for it certainly can be argued that the new Afro-American fiction began (especially as far as many women writers are concerned) with the publication of *The Bluest Eye*, and that by the time *Tar Baby* saw print, Morrison had not only many fellow-travellers but many rivals. We may be assured, however, that her place in Afro-American letters is secure.

This is so in part because while Morrison had created a number of totally fresh characters in the literature – think here especially of Sula Peace – she has been equally consistent in offering her own versions of established figures. Ajax in *Sula*, Son in *Tar Baby*, and perhaps, too, Cholly Breedlove in *The Bluest Eye* are all strong contemporary interpretations of the 'Long Gone' ramblin' man in both black and white American folklore, but especially in this instance in black songs and tales. It can also be said that Soaphead Church in *The Bluest Eye*, Shadrack in *Sula* and Pilate in *Song of Solomon* are significant, complex revisions of the conjure men and women found in the writings of Charles W. Chesnutt, Zora Neale Hurston, and Jean Toomer. Moreover, while there are vast differences between Morrison's Milkman Dead and Ralph Ellison's Invisible Man, it seems nonetheless that Milkman's story in *Song of Solomon* is quite possibly the most significant retelling of Invisible Man's tale we have, precisely because Morrison refuses to give in to current ideological fashion, and instead joins Ellison in starkly and perhaps belligerently portraying the enduring distinctions between cultural awareness and social responsibility. In this regard, if Ellison is one of the first true Afro-American modernists, Morrison is one of the last. This explains why, in part, as we complete the 1980s, she is as much a puzzle as a treasure for younger readers: in insisting, for example, that she can remember when the black community was called seemingly more simply the neighbourhood, and in writing as much about men as about women, she erects generational fences which create in turn several communities of readership at a time when many younger readers long to be the sole or favoured readership, and seem to insist on that when the writer is a woman.

What has been suggested so far about Morrison's male characters can be said about her extraordinary female characters as well. Even before the last two novels appeared, it seemed to me that Morrison was much in the tradition of Ann Petry in that both women seemed to have a mission to revise – indeed, to rehumanize – certain black female characters in Richard Wright's canon, including Bessie in both *Native Son* and *Black Boy* and Bigger Thomas's mother and sister. I would still argue that point. The McTear and Breedlove women in The *Bluest Eye* lead thwarted lives, and the Breedlove women appear particularly maimed as a result. But there is a complexity to their lives in Morrison's novel which Wright has difficulty in attributing even to the character who is his mother in *Black Boy*. The family of Peace Women in *Sula* and the two aggregations of women in *Song of Solomon* (Pilate and her daughters; Ruth Foster Dead and hers) advance this point further. While we would never wish to deny the intense individualism of a Sula, Nel, Reba, Hagar, Pilate or First Corinthians, just to name a few of these women, it can be said that each family of women devised by Morrison is a collective portrait of a multifaceted black woman, a *heroine* who is as protean and occasionally as problematic as any of the black heroes commonly offered in other fictions.

Much of what I am describing here bears on the nature of the evolving portrait in the new fiction of a politically controversial entity, the black American matriarchial family. The families headed by Eva in *Sula* and Pilate in *Song of Solomon* are quite different from those portrayed in *Native Son, Black Boy*, or even Hurston's *Their Eyes Were Watching God*. In Wright and Hurston, the matriarchical family is part of the problem, part of what the protagonist – male in Wright, female in Hurston – must be liberated from; it is as if both of these writers were intent on writing early drafts of the now notorious Patrick Moynihan Report. In Morrison, while aspects of this pattern continue in *Sula*, the prevailing idea is that while families headed by women can suffer, they can also survive – and love and nurture.

For Morrison, this is a major theme but no more than that; for some of the women writers following her – Alice Walker and Gloria Naylor, for example – it is virtually an ideology, at times broadly feminist, at others more narrowly individuated, the latter being evident in Walker's personal distinction between womanist and feminist perspectives on many vital matters, including presumably female and familial portraiture in literature. Somewhere in between these two camps lies the work of our next writer, Gayl Jones, who is less well known than Walker (and now in the 1980s, than Naylor) but who, within my teaching experience, is easily the more provocative writer.

One thinks of Jones along with Morrison, partly because as a senior editor at Random House Morrison is, or has been, Jones's editor. Certainly, all three of Jones's books to date – *Corregidora* (1975, Random House), *Eva's Man* (1976), and *White Rat* (1977) – were edited and in that sense nurtured by Morrison. I note this because one of the most interesting aspects of the evolution of Afro-American literature in our time has been the assembly at Random House of a group of younger black writers: Morrison and Jones obviously, but also Toni Cade Bambara, Lucille Clifton, Maya Angelou, Leon Forrest, Ishmael Reed (shared with other houses, including his own), Ernest Gaines (his last two novels), and the late

Henry Dumas. About half of the names mentioned are those of women, and unfortunately that has been remarked upon disparagingly by some male writers. Reed and Steve Cannon at one point led the attack, complaining that doors were being closed against the black male writer, and suggesting that women including Morrison were making sure of the locks. This is one way to view the matter; I prefer another: the Random House entourage reflects in microcosm the healthy, balanced state of a literature embracing male and female voices alike. Moreover, it is to the good that a large group of major black writers have had really for the first time, a black senior editor at a dominant publishing house to whom they can turn and get support. More must be in place for a whole literature to prosper, but this is at least a start: the politics of publishing is now as before an integral part of the 'politics' of white *and* black reader response and hence of various canon formations.

Of course, there is much to say about Gayl Jones that extends beyond her affiliation with an editor and a publisher. Though not yet 40, she is already impressive as a contributor to at least two strains within modern Afro-American literature. On the one hand, like Hurston and later, Morrison, she creates extraordinary women (Ursa in *Corregidora*, Eva in *Eva's Man*) and then studies them in prolonged, bittersweet heterosexual relationships which are, in a phrase, blues in prose. On the other hand, like Hurston but much less like Morrison than, say, Ernest Gaines, she seeks to achieve a parity between folk and written traditions in fashioning these blues passages. Consider, for example, the fusion of the vernacular and the written as well as the simulation of blues mood and form in this conversation!

> *'What bothers you?'*
> *'It bothers me because I can't make generations.'*
> *'What bothers you?'*
> *'It bothers me because I can't.'*
> *'What bothers you, Ursa?'*
> *'It bothers me because I can't fuck.'*
> *'What bothers you, Ursa?'*
> *'It bothers me because I can't feel anything.'*
> *'I told you that nigger couldn't do nothing for you.'*
> *'You liar. You didn't tell me nothing. You left me when you threw me down those . . .'*[1]

In *Corregidora*, parity of this sort is also managed through the presentation of Ursa as a consummate blues singer. I don't recall that Ursa ever sings these famous blues lines, 'I love the life I live / And I live the life I love,' but they are apt in that they express the full measure to which her love life is her blues life, and to which both of these lives in turn are entwined with her personal and familial history. While the blues poem has possibly run its course, the blues novel most certainly has not. More work will be done in this area, and Jones will complete some of the best of it.

[1] Gayl Jones, *Corregidora* (New York, Random House, 1975), p. 90.

In citing the authors who have influenced her work, Jones often mentions Ernest Gaines. She admires him because he is a good storyteller; I would expand that slightly and say that he is in one of the best senses of the word, traditional. In book after book, including his four contributions to the literary decade under review (*Bloodline* (1968, Dial), *The Autobiography of Miss Jane Pittman* (1971), *In My Father's House* (1978) and *A Gathering of Old Men* (1983)), Gaines sets his stories in a traditional southern black community – Bayonne, Louisiana and its environs – and fashions narrators who tell stories in a traditional way, by which I mean in part an inventive, shared folk idiom. It was Sterling Brown who said, 'Negro speech is not dis and dat and a split verb, but "been down so long that down don't worry me" or "me and my baby gonna shine, shine." ' [2] As much as any other Afro-American writer of our time, Gaines understands Brown's point and writes accordingly. No one has a sharper ear for the spoken word, no one produces better dialogue.

As I review Gaines's canon, I cannot help but notice that the best stories are told either by the very old, which is expected, or by the very young, which is not. Even in the first, 'expected' category much innovation goes on. In *Bloodline*'s title story, for example, Felix's story quite unexpectedly probes the present not the past, as most tales from elders do. More to the point, it is a tale of the future: what indeed *will* happen if Mr Frank dies and his property goes to his white niece or, much less likely but possibly, to his black nephew? Beyond this, one notes the orchestrated, almost ritualized give-and-take between Felix and Mr Frank. Every time Mr Frank barks a command and Felix edgily replies, 'you the authority', and every time Mr Frank inquires if Felix reacts to fear, and Felix says, 'no, I respond to respect', we sense the extent to which these two old southern men – one black, one white – *share* the act of storytelling. Together, they create in Gaines's fiction a primary scene – a socially responsible action – that is repeatedly rehearsed and occasionally improved upon, such as in the singular conversations between (white) Mr Jules and Miss Jane Pittman. All of these characters – Felix, Frank, Jules, Jane, and their variants – in their 'antagonistic cooperation' with each other, as Ralph Ellison would remark, stand as a metaphor for much of what was always interracial in the American South before integration was legislated.

Multiple narration of another, sharing kind is also found in the novels. In *The Autobiography of Miss Jane Pittman*, for example, Gaines tells us a great deal about the mood and form he hopes to achieve when he has the young history teacher tell us,

When she was tired, or when she just did not feel like talking any more, or when she had forgotten certain things, someone else would always pick up the narration. Miss Jane would sit there listening until she got ready to talk again. If she agreed with what the other person was saying she might let him go on for quite a while. But if she did not agree, she

[2] Sterling A. Brown, 'A Son's Return', in Michael S. Harper and Robert B. Stepto (eds.) *Chant of Saints* (Urbana, Illinois, University of Illinois Press, 1979), p. 18.

would shake her head and say: 'No, no, no, no, no.' The other person would not contradict her, because, after all, this was her story. . . .[3]

The mode of narration suggested here is at once valid from the point of view of folk culture and sophisticated from that of modern novelistic technique. Even better, it allows a small but intimate group of black kith and kin to reach across the generations and raise its collective voice. In contrast, multiple telling in the latest book, *A Gathering of Old Men*, is less intimate and distinctly biracial. That throws us back to 'Bloodline' in one sense but not in another: most of the voices in *A Gathering*, young and old, are black, and an intact though ageing black community is thus created in the midst of an integrated Louisiana, figured in the new biracial composition of the state university's football team.

One should note that Gaines's fiction is often about fathers and sons, and about manhood. In an early novel, *Of Love and Dust* (1967), Marcus locks horns with the Cajun overseer, Sidney Bonbon, and while Bonbon attempts to work him to death, Marcus courts Bonbon's wife *and* mistress. The first *Bloodline* story, 'A Long Day in November', tells how Eddie Howard's situation with his wife is compounded by the fact that his manly indifference toward what the community thinks of him is in conflict with that community's rigid idea of what is a man. In the second *Bloodline* story – the one selected for the recent PBS television series on The American Short Story – 'The Sky is Gray', James must endure his toothache and also undergo rigorous lessons in manhood since his father is far away in the army. While in 'Bloodline', Christian 'Copper' Laurent returns home to demand his birthright from his white father, in *In My Father's House*, a son returns to insist on the recognition his black father – now a successful preacher – never gave him.

These are 'male' stories but decidedly not of the stripe presumably initiated by Richard Wright and other 'Protest' novelists of the 1940s and 1950s. This explains in great part why Gaines has not achieved an astounding success: some readers of black fiction still want portraits of blacks as utter victims, crippled or further crippled or annihilated, while others desire new fantasies of uplift different from those of Booker T. Washington yet grounded still in visions of a new-born black society. Gaines's work satisfies neither camp. What he does do, especially in the 'male' stories and episodes, is to create a repetition or near-repetition of narrative circumstance that allows his work to layer or amass in an effective way; for many of the same reasons, his canon, like Faulkner's, is profitably read whole. Second, more than most of the other writers, Gaines provides us with a full complement of black boys and men to set beside the many new black girls and women in our fiction. My point here is not about matchmaking but about seeing a people and culture in some semblance of its entirety: one may begin to accumulate a full set of images of blacks in the new South if one reads, for example, both Gaines *and* Walker, not one or the other.

[3]Ernest J. Gaines, *The Autobiography of Miss Jane Pittman* (New York, Dial, 1971), p. ix.

James Alan McPherson figures in this discussion partly because he, like Morrison, has been a prize winner in our time (his story collection *Elbow Room* (Atlantic/Little Brown) won the Pulitzer in 1977), and partly because he bears much the same artistic relationship to Gaines that Jones has to Morrison. What I mean is that much as Morrison is an elder sister to Jones, so Gaines is an older brother to McPherson. Of course, among artists, as among actual kin, there is such a thing as sibling rivalry. This may explain some of the differences in interests and in artistic posture between Gaines and McPherson.

Like Gaines, McPherson is a southerner for whom the word 'country' has special dynamic complexities. As a black Georgian, McPherson is one of the two extraordinary young black writers to come from that region, the other being of course Alice Walker. However, unlike Gaines or Walker, McPherson is not consumed by a sense of southern birthplace, and hence does not appear to be interested in fashioning out of his native Georgia anything comparable to Hurston's Eatonville, Faulkner's Yoknapatawpha, or Gaines's Bayonne. What we see instead is a kind of Whitmanesque impulse to sing America, especially in that tune that has been syncopated by Ralph Ellison.

The variety of settings for the *Elbow Room* stories supports this point. 'Why I like Country Music' is a southern, country story about a childhood episode the southern black narrator has related many times to his northern-bred wife, partly to delight but mostly to instruct. 'The Story of a Dead Man' seems rightly situated in Chicago; 'The Faithful' could be set in many places but works especially well in Harlem; 'Widows and Orphans' is a tale of black Los Angeles; 'Elbow Room' sensitively evokes what made San Francisco a mecca for hordes of American young people, black and white, in the volatile 1960s. All this has something to do with what makes McPherson's work unique, and much to do with what makes it traditional.

Earlier in this discussion, I referred to the folk figure of the 'Long Gone', the man who, as Sterling Brown has described him, sings a song like this:

> I is got to see some people
>   I ain't never seen,
> Gotta highball thru some country
>   Whah I never been.
>
> Ain't no call at all, sweet woman
>   fo' to carry on –
> Jes' my name and jes' my habit
>   To be Long Gone. . . .[4]

I mention this figure once again because McPherson strikes me as being one manifestation of the Long Gone as author. One should always be careful

---

[4]Sterling A. Brown, 'Long Gone', in Michael S. Harper (ed.), *The Collected Poems of Sterling A. Brown* (New York, Harper & Row, 1980), pp. 22–3.

about linking an author's personal experiences with features of his or her art, but it is reasonable to say that McPherson's adventures as a waiter for the Great Northern Railroad immersed him in a tradition of black American wanderlust which is unquestionably of the Long Gone strain. He sings of America because he never goes home, never stays put, and never stays put partly because, to paraphrase Brown and McPherson, he has to hear *stories* he ain't never heard. In this particular regard, there is much of McPherson in the narrator of 'Elbow Room', and possibly much of the *raison d'être* for McPherson's sojourn in California in the 1970s in the following declaration offered by that narrator:

> I went to the territory to renew my supply of stories. There were no new ones in the East at the time I left. Ideas and manners had coalesced into old and cobwebbed conventions. The old stories which were still being told, but their tellers seemed to lack confidence in them. Words seemed to have become detached from emotion and no longer flowed on the rhythm of passion. Even the great myths floated apart from their rituals. Cynical salesmen hawked them as folklore. There was no more bite in humor. And language, mother language, was being whored by her best sons to suit the appetites of wealthy patrons. There were no new stories.[5]

In light of these sentiments, it seems hardly surprising that while McPherson is unquestionably a culture bearer – a traditional artist whose stories are often about stories or about storytelling – he is also a cultural innovator, a traditional artist in search of new radicals of presentation that are nonetheless 'culturally correct'.

Evidence of this appears in his first story collection, *Hue and Cry* (1969), but especially in *Elbow Room*. Both volumes offer stories in which elder black storytellers educate or attempt to educate younger black, not white, listeners – this being a persistent feature of the storytelling literature of this century in contrast to that of the nineteenth. Gaines, for example, pursues the same task in *The Autobiography of Miss Jane Pittman*. On the other hand, as we see in *Elbow Room*, McPherson repeatedly proves himself capable of devising fresh versions of this story type. Far from being a wise elder, the black narrator in 'The Story of a Dead Man', for example, is young, insecure, fairly naive, and above all a striver complete with a schedule-for-life – in short he is a Benjamin Franklin or Booker T. Washington *manqué*. William, for such is his name, barely knows what to make of the stories his cousin Billy (obviously the master storyteller) tells, or of the exuberant folklore about Billy, chiefly because these tales only seem to disrupt William's plans for orderly self-uplift. Yet he relates the stories, and does a wonderful job of it, presumably because he, like Billy's other black listeners, is as attracted to the stories as he is repelled by Billy, who has a way of coming on like a crazy, 'Stagolee' type of Negro of the most pungent sort. Of course, part of what McPherson explores here is just

[5]James Alan McPherson, 'Elbow Room', in *Elbow Room* (Boston, Atlantic – Little, Brown, 1977), p. 219.

how complicated the kinship between storytellers and storylisteners can be, especially when they are actual kin, and when admiration and respect for the storyteller is for all sorts of supposedly sanctioned reasons elusive. Matters are suitably complicated further by the fact that William and Billy share the same name, each having been named for their paternal grandfather, a 'jackleg' preacher known as Willie Joe Warner. So is it William or Billy who is the true heir to Willie? Which man or plan or story-teller posture sustains the family, the culture, the race? Merely in posing these questions, however implicitly, McPherson pumps blood into the old stories which seemed so limpid to his 'Elbow Room' narrator/persona.

I have focused so far on Morrison, Jones, Gaines, and McPherson because they are as interested in storytelling as they are in fiction making and have thereby made significant advances in how certain key aspects of American expressive culture, black and white, can be sustained in written art; unlike so much Afro-American writing of the 1960s, theirs is an art in which the vibrant, performative features of vernacular life come to life on the page. Morrison and the rest thus help me to comprehend the Afro-American literary tradition and to organize fresh thoughts about why the last decade or so has been, above all else, a period of fiction writing. However, they are by no means the only fine writers of the era.

Among the men, one must cite immediately Ishmael Reed, whose third novel, *Mumbo Jumbo* (1972, Doubleday), stands at the beginning of the period as prominently as does Morrison's *The Bluest Eye*. Over the decade, Reed has produced several other fine titles – including *The Last Days of Louisiana Red* (1974), *Flight to Canada* (1976), and *The Terrible Two's* (1982) – though none, in my view, quite up to the high mark of *Mumbo Jumbo*. The book is many things at once: a detective story of the romping, hilarious sort associated with writers as various as Donald Westlate and Malcolm Bradbury; a thinly veiled satire of the Harlem Renaissance social and cultural scene – Hinckle Von Vampton is surely Carl Van Vechten, as Nathan Brown is Countee Cullen; a revisionist cultural history complete with bibliography, illustrations, etc., that is as serious as it is mischievous, especially in introducing the iconoclastic historiography of J.A. Rogers partly so that new 'black answers' may be proffered for old enduring questions such as 'What caused the Depression?' In the 1980s, one hears less about *Mumbo Jumbo's* daring and verve than about the ways in which it portrays, with surprising accuracy, the modes and methods of African syncretism in the New World. It has become in short a prescursing text of a kind for neo-Black Aesthetic analyses of trans-Atlantic black culture, as we see most evidently in the burgeoning work of Henry Louis Gates, Jr. Of course, there is much irony in this since many Black Aestheticians of the 1960s – Addison Gayle, Houston Baker and Amiri Baraka (in his nationa-list phase) – were as likely to dismiss Reed (as cute, frivolous, apolitical, etc.) as he was to parody and otherwise attack them.

As a California writer, Reed has much to say (all of it acerbic) about literary politics and the insufferable ways in which Eastern writers and publishers manage to dominate American literary life. These views have prompted the castigations of women writers and their publishers mentioned earlier, but have also led to more constructive activities including the mounting of literary journals – *Yardbird, Y'Bird, et al.* – and publishing ventures (one of these is whimsically called I. Reed Books). One result of these efforts has been the creation of greater publishing opportunities for ethnic Americans of colour, including especially the Chinese, Japanese, Filipinos, Chicanos, Afro-Americans and Native Americans comprising the 'gumbo culture' of the San Francisco Bay Area. Another result is that one can say that in the 1970s Reed (along with various co-editors – usually Shawn Wong, Bob Callahan, Victor Hernandez Cruz, and Al Young) was already producing new, canon-debunking collections of American writing of the sort scholars would call for in the 1980s.

Of the writers just cited, Al Young, deserves a further note. He is a poet and screenwriter but also a novelist whose three most recent books – *Sitting Pretty* (1976), *Who is Angelina?* (1976) and *Ask Me Now* (1980) – are wrongly unacclaimed. I think this is so because they are neither freshly absurd in the Reedian vein (of course I mean 'absurd' in the generic sense) nor obsequiously indebted to Protest writing. In short, even more than most of Gaines's novels (the obvious exception being *The Autobiography of Miss Jane Pittman*), Young's books refuse to conform to what many readers and publishers narrowly seek from black male writers. While Young occasionally indulges in parody (consider for example his scathing portrait of a 1960s style black-is-beautiful poet, O.O. Gabugah), his humour and hence his fiction is broadly, gently comic: the accent falls on what is funny-sad about growing up or feeling a little old rather than on what may be comic about duping the powerful. Curiously enough, an audience for Young is being created, not by the books of other writers but by television. Most of the popular 'black' shows I can think of, ranging from *Sanford and Son* to the *Cosby Show*, concentrate on the sort of family, work and ageing crises that have been the stuff of Young's fictions for 20 years. Perhaps viewers will become readers, and perhaps as readers they will be more accepting of those pleasing moments when fiction by men meanders beyond the 'stops' imposed by the conventions of literary Protest.

As I travel East in my mind from California, I come to Wyoming, where John Edgar Wideman resides. He has been prolific in the decade under review: six books of fiction have seen print, including *A Glance Away* (1967) and more recently the three popular Avon volumes – *Damballah* (1981), *Hiding Place* (1981) and *Sent For You Yesterday* (1983; winner of the PEN/Faulkner Award for fiction, 1984). More recent still is the publication of *Brothers & Keepers* (1984, Holt Rinehart & Winston), a biography of Wideman's incarcerated brother, Robby, that is by way of intentional narrative strategy Robby's autobiography and John's autobiography as well. (On the jacket and elsewhere, John appears as the sole author, yet multiple authorship is suggested in the text and curiously enough in the Library of Congress Cataloging note: '1. Wideman, Robert

Douglas, 1950. 2. Wideman, John Edgar. 3. Afro-American Criminals – Biography. 4. Brothers – United States – Biography.'

If the decade we are observing comes to be known (as it might) as the 'Roots Decade', the label will be justified not by the enormous popularity of Alex Haley's family saga but by the more imaginative quests for heritage found in the fiction of Morrison, Walker, Bradley and Wideman. (Of course this list is hardly inclusive.) Wideman offers a particularly interesting study in this regard, chiefly because each of his fictions is to some degree an artful and deeply personal homecoming to a Pittsburgh neighbourhood aptly – and actually – named Homewood. What he comes home from is all that is mundane and impersonal in a western territory of possibility (one senses that Wideman's Wyoming is the Twainian *and* Ellisonian 'territory' demythologized); what he comes home to is a store of family tales, a heightened sense of personal history, a more familiar and familial vernacular, and a stormy weather less seasonal than social and economic. All of the volumes in the Avon series in particular contain flints and shards of the Wideman family past: a family tree prefaces *Hiding Place*; a begat chart appears in the first pages of *Damballah*; names from both of these lists are transformed into full-fledged fictive characters, products of Wideman's imagination to be sure, but also of his vivid, familian memories. All of these texts, including *Brothers and Keepers*, can be read together as a series of interrelated fictions portraying a family, a community, and a socio-cultural moment; however, the most enduring portrait provided is that of John Wideman himself, sifting through his vast hoard of private materials on the one hand and of writerly strategies on the other in order to gain a lasting intimacy – with who he is, with what manner of kith and kin he has sprung – that previously has been distressingly elusive.

If Ishmael Reed is right about how the Eastern regions of the country dominate contemporary American writing, I should have many Midwest fiction writers to cite. In point of fact, however, I am moved only to mention a few male fictionists: Cyrus Colter of Chicago, whose novels include *The Rivers of Eros* (1972) and *Night Studies* (1980), and whose short story collection, *The Beach Umbrella* (1970), deservedly won the Iowa Prize; Leon Forrest, also of Chicago, whose fiction is as exhausting as it is exuberant – only devotees stray beyond his first and best book, *There is a Tree More Ancient Than Eden* (1973); John McCluskey, formerly of Cleveland, now of Bloomington, Indiana – his novels (*Look What They Done to My Song, Mr America's Last Season Blues*) and stories are appropriately linked with Al Young's in terms of how they pursue a 'positive, lyrical spirit' largely antithetical to the 'unrelieved gloom and despair' found elsewhere in Protest and neo-Protest writings.[6] (Is there a 'Stanford Connection' worth acknowledging here? Is it just a mere coincidence that so many of the black male 'positive lyricists' – Gaines, Young,

[6]See Charles Johnson, 'Whole Sight: Notes on New Black Fiction', *Callaloo* 7 (Fall, 1984), p. 5.

McCluskey, and more recently Nathaniel Mackey – came through that university's writing programme?)

Turning finally to the East Coast, I find myself drawn less to authors as such as to two particular novels, David Bradley's *The Chaneysville Incident* (1981, Harper & Row; winner of the PEN/Faulkner Award, 1982) and John A. Williams's *!Click Song* (1982). There are ways in which these two books can be lumped together: both are unabashedly about men; both study what might be called the Afro-American practice of humanistic vocations – Bradley's hero is a historian, Williams's a writer. Both strive to be encyclopedic and probing while examining – or better, imagining – specific historical episodes such as the careers of the Underground Railroad and the Civil Rights Movement. On the other hand, the books are quite distinct, chiefly because historians and writers, even when they are characters in novels, are not ultimately up to the same business.

From what I can tell, what I admire in these books is not what is most often discussed. Charles Johnson, for example, describes *The Chaneysville Incident* as a 'wondering . . . over the meaning of history as a shamelessly hermeneutic art-form,' which leads him to praise it as 'one of the most intellectually interesting novels to come along in years.'[7] When Susan Blake and James Miller interviewed David Bradley in 1983, their questions were mostly about the 'pull' of history and the extent to which the novel's historian-hero, John Washington, is Bradley himself.[8] History *is* a force in *The Chaneysville Incident*, and one can laud the book simply for its vivid imaging of the perils escaping slaves faced even after crossing the Mason–Dixon Line. However, storytelling is an even stronger force – as a subject and, if you will, as a method of research. Thus it is not surprising that the solution of the novel's historical puzzle results not so much from John Washington becoming a better historian as from his becoming a better story-listener and eventually a *good* storyteller. While I admire this valorization of storytelling, even to the point of rejoicing secretly (as other scholars probably do not) when Washington finally burns his 3 x 5 cards, what I value most is Bradley's deft orchestration of the many strategies for storytelling in written texts. Quite to the point, a glory of the book is that as it becomes in effect a nineteenth-century tale it adopts the features of a nineteenth-century storytelling fiction, including all of the postures of distrust inherent when the teller is black and the listener white.

!Click Song's story is compelling enough, but for me the significance of the book lies in passages such as the following in which Williams's hero, Cato Douglass, muses about what goes on in the heads of white interviewers of black novelists:

> These interviewers, critics, and reviewers . . . regarded almost every work by a nonwhite author as a political action. They were almost correct . . . but failed to understand the politics – or, conversely,

[7]Johnson, 'New Black Fiction', p. 4.
[8]Susan Blake and James A. Miller, 'The Business of Writing: An interview with David Bradley', *Callaloo* 7 (Spring-Summer 1984), pp. 19–34

understood them perfectly. They did seem to comprehend, along with some like-minded editors, that they were functionaries of the cultural mechanisms of the West, a gemot whose verdicts became, if not the law, the practice. How could they then allow certain other people into their ranks on other than a temporary/token basis? To be sure, they admired Latin writers – but those in Latin, not North, America; they admired black writers, but many of those were from Africa and, in the case of Afro-Americans, dead; from the Caribbean they much adored, obversely, the minority rather than the majority writers, those who deplored, laughed at or debased the island societies of which they were a part; they exulted when good works on the Indian experience appeared, though not those written by the Amer-Indian himself, and they preferred Asian female writers to all like John Okada.[9]

Outbursts of this sort abound in *!Click Song*, and while we might want to quibble with one or two of Cato's points (when we are not otherwise engaged in identifying the writers to whom he refers – in this instance, Garcia-Marquez? Achebe? Wright? Naipaul? Neihardt? Kingston?), we silence ourselves and listen on, largely out of respect for the justness of his rage. *!Click Song*, more than any other novel I know, clarifies the recent history of how and why black writers are published and on what terms. A boom in Afro-American fiction is there, but one should not be deluded into thinking that it is altogether the result of writers composing good books, or of publishers seeing with sudden and resolute clarity the aesthetic achievement of the manuscripts thrust into their hands.

I have discussed several male writers to give them their due, but the most significant development of the decade has been the emergence of many black women writers as major voices in the literature. In mentioning Toni Morrison and Gayl Jones I have already cited two of the most remarkable black women writing fiction. Any list must also include Toni Cade Bambara (*Gorilla, My Love; The Salt Eaters*) and Paule Marshall, whose 1983 novel, *Praise Song for the Widow*, was her first since *The Chosen Place, The Timeless People* (1969). Colleen McElroy and Rita Dove regularly place new fiction in journals such as *Callaloo*; Dove's story collection, *Fifth Sunday*, will appear shortly in *Callaloo*'s fiction series. Gloria Naylor is another young writer who bears watching: her *The Women of Brewster Place* won the 1982 American Book Award for best first novel; her new novel, *Linden Hills* (1985), is one of the very few black-authored texts in Penguin's Contemporary American Fiction series.

Despite the presence of these and other fine women writers, the decade seems to be dominated, at least in terms of popularity and visibility, by Alice Walker. Her career in fiction began with *The Third Life of Grange Copeland* (1970) and took another leap forward with *Meridian* (1976), the first major 'civil rights' novel to follow Gaines's *The Autobiography of Miss Jane Pittman* and arguably the best we have. There have been volumes of remarkable stories, *In Love and Trouble* (1973) and *You Can't Keep A*

[9]John A. Williams, *!Click Song* (Boston, Houghton Mifflin, 1982), p. 179.

Good Woman Down (1981), and recently we all benefited when Walker's essays were finally collected in *In Search of Our Mothers' Gardens* (1983). Of course, if people around the world are today reading (or re-reading) the titles just cited, it is because they have been either enthralled or enraged by Walker's most recent novel, *The Color Purple* (1982, Harcourt Brace Jovanovich), or comparably agitated by the Steven Spielberg film based upon it.

Critics including Trudier Harris have rightly argued that the entire Color Purple episode (the book, the film, the publicity for both – including the printing and vending of Alice Walker calendars and date books) raises questions about how black authors and books are promoted (Harris writes, 'Now, Alice Walker has been chosen for the media, by its very racist nature, seems to be able to focus on only one black writer at a time'), and about how some black authors collude in this.[10] There has also been enormous controversy over the rather harsh portrayal of black men in both the book and film. All such matters need to be debated, but not in a way that distracts us from considering the literary strivings and achievements of Walker's text. Consider, for example, the revisions of American writerly practice achieved in Walker's presentation of Celie's letters, which are those that have prompted the most thoughtful praise of *The Color Purple*'s ambitions.

Celie, whom we have to call the central character even though she is not always the most fascinating one, writes letters to God; there are also letters from Celie to her sister, Nettie, from Nettie to Celie, and at the end, Celie writes to God and the whole world (that letter begins, 'Dear God. Dear stars, dear trees, dear sky, dear peoples. Dear Everything, Dear God.')[11] There are several remarkable features to Walker's use of this strategy, one being the full measure to which an American vernacular is successfully presented in writing, chiefly because the character 'voicing' the vernacular *is* writing. Walker *seemingly* removes herself from the narrative and in this way refuses to mediate in any outward fashion between Celie's voice and the reader. One key effect is that we are denied what has been the distinctively American readerly pleasure of questioning the motives *and* skill of authors (or authorial personae) who claim access to or intimacy with a black vernacular voice – and claim as well that their writerly representations of that voice are authentic and unprejudiced. (A convention in American acts of reading is not accommodated quite simply because a convention in American writing is not pursued.) Another effect is that we readers are forced to confront, far more than we would be otherwise, what *is* there, namely, the *writerly* voice of an under-educated rural black woman, which proves to be more powerful than that of her more educated and more worldly sister, and quite capable of telling a tale without the aid of an editor, amanuensis, etc.

To say that Walker absents herself from the narrative of *The Color*

[10]Trudier Harris, 'On *The Color Purple*, Stereotypes, and Silence', *Black American Literature Forum*, 18 (Winter, 1984), p. 155.
[11]Alice Walker, *The Color Purple* (New York, Harcourt Brace Jovanovich, 1982). p. 242.

Purple is not to argue, however, that she has no interest in authenticating it. Absence *is* a strategy for authentication, especially when one wishes to convince a readership that a vernacular voice has not been mediated and that the diacritical representations of that voice have been in no way adulterated. But Walker is up to something else as well: a strategy by which the femaleness of her storyteller may be authenticated in features of narration as much as they are confirmed in those of episode.

As a woman and a storyteller, Celie's primary condition – the one to be repaired in the course of the novel – is her *audiencelessness*. This is conveyed repeatedly whenever Celie writes to God, who is an audience to be sure, but one from whom a reply is traditionally and otherwise a miracle. So, too, is this conveyed whenever Celie writes Nettie: a reply is altogether possible but there is always a question as to whether Celie's letters are ever received. The absence of an authorial persona from the novel's narrative design is yet another means by which Celie's condition may be portrayed: no 'author' received the letters, found them, had them read to her – or him – or seemingly took the slightest interest in them. While it may be sufficient to say that Celie's circumstance is female in that it is caused in great part by Albert who, as a man and her husband, has the power to disrupt her correspondence (that of course is putting the matter politely), is seems necessary to add that it is female in its resolution: audience appears in *The Color Purple* not in the discovery of an author from afar (such as an editor, an amanuensis, an accomplice who usually assists a 'voice' in escaping to *their* world and finding a readership *there*) but in that of male-and-female kinship at home. Celie writes not to produce a voice (as if one weren't there if she didn't) but to create a reunion, a homecoming, and while all such activity is ultimately shared across gender lines, that activity is most often initiated, however elliptically, by womenfolk.

In shaping all this up, Walker self-authenticates herself as a female author, and possibly as a black female author, as well. To assert in many narrative strategies that Celie doesn't need to enter her author's world, which stands synecdochially for ours, in order to gain the power with which to be respected 'at home', is to say that women of Celie's circumstances *can* be self-sufficient, that people in the environments in which the Celies of this world live *are* capable of turning things around and responding to the Celies, and that the traditions of thinking otherwise, along with the conventions of writing and reading emanating from those traditions, are essentially male traditions that Walker will no longer (if she ever did) countenance in her fiction. What may be female *and* black in all of this has to do with the long history in American letters of white women joining white men in laying editorial hands on the texts (real and imagined) of our society's lowly while often pursuing a 'hands off' policy regarding almost any text produced by someone of the literate class as that is usually construed. In keeping her hands off Celie's letters, or at least in creating the impression that she had done so, Walker strategizes an authorial position quite different from that of most American writers, one which I will call that of the 'womanist' writer, in deference to the terms Walker devises in *In Search of Our Mothers' Gardens*.[12]

In shattering the usual ways in which 'found' documents such as letters are presented to American readers when the authors of those documents somehow represent the 'Other' in society, Walker achieves much as a literary revisionist – much that is obscured by the weaker, more preyed-upon features of *The Color Purple*, and by the extra-literary controversies the novel has generated. We best honour what she (among others) has achieved by recognizing fully the male and female strains within the Afro-American literary tradition while resisting the temptation to allow that act of recognition to be a confrontational, polarizing activity. The Afro-American South embraces equally Walker's Georgia and Gaines's Louisiana; urban black America is certainly various enough to include the San Francisco of Al Young and James McPherson as well as the New York of Paule Marshall and Gloria Naylor. Afro-American art-making and culture-bearing have developed ways of at times transcending the barriers of region, class and gender while at others respecting them. This singular artistic freedom has allowed Afro-American literature to prosper – indeed, to boom.

[12]Alice Walker, *In Search of Our Mothers' Gardens* (New York, Harcourt Brace Jovanovich, 1983), pp. xi–xii.

Note

The pioneering study of what George Bluestone calls 'the metamorphosis of fiction into cinema', is his *Novels into Film* (Berkeley: University of California Press, 1957), which proposes a methodology for such studies with detailed examples based on six classic films produced between 1935 and 1949 – *The Informer, Wuthering Heights, Pride and Prejudice, The Grapes of Wrath, The Ox-Bow Incident, Madame Bovary*. His book has been supplemented by Gerald Peary and Roger Shatzkin, eds., *The Classic American Novel and the Movies* (New York: Frederick Ungar, 1977), which contains 27 essays by various critics, discussing film versions of novels written before 1930 from *Moby Dick* to *The Sound and the Fury*. The same publisher has also launched the Ungar Film Library, a continuing series of books about adaptations of the works of famous novelists and playwrights, including Bruce Kawin, *Faulkner and Film* (1977), Gene D. Phillips, *Hemingway and Film* (1980), and Joseph Millichap, *Steinbeck and Film* (1983). A more general study of cinematic adaptations of all literary forms is Robert Richardson, *Literature and Film* (Bloomington: Indiana University Press, 1969). Since January, 1973, *Literature/Film Quarterly*, eds. Thomas L. Erskine and James M. Welsh, has been devoted to articles on the theory and practice of literary adaptations and comparisons of films with their literary sources.

7

Fiction vs Film, 1960–1985

Warren French

Suddenly I realized that in the quarter century since the making of the films that George Bluestone discusses in *Novels into Film*, there had been occuring on a vast battlefield a war between words and images that has left behind it a litter – not just of corpses (though these are frequent enough in many films) – of winding miles of discarded film and heaps of debauched books.

The whole scene from Sundance to Starnberg, from the Apple and Mayor Koch's enticements to Yugoslavia's mimicking landscapes is too colossal (to use a favourite term of filmland) to contemplate; one can only zoom in on a few of the most spectacular effects of this still unresolved conflict.

Namedropping

The 1950s were the *belle époque* when the courtesans of the dream factory (as sociologist Hortense Powdermaker dubbed Hollywood) sought to feather their boas by liaisons with the commanding masters of fiction, but even then too many bombs were dropping.

In retrospect 1949 appears to have been the peak year when the work of two artists on their way to Nobel laureateships promised to establish the American novel and narrative film as twin products of the visions of the same geniuses. John Steinbeck wrote the script for director Lewis Milestone's *The Red Pony*, in which the four parts of the short-story cycle were translated into a narrative with a unified structure; and Clarence Brown's adaptation of William Faulkner's *Intruder in the Dust* was filmed on location in Oxford, Mississippi, under the surveillance of the author. Also Hollywood showed new daring in tackling a controversial political subject in Robert Rossen's version of Robert Penn Warren's novel *All the King's Men*; and it would be followed two years later by George Stevens's much praised treatment of Theodore Dreiser's *An American Tragedy*, retitled *A Place in the Sun*.

Both Faulkner and Steinbeck had more extensive experience as script-writers and film-makers than most. Steinbeck had studied documentary film-making with Pare Lorentz (*The Plow that Broke the Plains*) and had gone on location in Mexico with Herbert Kline's company to film the novelist's script *The Forgotten Village* (1940). He later wrote the script for the film version of his popular novel, *The Pearl*, also filmed in Mexico in English and Spanish versions; and in 1952 he would write the script for Elia Kazan's film about a Mexican revolutionary hero, *Viva Zapata!*. That venture, however, marked the abrupt end of what had been developing into a distinguished career as a scriptwriter, and Faulkner's much longer connection with Hollywood also ended in the early 1950s. Though in the 1930s, promising novelists like Nathanael West, Dalton Trumbo, and Daniel Fuchs had abandoned these careers to devote themselves to scriptwriting, after the early 1950s none of the promising young American novelists were lured to join Hollywood's poolside set. Norman Mailer's brief career as an independent producer-director of three films that have fallen into obscurity added nothing to his reputation as an artist.

After 1952, however, film-makers' exploitation of the treasure horde of American novels intensified, although the original authors were no longer prominently involved. Faulkner's *Pylon* (retitled *Tarnished Angels*), *The Hamlet* (retitled *The Long, Hot Summer* after one of its sections), and *The Sound and the Fury* all flashed on screens in 1958 as the work of trendy directors Douglas Sirk and Martin Ritt. Tony Richardson's *Sanctuary* (1961) brought this short-lived fashion to an especially dismaying conclusion.

Elia Kazan returned to Steinbeck's work in 1955 to fashion *East of Eden* from the last section of that mammoth novel as a vehicle for doomed superstar James Dean; and an obscure figure named Victor Vicas turned *The Wayward Bus* into a vehicle for doomed superstar Jayne Mansfield (1957).

A third Nobel laureate's works were even more extensively looted. Hollywood developed a mounting infatuation for the virile tales of Ernest Hemingway beginning with Sam Wood's inspiring version of *For Whom the Bell Tolls* in 1944. (Frank Borzage's tear-jerking *A Farewell to Arms* from the early days of the talkies had been forgotten if never forgiven.) A much altered *To Have and Have Not* as a vehicle for torrid lovers Humphrey Bogart and Lauren Bacall followed in 1944. *The Killers* served as the vehicle for the striking screen debut of Burt Lancaster (1946), and Zoltan Korda's *The Macomber Affair* (1947) provided what Andrew Sarris calls 'the best stretch of Hemingway ever put on the screen.'[1]

Quantitatively 1950 proved Hemingway's biggest year in the movie houses with his stories providing the basis for two of the last three films of ageing tough guy John Garfield: *Under My Skin* from the short story 'My Old Man' and *The Breaking Point*, another version of *To Have and Have Not*, closer to the original, but with the action moved from Florida to California. In 1952 one of Hollywood's rugged new heroes, Gregory Peck, took on *The Snows of Kilimanjaro*. Then the two major early novels on which Hemingway's reputation had been founded came in rapid succes-

[1]Andrew Sarris, *The American Cinema: Directors and Directions* (New York: E.P. Dutton, 1968), p. 182.

sion – the first filming of *The Sun Also Rises* (1957) and a remake of *A Farewell to Arms* (1958), the same year that Spencer Tracy translated to the screen the tribulations of the fisherman Santiago in *The Old Man and the Sea*, a film to be mentioned briefly as an ill-advised experiment later in this article.

The last gasp of what had become virtually an exploitative sub-genre was emitted in 1962 in the form of a curious concoction called *Hemingway's Adventures of a Young Man*. Hemingway had never used this title, although ironically John Dos Passos had for his novel about the Spanish Civil War that alienated him from Hemingway. The script had been carpentered for Martin Ritt's film from several early Hemingway stories. The promotional emphasis had shifted from the original fiction to the celebrated author, who had committed suicide just the year before.

Not only the works of these three luminaries were seized upon during the decade after *A Place in the Sun*. That film was followed up by William Wyler's much less successful treatment of Dreiser's *Sister Carrie* (*Carrie*, 1952). F. Scott Fitzgerald's short story 'Babylon Revisited' was transformed into *The Last Time I Saw Paris* (1954), and his *Tender Is the Night* became a vehicle for Jennifer Jones (1962). Hollywood found at last the courage to film Sinclair Lewis's satirical attack on questionable evangelists, *Elmer Gantry* (1960), while popular romance writers fared even better. Herman Wouk's *The Caine Mutiny (1954) and Marjorie Morningstar* (1958) both fared well at the box office, while Edna Ferber's sprawling costume tales provided the most dependable sources of those rare films that sold more tickets than popcorn. Ferberfare was quite steadily available with remakes of *Showboat* (1951) and *So Big* (1953), followed by lavish big-screen treatments of the new *Giant* (1956) and *Ice Palace* (1960), and the old reliable *Cimarron* (1960).

The less said about most of these adaptations of the works of celebrated novelists during the 1950s the better. A quotation from one of Bosley Crowther's fulminations in the *New York Times* is enough to recall the tone of the period:

> Irving Ravetch and Harriet Frank, Jr have written a formless, spongy script and Martin Ritt has directed with an eye to the dazzle of the scenes . . . and little feel for the texture of the whole. . . . It's like Alex North's jazzy musical score – sentiment-dripped and synthetic. Big-screened and colored, but no content, that's all.[2]

Hollywood was interested in exploiting the reputations of the novels and their celebrated authors as one of the desperate efforts during a trying decade to meet the increasing challenge from television. The adaptations showed steadily decreasing interest in the challenges posed by the fictions, as the films became only another effort, like the abortive move to 3-D and the shift to bigger screens and more expensive productions, to hold a

---

[2]Review of *The Long, Hot Summer*. *New York Times*, 4 April 1958, p. 16.

constantly dwindling audience that found it cheaper and more comfortable to sit at home and watch the glowing tube.

Most of the novelists involved were writers of traditional 'realistic' works who had achieved their reputations during the 1930s. Relatively few efforts were made to draw upon the less conventional works of writers who had emerged since World War II. Norman Mailer's *The Naked and the Dead* had been in print 10 years before it was filmed in 1958, and of his other works only a comparatively little-noticed film version of *An American Dream* turned up in 1966. Utilizing the talents of Peter Sellers and James Mason, Stanley Kubrick stunned scoffers by making an intriguing *film noir* of Vladimir Nabokov's seemingly unfilmable *Lolita* (1962), but his example resisted emulation.

After Samuel Goldwyn's trashing of 'Uncle Wiggily in Connecticut' as *My Foolish Heart* (1950) increasingly alienated J.D. Salinger, though a fan of 1930s films, he refused to sell rights to any of his other works. After a surrealistically distorted version of new cult idol Jack Kerouac's *The Subterraneans* (1960), which turned the black heroine white, was denounced by Beats and Squares alike, no further adaptations of his books were attempted.

None of Saul Bellow's highly esteemed novels have been filmed, and only two of prolific Bernard Malamud's novels made it to the screen, many years apart *(The Fixer*, 1968; *The Natural*, 1984 – from a 1952 novel). Only John Barth's most nearly conventional novel, *The End of the Road*, reached the screen in 1970 in a highly stylized version that received little distribution and remains almost unknown. Of John Updike's many works only his popular *Rabbit, Run* became a mediocre film (1970): and even from among John Cheever's traditionally realistic portrayals of contemporary suburban life only one short story, 'The Swimmer', has been filmed (1968) as a somewhat bizarre vehicle for Burt Lancaster.

Of Kurt Vonnegut's popular satires only *Slaughter-House-Five* (1972) has reached the screen; Robert Altman's plans to film *Breakfast of Champions* fell through. Joseph Heller's *Catch-22* was filmed by Mike Nichols (1970), but his later works have been ignored; and selections from the work of our most prolific novelist of contemporary manners, Joyce Carol Oates, have been seen only in TV-films (a still chaotic genre that it is impossible to consider here because of the ephemeral nature of many specimens and technical differences from theatrical films).

As for the most recent generation of avant garde writers, the situation is even more bleak. Jerome Klinkowitz, the most conspicuous critic-historian of these 'experimental realists', cites as the leaders Walter Abish, Donald Barthelme, Don DeLillo, Stephen Dixon, Raymond Federman, Kenneth Gangemi, Steve Katz, Clarence Major, Gilbert Sorrentino, and Ronald Sukenick.[3] None of their works has been filmed.

[3] See Jerome Klinkowitz, 'Fiction: The 1950s to the Present', *American Literary Scholarship 1983*, ed. Warren French (Durham, N C: Duke University Press, 1985), pp. 289–90, 319–21.

When Hollywood does turn to fiction today for its inspiration, it is generally to pay homage to neglected masterpieces from the past, as in David Lean's opulent metamorphosis of E.M. Forster's *A Passage to India* (1984), which transforms the remaining motion picture palaces into temples where a sacred ceremonial is being enacted. Another veteran director, John Huston, has been more honoured than rewarded for some recent daring ventures. His hell-fire version of Flannery O'Connor's *Wise Blood* (1979) proved too strong medicine for attenuated American sensibilities, while, despite a powerful cast, Malcolm Lowry's *Under the Volcano* (1984) proved, as those who had failed earlier to find suitable film form for it predicted, too static and cerebral for a picture that was adequately *moving* – either physically or emotionally.

The novels of two recent writers whose montage techniques have been heavily influenced by the cinema gave rise to fleeting hopes that fiction and film might be finding some mutual ground for reinforcement rather than hostility. George Roy Hill's production of John Irving's *The World According to Garp* and Milos Forman's evocation of E.M. Doctorow's *Ragtime* (both 1982), although not necessarily satisfying to admirers of the originals, proved exciting screen fare that attracted large, enthusiastic audiences; but efforts to follow up with screen versions of Doctorow's *Book of Daniel* (Sidney Lumet's *Daniel*, 1983) and Irving's *Hotel New Hampshire* (1984), proved disastrous. Something had happened around 1960 that has for at least a quarter-century ended film-makers' dependence on the works and names of celebrated fictionists as a principal source for their most prestigious vehicles.

The Age of Auteurism

That *something* was the rise of the *auteur*. Prior to World War II, most filmgoers rarely knew or cared who had directed the films they watched – the product was sold principally on the basis of its stars, or perhaps its literary or theatrical source. Even the best informed film buffs were lured into the darkness only by a few names like Cecil B. DeMille – famed for his lush epics – and, after *It Happened One Night* (1934) was the first film to win all the major Academy Awards, Frank Capra, who justifiably called his autobiography *The Name Before the Title*. The situation began to change at the beginning of the 1940s with the highly publicized arrivals in Hollywood of Alfred Hitchcock from England and Orson Welles from Broadway.

After World War II, Europe had a difficult time recapturing a world market for its films. The American market for imported films was never large. Anatole Litvak's drama of doomed passion, *Mayerling* (U S release 1937) was the first subtitled film to enjoy national distribution to neighbourhood theatres. After World War II, however, an art theatre circuit developed, at which pre-war classics were revived. Gradually films from redeveloping industries in France, Italy and Germany (as well as Japan) were introduced, so that by the time a new generation of intensely idealistic film-makers began to assert themselves, an audience was ready for a kind of cinema that the American industry would not provide.

The complete story of the Eurasian invasion of American moviehouses is too long to tell here and of only limited relevance to the particular subject of this chapter. Suffice it to say that with the arrival of French New Wave leader François Truffaut's *The 400 Blows* in New York in November, 1959, a new product commanded the patronage of film connoisseurs. The films that still dominate Ingmar Bergman's repetoire – *Smiles of a Summer Night, The Seventh Seal, Wild Strawberries, The Magician* – had already premiered in New York between 1957 and 1959, as had several of Federico Fellini's early films; but it was the opening of Fellini's *La Dolce Vita* in April, 1961, at a commandeered Broadway playhouse on a reserved-seat basis that confirmed the triumph of the *auteurs*, who would continue to dominate American art circuit fare for two decades. (With the rise of the videotape, art house audiences have declined alarmingly, but Bergman's *Fanny and Alexander* enjoyed long runs as late as 1983.)

What is relevant about *auteurist* cinema to our subject is that the most influential *auteur* directors generally avoided adapting important works of fiction for the screen and preferred instead to generate their own scripts or to work with teams of continuing collaborators. Despite tedious arguments over the relative contributions of the members of the company involved to the creation of films, the significant *auteurs* – including a frustrated few like Robert Altman in the United States – exercised effective control over every detail of their productions. Sometimes they started from published fictions as Truffaut did from the obscure novels of Henri-Pierre Roché or the American detective stories of William Irish; but the film-makers did not rely upon the reputation of their sources to attract audiences. Sometimes, as in Fellini's treatment of an Edgar Allan Poe short story for his contribution to *Spirits of the Dead* (1968), such films bore almost no relationship to the sources that had provided only an inspiration. Auteurists' insistence on developing films from their original visions was certainly a major reason for fictionists rarely being called upon during the 1960s and 1970s by the film-makers. Except for Norman Mailer, the fictionists, on the other hand, either had little interest in using their visions as the basis for cinematic works or else they lacked the resources for carrying out such ambitions.

The Case of John Fowles

One conspicuous and outspoken exception to this tendency of fictionists to ignore the cinema was John Fowles, and the history of his relationship to the motion picture industry, as he has himself details it, provides an instructive insight into the relationships between contemporary fiction and film during the 1960s and 1970s.

On the basis of his statement that he had seen a film a week since he was six years old,[4] we might have expected Fowles to pursue a career as a script-writer rather than a novelist. The title character in one of Fowles's novels, Daniel Martin, is, in fact, tempted into pursuing such a course until his better senses prevail; and Fowles himself became involved in the production of a film version of his novel *The Magus*, even playing a small role in what turned out to be a notoriously bad film that seriously disillusioned the novelist about film-making.

Fowles recognized earlier than his fictional creation a fundamental cleavage between the media that serves to explain not only his personal discomfort but also the diverging of the paths of fiction and film during an age when the word is being overshadowed by the visual image.

Throughout this essay fundamental similarities between fictional prose and fictional film as modes of narration have been minimized. Although their importance had probably been recognized even before Sergei Eisenstein's comments in the 1930s on Dickens's importance to D.W. Griffith in the development of techniques of montage, and the complementary influence of cinematic techniques upon novels like John Dos Passos's *USA* have been generally acknowledged, basically all that can be said about the mutual interdependence of these methods of getting the story told is summed up in Fowles's admission of the fundamental importance of cinematic techniques to his own artistic development:

> How can so frequently repeated an experience not have indelibly stamped itself on the *mode* of imagination? At one time I analysed my dreams in detail; again and again I recalled purely cinematic effects . . . panning shots, close shots, tracking, jump cuts and the rest. . . .

Fowles, however, goes on to point out that

> there is an essential difference in the quality of the image evoked by the two media. The cinematic visual image is virtually the same for all who see it, it stamps out personal imagination, the response from individual *visual* memory. A sentence or paragraph in a novel will evoke a different image in each reader. This necessary cooperation between writer and reader, the one to suggest, the other to make concrete, is a privilege of *verbal form*, and the cinema can never usurp it (p. 170).

Fowles goes further in his pinpointing of the distinctively evocative quality of fiction when he foreshadows Eudora Welty's self-examination of the development of a fictionist in *One Writer's Beginning*. Discussing her early experiences as a photographer, Welty, in the final section of her book, called 'Finding a Voice', writes: 'I felt the need to hold transient life in *words* – there's so much more of life that only words can convey – strongly enough to last me as long as I lived. The direction my mind took was a writer's direction from the start, not a photographer's, or a

---

[4]John Fowles, 'Notes on an Unfinished Novel', *Afterwords: Novelists on Their Novels*, ed. Thomas McCormack (New York: Harper & Row, 1969), p. 170. Subsequent page references in text.

recorder's.'⁵ Fowles observes, 'The most difficult task for a writer is to get the right 'voice' for his material.' He continues: 'I have heard writers claim that [the] first-person technique is a last bastion of the novel against the cinema, a form where the camera dictates an inevitable third-person point of view of what happens, however much we may identify with one character' (pp. 166–7).

In support of Fowles, one must observe that cinematic attempts to retain a novelistic effect by employing an overvoice narrator as in the film versions of Hemingway's *The Old Man and the Sea* and Steinbeck's *Cannery Row* (1982) have proved artificial and ineffective; even in the most effective uses of first-person flashback technique, as in Alfred Hitchcock's *Rebecca*, the viewer soon forgets the would-be controlling voice in an absorption in the concrete visual image immediately before him. (One of cinema's most nearly novelistic episodes is the flashback-within-a-frame story in *Rebecca*, during which Laurence Olivier as Maxim de Winter describes the events of the night of his first wife's death while the camera roams a dark beach cottage challenging the viewers to evoke the scene that transpired there.) While some viewers were enchanted by Louis Malle's *My Dinner with André* (1982), others walked out in bitter disappointment from a film in which the most dramatic events involved are simply talked about by two diners who never leave the table.

Fowles is led by this contemplation of the difference in the modes of imagination required by fiction and film to articulate the difference between the fictionist and even the most privileged auteurist/director as he recalls his experiences on the set during the filming of *The Magus* in Majorca:

> Yet it is interesting to watch, on a big film production, how buttressed each key man is by the other key men; to see how often one will turn to the other and say 'Will it work?' I compare this with the loneliness of the long-distance writer; and I come back with a sort of relief, a reaffirmation of my faith in the novel. For all its faults, it is a statement by one person. In my novels, I am the producer, director, and all the actors; I photograph it. . . . [T]here must be a virtue, in an age that is out to exterminate the individual and the enduring, in the individual's attempt to endure by his own efforts alone (p. 169).

Fowles's eloquence is coloured, of course, by his arguing for the superiority of the lonely novelist to the team of film collaborators; but objectively his remarks can provide a basis for discussing whether the novelist's and the film-makers' relationship to the audience can be compared except on a superficial phenomenological basis.

Fowles is finally not too happy about the use that his novelist contemporaries have made of their unique position. In his novel *Mantissa* (1982), he has a novelist at odds with his milieu observe sarcastically, 'Serious modern

---

⁵Eudora Welty, *One Writer's Beginnings*. (Cambridge, Mass.: Harvard University Press, 1984), p. 92.

fiction has only one subject: the difficulty of writing serious modern fiction' and then deliver to his muse a diatribe against 'postmodernism', the most important tenet of which he asserts is that 'at the creative level there is in any case no connection whatever between author and text. They are two entirely separate things. Nothing, but nothing, is to be inferred or deduced from one to the other, and in either direction. The deconstructivists have proved that beyond a shadow of a doubt.' Thus, he concludes, 'If you want story, character, suspense, description, all that antiquated nonsense from premodernist times, then go to the cinema. Or read comics. You do not come to a serious modern writer. Like me.'[6] While praising the cinema for preserving qualities lost in postmodernist fiction, he, on the other hand, shows a condescending attitude towards it through his comparison of it to comic-strips.

The Loneliness of the Long-Distance Runner

Without getting trapped in the quagmire presented by Fowles's denunciation of 'serious modern fiction', we may find in his views a basis for isolating an irreconcilability between fiction and film that prevents all 'translations' of verbal icons to visual images from ever being more than works 'suggested by' others, as some film-makers concede.

It seems hardly likely that one so well informed about both fiction and film as Fowles would have used accidentally the phrase 'the loneliness of the long-distance writer' to describe his conception of the position of the virtuous individual who resists ever increasing collective homogenization. The original version of Alan Sillitoe's novelette *The Loneliness of the Long-Distance Runner* and its film adaptation with the same title (1962) offer a most unusual opportunity for the study of an effort to convert a work of fiction into a film. The original writer was given a free hand with the script by a sympathetic director, Tony Richardson, who was just establishing his reputation for memorable films from stories about outsiders by England's rising generation of Angry Young Men, *Look Back in Anger* (1959) and *A Taste of Honey* (1962). *The Loneliness of the Long-Distance Runner*, adapted from a tightly unified story of 50-odd pages, was ideal for screen treatment and proved also a memorable film, as would Richardson's *Tom Jones* (1963), from Fielding's classic novel, and *The Loved One* (1965), from Evelyn Waugh's scathing satire of the American way of dying. Yet despite the same characters, the same setting, the same central conflict, the film was not faithful to the novel. Despite similar conclusions, the works left totally different impressions. Under the circumstances, the question is, could the result have been otherwise?

Two analyses printed in *Literature/Film Quarterly* in 1981,[7] both

---

[6] John Fowles, *Mantissa* (Boston: Little, Brown, 1982), pp. 118–19.
[7] Eugene F. Quirk, 'Social Class as Audience: Sillitoe's Story and Screenplay *The Loneliness of the Long-Distance Runner*', *Literature/Film Quarterly* IX (1981), pp. 161–71; Jane Buck Rollins, 'Novel into Film: *The Loneliness of the Long-Distance Runner*' follows, pp. 172–88.

starting out from Peter Harcourt's 1962 review notes in *Sight and Sound*, present the most recent views of the differences between Sillitoe's fiction and Sillitoe/Richardson's film. Eugene Quirk attributes the changes principally to Sillitoe's script and argues that 'instead of re-creating the picture of a hardened, anti-social criminal [whom Quirk later calls a "nihilistic revolutionary"] he creates a heroic, romanticized boy who could have been much except for the "raw deal" dealt him by an uncaring society.'[8] Quirk further attributes this 'defusing' of the character to 'the politics of mass media art and the necessity to comfortably appeal to the audience of that art (especially in the light of the need to recoup the vast economic investments required of a film producer)' (p. 162). Quirk attributes the need for these changes to 'the difference in audience between fiction and film', arguing that 'the audience for serious fiction is a necessarily elite' one, limited to the 'upper middle class'. He thus reads Sillitoe's novel as a cautionary tale, 'an enlightenment, perhaps even a warning to the insulated . . . audience' (p. 168). If this Smith were reproduced in the film, he would become 'a symbol not simply of sullen alienation but of overt rebellion', who might 'incite' a lower-class audience 'to vent their own anger at their oppression' (p. 169). Thus Quirk reasons that the changes from fiction to film were 'inevitable, given the methods of production and the social role of the mass entertainment as 'safety values' to protect the existing social order' (p. 170).

Janet Buck Rollins's somewhat more sophisticated approach avoids the question of the reasons for the changes and concerns itself principally with putting down Peter Harcourt's position, which she takes to be that 'artful cinema, when based upon novels or stories, is a process of translation or paraphrase', because she feels that 'the adaptation process is better explained as a transformation.' She is content to describe both embodiments of Sillitoe's vision as presentations of 'a social statement and a timeless comment on the plight of youth in its quest for identity and happiness'.[9] Her initial point is that 'the collaborators have effectively balanced social criticism with a touching study of individual inspiration' (p. 173), and that 'running is the paramount symbolic action of the story' (p. 180). She attributes most of the changes to Tony Richardson, whose film adaptation, she concludes, 'offers a negative vision of postwar Europe and capsulizes Sillitoe's view of working-class life' (p. 186).

Rollins appears better informed about the technicalities of film-making than Quirk, and she produces a carefully detailed account that provides a useful basis for the comparison of this 'transformation'. Neither she nor Quirk, however, appear to have perceived what is really 'the paramount symbolic action of the story', so that neither account comes to grips with the underlying theme or the spirit of the work undergoing transformation.

Quirk, in passing, makes a sweeping and erroneous generalization that provides the clue to perceiving the particular difficulties that Sillitoe faced

---

[8]Quirk, p. 161. Subsequent page references in text.
[9]Rollins, p. 187. Subsequent page references in text.

in adapting his novelette to the screen. Quirk believes that some of the changes from story to script 'are necessary due to inability of film to present a first-person narrative' (p. 166): but while admittedly difficult, this is not impossible. I have already commented on the static artificiality of films with voice-over narrations, and probably the only way that the film of *Loneliness* could have been shaped by the same kind of voice that tells the story would have been to use the technique of substituting the camera's eye for the narrator as Robert Montgomery did in filming Raymond Chandler's detective story *The Lady in the Lake* (1946). Had this device been used, the audience would never actually see Smith, but only what he sees in the way (possibly quite distorted) that he sees it. One result of this presentation would have been that the sequences of his practice runs that are essential to the story would have become intolerably dull travelogues. As soon as the audience sees Smith, however, especially as portrayed by tall, gaunt Tom Courtenay, he becomes a formulaic figure. As Quirk points out, 'an agres-sively nihilistic anti-hero' in the novel is 'transmuted into a stock figure, the downtrodden urban working man who, beneath his unkempt exterior, and defensive posturings is a decent, sympathetic figure' (p. 167). The problem is that Smith, as Sillitoe presents him in the novelette, is not such a stock character of the kind that Quirk traces back to Stephan Blackpool in Dickens's *Hard Times*; and, as I shall now argue, there is no way we can see Smith as he sees himself unless a first-person narrative is used to let him inform us who he is.

The generically named Smith (Quirk points out that he has no first name in the novelette) is not as Quirk would have it 'an aggressively nihilistic anti-hero', nor, as Rollins announces, is running (in the strictly literal sense of an athletic event) 'the paramount symbolic action of the story'. Smith is less interested in either the running itself or the use that he makes of it to embarrass the governor of the Borstal than he is in *writing about the episode*. The fiction ends with Smith's confession that he has given his manuscript to a pal 'to put in a book or something, and that he would like to see the governor's face' if it is published. This is the same kind of ending as we find in Jack Kerouac's novel *The Subterraneans* (1958), about a frustrated love affair that is not really the narrator's principal concern: 'And I go home having lost her love. / And write this book.'[10]

Neither Quirk nor Rollins recognizes the importance, either, of Smith's confiding to the reader at the beginning of his narrative that 'cunning is what counts in life'. Rollins does not investigate the implications of the statement; and while Quirk does point out that it indicates Smith's con-scious dedication to 'a life of criminal rebelliousness', he does not recog-nize it as a literary echo of Stephen Dedalus's avowal in James Joyce's *A Portrait of the Artist as a Young Man*: 'I will try to express myself in some mode of life or art as freely as I can and as wholly as I can, using for my defence the only arms I allow myself to use – silence, exile and cunning.'[11]

[10]Jack Kerouac, *The Subterraneans* (New York: Avon, 1959), p. 126.
[11]James Joyce, *A Portrait of the Artist as a Young Man* in *The Portable James Joyce*, ed. Harry Levin (New York: Viking Press, 1947), p. 518.

While Joyce might be shocked to find Stephen's credo expanded to justify a life of criminal outlawry, Smith's behaviour is the ultimate logical consequence of oppressively conformist societies' continuing reaction to determinations like Stephen's.

Loneliness of the Long-Distance Runner might thus be used to prove again the bitter assertion in John Fowles's *Mantissa* that the only subject of serious modern fiction is the difficulty of writing it, or at least of becoming a serious modern fictionist. Sillitoe's novel is another portrait of the artist as a young man in the Joycean tradition; and adaptation of the fiction that does not bring out the protagonist's discovery of his vocation is indeed a 'transformation'. The recognition of one's vocation, however, is an internal development that could be dramatized only through a first-person narration; and, even leaving aside the meretricious box-office considerations that Quirk stresses, one must question whether such an action is indeed adequately *cinematic*. Even an attempted film adaptation of Joyce's own dynamic novel proved a dull visual experience.

No mention is made in the film version of *Loneliness* of the secret that Smith confides to his readers at the end of the novelette, so that he is seen indeed as a stock figure of underprivileged youth being exploited by the establishment. Neither Quirk nor Rollins, however, made as much as might be made of Smith's exploitation in the film because both overlooked a small but significant detail that polarizes an important difference between fiction and film.

In the novelette the governor is only a dimly perceived figure whom readers encounter entirely through Smith's eyes. In the film, however, viewers have to see the governor, so that he, too, becomes a kind of stock figure whom they can identify for themselves. I am not going to deal here with the recognition of veteran filmgoers that the governor is played by Michael Redgrave, who brings with him a 24-year tradition of an image shaped in his own right, although his being cast opposite newcomer Tom Courtenay could prompt a splurge of speculations. One detail about his presentation, however, requires attention. In the novelette, we can only guess what he looks like and *what he is wearing*, as he devises his scheme to win the cup for the long-distance race from the aristocratic public school that once a year condescends to compete with the Borstal team: but because of film's mercilessly indifferent exposure of whatever comes within the range of the camera's eye, viewers can see that the governor habitually wears a blazer emblazoned with the coat of arms of one of the public schools that train Britain's elite.

Viewers still do not understand what his motives are: a public school graduate could have decided to dedicate himself to the redemption of underprivileged youth, or he could have been forced by circumstances and incompetence into a position in the Borstal that his peers would regard with scorn. As Rollins argues, however, the addition to the film of a sub-plot involving Stacey, the less talented runner whom Smith displaces, exposes fully 'the hypocrisy of the governor's ambitions'. He does not care at all for the boys themselves; he favours the new boy only because he 'promises to be a winner' (p. 177). The tiny detail of the governor's adolescent clinging to his blazer emblem (accompanied always by an old school tie), which is lost on American audiences, signals to audiences versed in British traditions how the governor is to be judged. Who was responsible for the choice of this telling detail in the film probably can't be found out, but I suspect Tony Richardson. In any event, the Joycean fiction of a fledgling artist's revengeful thwarting of establishment exploitation, a private drama that only its author can appreciate until he communicates it to readers, has become in the film a social drama, because, as John Fowles argues, what fiction suggests, film makes concrete and, we may add, stereotypical. Could the situation be otherwise?

Perhaps the last word should go to a writer who would not generally be acknowledged as the author of 'serious modern fiction', but of a transiently popular sensational costume melodrama. For a poll reported in 1978, but conducted some time earlier, graduate student James R. Messenger wrote to all the authors whose addresses he could find, asking their opinions about cinematic adaptations of their works. Nineteen replied, and the statement of greatest interest for purposes of this discussion was to the question 'Do you feel film-makers should be obliged to adhere strictly to a literary piece when adapting it for the screen in view of the differences between the medium of the novel and the medium of the film?' Kathleen Winsor, author of a once scandalous best seller, *Forever Amber* (1944), replied: 'I should think that a direct translation from the printed page to the screen would be impossible. In fact, I have always wondered why they continue to try doing it, since it is always ridiculous in the final result. It would seem to me that scripts written directly for the screen would have a much better chance of adapting to the screen than something written in a medium so different as the novel.'[12]

Film into Fiction

The matter might rest here, as it might also with George Bluestone's conclusion in the pioneering study of film adaptations of fiction, 'the filmed novel, in spite of certain resemblances, will inevitably become a different artistic entity from the novel on which it is based';[13] but finally notice must be taken of a phenomenon that may shed further useful light on the insurmountable difference between verbal and visual media – the practice of releasing or even preparing a printed version of the story after a film made from a script written originally for the screen has become a financial success.

I am not speaking of the long-standing practice, dating back to the earliest days of feature films, of coordinating new reprints of recently filmed novels with the release of the film version, even though – as with a

[12]James R. Messenger, 'I Think I Liked the Book Better: Nineteen Novelists Look at the Film Version of Their Work', *Literature/Film Quarterly* VI (1978), pp. 131–2.
[13]George Bluestone, *Novels into Film* (Berkeley: University of California Press, 1957), p. 64.

1926 edition of *Moby Dick* – the book might be illustrated with stills from the film of scenes not described in the novel or even of characters invented for the film. The new practice is rather to have a fictionalization developed from (presumably) the shooting script, although some earlier version may be used that creates discrepancies between the narrative and the film as exhibited in theatres.

The problems of moving from a concrete medium like film to an evocative one are suggested by the comments of Donald Mott and Cheryl Saunders on the fictionalization of a film that remains at present writing the biggest-grossing American attraction of all time, Steven Spielberg's *E T: The Extra-Terrestrial*. These authors of a critical study of Spielberg's astoundingly profitable work observe that 'a lack of exposition and point-making . . . create minor flaws in the film, at least from the standpoint of the audience totally understanding events. . . . [E T's sudden turn for the worse near the end of the film might be his depression at not being able to get home. Is he grieving himself to death or is there another reason? William Kotzwinkle's novelization of the screenplay gives us the hint that it is a combination of depression, poor diet and the effects of gravity that cause E T to wither and die.'[14]

E T recovers, however, and Mott and Saunders observe, 'He has apparently healed himself, but we don't know how or why'; and they follow with a long quotation from the novelization in which Kotzwinkle 'fills the reader in with [a] rather oblique explanation' that something 'calling from the beyond', touched E T's healing finger and 'caused it to glow'. The novelization also provides information lacking in the film because of E T's inability to speak English adequately by referring to his 'communication via ESP to plants . . . and later animals'.

The viewer of the film is likely, however by this point to be so caught up empathetically with E T that this lack of information doesn't matter. As Mott and Saunders observe, 'Whatever appears missing to the viewer seems unimportant to the friendship between Elliott [the young boy in the film] and the alien or the final climax of E T's adventures on Earth – we either take it for granted or let our own imaginations fill in the blanks.'

The important point here is the implied claim that even with all its concreteness film, like fiction, is an evocative art form. Viewers may not know the causes of the events that they are observing, but they can gather the effects from visual signals and that is all that matters to them. The difference from fiction is that the signals are likely to be stereotypes triggering similar responses in the mass of sympathetic viewers; and it is clear, at the end of E T, for example, that this outsider must get home to survive. His crisis is not ideological but physical, the result not of individual feelings but of oppressive human bureaucracies that will not allow him to make his way home to regain his health. Again the confrontation is between the individual and external forces; the viewer does not need to

---

[14]Donald Mott and Cheryl Saunders, *Steven Spielberg* (Boston: Twayne Publishers, 1986). Quotations are taken from uncorrected galley proofs.

understand E T's internal chemistry to sympathize. What we may need to ponder is whether just as in filming a fiction, evocative elements from the original must be replaced by concrete symbols, so in making a verbal narrative from a film the meaning of evocative symbols from the visual medium must not be concretely spelled out.

Note

The works of Chris Bonington and Martin Green, cited in the footnotes to this essay, contain useful, up-to-date bibliographies on quest and adventure. In addition to the literary works discussed in the essay, here are a few, among many others, of diverse interest: Michael J. Arlen, *Exiles* and *Passages to Ararat* (New York, Farrar, Straus & Giroux, 1975), Edward Hoagland, *African Calliope* (New York, Random House, 1979), Peter Matthiessen, *Far Tortuga* (New York, Random House, 1975), Cormac McCarthy, *Blood Meridian* (New York, Random House, 1985), Robert M. Pirsig, *Zen and the Art of Motorcycle Maintenance* (New York, William Morrow, 1984), Paul Theroux, *The Great Railway Bazaar* (Boston, Houghton Mifflin, 1975), Tom Wolfe, *The Right Stuff* (New York, Farrar, Straus & Giroux, 1979), and Paul Zweig, *Three Journeys* (New York, Basic Books, 1976).

8

Quest: Forms of Adventure in Contemporary American Literature

Ihab Hassan

I

Quest? Adventure in the waning years of the twentieth century? In this era of satellites and supersonic jets, of the ubiquitous McDonald's and pervasive Panasonic? In our jacuzzi culture, in our cybernetic if not yet cyborg society, where *accidie* measures lives between hype and fix? Indeed, the very topic of quest seems now rather quaint, lacking, in academic circles at least, the glamour of feminism or poststructuralism, lacking even the glitz of Marxism.

Yet the subject endures, boasting a venerable pedigree. Think of Magellan and Drake, Marco Polo and Odysseus. Think, more recently, of Burton, Doughty, T.E. Lawrence and Freya Stark. Their tradition reaches, in postwar England alone, to Wilfred Thesiger, Francis Chichester, Chris Bonington. From rain forests, across oceans, steppes, savannahs, saharas, to the heights of the Andes or Himalayas, men and women still test the limits of human existence. They test spirit and flesh in a timeless quest for adventure, for meaning really, beyond civilization, at the razor edge of mortality. And they return, with sun-cracked skin and gazes honed on the horizon, to tell us all.

Adventurers can be eloquent, even loquacious. I shall, therefore, limit myself here to contemporary American prose writers whose work absorbs the traditional forms of quest, adventure, and autobiography into a somewhat esurient genre. And I shall address mainly one large query: what kind of symbolic option does this genre provide at the present time? So vague a query may be focused into three discrete questions:

(i)   what are the literary features of the genre?
(ii) what is its historical motive in the American experience?
(iii) what does the genre finally reveal about contemporary individuals and their society?

Even then, our answers will remain probative, at very best, small, vicarious ventures into the lives we lead, dream to lead, in the closing moments of our century. The answers, in any case, will lead us from some general considerations of quest to selective literary examples.

II

The genre in which autobiography, adventure, and quest meet remains mapless. It draws on a wide region of experience, which we can try gradually to imagine, if not to define.

Consider autobiography first, now so abundant. Why this rage for self-witness? Perhaps because we live in a self-regarding age; perhaps because through autobiography we deny the obsolescence of the self in mass society, and hope to refute Nietzsche who proclaimed the self a fiction; perhaps because we lack consensus in our values, and so must ground our deepest articulations on the self, on death itself, the invisible ground of every autobiography. But perhaps, too, we choose autobiography because it expresses all the ambiguities of our postmodern condition.

Autobiography is, of course, literature itself, the impulse of a living subject to testify in writing, as the Greek etymology of the word shows. But in the current climate of our ironic self-awareness, autobiography loses its innocence; it becomes the vehicle for our epistemic evasions, our social and psychic vexations. The innate contradictions of autobiography emerge to confirm the cunning of our histories. This is evident in the questions that theoreticians of autobiography now ask. For instance:

(i)   Can a life ever be translated into words? Is there no irreconcilable tension between word and deed? Was St John or Goethe right about 'the beginning'?

(ii)   Can a life still in progress – the dead don't write autobiographies, they only have biographies written about them – ever grasp or understand itself? Isn't autobiography doubly partial, twice biased, in the sense of being both personal and incomplete, partisan and fragmentary?

(iii) Can we clearly distinguish between fact and fiction in autobiography, any more than we can in news media? Isn't memory a sister to imagination, kin to nostalgia or self-deceit?

(iv)   Isn't autobiography, therefore, itself a quest rather than the record of a quest, a labour of self-cognizance no less than of self-expression?

(v)   And doesn't this quest, this labour of self-discovery, in turn affect the real, living, dying subject? Put another way, isn't autobiography shifty in that a first-person present (I, now) pretends to be a third-person past (he/she, then), and in the process alters both persons' character?

(vi)   To that extent, isn't all autobiography both an act of dying (pretending to round off one's life in writing) and also a wager on immortality (aspiring to remembrance through print)? A false ending as well as a pseudo-eternity?

(vii) Lastly, how does autobiography transform the most private confession into public expression? Doesn't autobiography – however idiosyncratic, indeed, often *because* it is idiosyncratic – offer us the best mirror of a society, even of an age?

These conundrums of autobiography betray our graphomania, betray even denser complexities of our self-conscious age. Still, all the difficulties fail to inhibit the primal powers of adventure and quest, so frequently interactive. For if autobiography is the central impulse of literature, adventure and quest both revert to myth, which prefigures literature and still breathes life into all its shapes. Originally, adventure and quest related to such mythic narratives as the shamanistic flight, the hero's night journey, his trials in search of ultimate knowledge. Later, these narratives provided the structures and archetypes of epic, romance and novel. To this day, they inform the gothic novel, science fiction, the detective story, all manner of travel and action tales, which find rich analogues in the *Mahabharata* or the *Gilgamesh*.

Yet raw action is not really their point. In the most resonant adventures we find a spiritual element, a mystic or ontic affirmation, a sense of the sacred that confirms the order of Creation. As Paul Zweig remarks: 'The gleams of intensity which invest [these moments of being] have an otherworldly quality, as if a man's duel with risk were not a 'vocation' at all, but a plunge into essential experience. . . . Adventure stories transpose our dalliance with risk into a sustained vision.'[1]

We can suppose, then, that autobiography, adventure, and quest coalesce in a contemporary genre that conveys both the perplexities of the postmodern condition and the ancient, visionary powers of myth. This genre, defying any comfortable distinction between fiction and fact, employs the sophisticated resources of narrative to raise fundamental problems of human existence, problems personal, social and metaphysical. At its centre stands the 'hero with a thousand faces', as Joseph Campbell called him, an ontological voyager, a doer, prophet, and over-reacher, at once an alien and founder of cities, with whom we can still identify. Thus the 'I' that speaks to us through contemporary quests – henceforth I will use quest and adventure interchangeably – is both knowing and naive, historic and primordial, worldly and insubstantial. Its words constitute reality even as they confess its entrapments; its confessions draw us into a circle of experience which remains perilously distant from ours. In a sense, then, this is a genre of literature that hints its own abolition – in death, in silence, in extreme spiritual risk, in all those final conditions that make literature superfluous. Moments of pure being, like the 'great adventure', leave us mute.

III

But it is time now to engage the second question, regarding quest in its historic assumptions, its American milieu. Certain commonplaces of criticism offer us rough clues. American literature, critics have maintained, is largely autobiographical, a literature of the Self, from Poe's Arthur Gordon Pym

---

[1]Paul Zweig, *The Adventurer: the Fate of Adventure in the Western World* (Princeton, N J, Princeton University Press, 1974), p. 4.

through Melville's Ishmael, Twain's Huck Finn, and Whitman's Myself, to Salinger's Holden Caulfield or Bellow's Augie March. It is also a symbolic, visionary literature, less social than metaphysical, with a penchant for myth and romance. As such, it is an 'Adamic literature', with a bias for innocence and wonder, as the titles of even scholarly books intimate: *The American Adam*, *The Reign of Wonder*, *The Virgin Land*, *A World Elsewhere*, *Radical Innocence*. Finally, it is literature, though Adamic, of extremity, of intense and brooding modernity. Thus D.H. Lawrence notes in what remains the best book on the subject: 'The furthest frenzies of French modernism or futurism have not yet reached the pitch of extreme consciousness that Poe, Melville, Hawthorne, Whitman reached. The great Americans I mention just were it. Which is why the world funks them, and funks them today [1923].'[2]

Such critical commonplaces indicate that quest is very much in the American grain. Its motive is in the wilderness, in the eternal search of misfits, outlaws scalawags, crackpots, vagrants, visionaries, individualists of every stripe, for something they can hardly name: Eldorado, the New Jerusalem, the Earthly Paradise, the Last Frontier. 'Philobats' (walkers on their toes), as Gert Raiethel argues in his psychohistory of *voluntary* American immigrants, they form weak attachments to objects, persons, places; they relish movement, exposure, transgressive fantasies.[3] Yet Americans no more exempt themselves from history than anyone else. Their quests, therefore, reveal certain social attitudes, historical patterns, that we also need to ponder.

Here Martin Green's *The Great American Adventure*, which reviews a series of classic stories from Cooper through Dana, Melville and Parkman, to Hemingway and Mailer, proves relevant. Green contends that such stories manifest certain dispositions – I would not hesitate to say manners. These include a pagan, anti-intellectual, anti-pacifist outlook; a masculinist, often mysogynist, stance; a concept of manhood linked to nationalism, patriotism, America's Manifest Destiny; and a strong sense of caste, if not class, led by military aristocrats *and* democratic woodsmen (hunters, trappers, Indian fighters) who magnificently possess the frontier virtues of valour, self-reliance, knowledge of the wilderness, and, above all, a rude *ecological ethic*. This prompts Green to conclude that venturesome quests mark 'the highest achievement of American literature', indeed, offer 'the equivalent of the Great Tradition that British critics [like F.R. Leavis] found in the line of great novelists beginning with Jane Austen'.[4]

The thesis is suggestive, the social analysis moot. In any event, though adventure became secular and non-sectarian in the last century, possibly even 'anti-Christian' as Green insists, it often took a spiritual, even mystic, turn. Green understands this; he says: 'Although hunting is an activity of

---

[2]D.H. Lawrence, *Studies in Classic American Literature* (Garden City, N Y, Doubleday Anchor, 1955), p. 8.
[3]Gert Raiethel, 'Philobatism and American Culture', *Journal of Psychiatry* VI (1979), pp. 462–96.
[4]Martin Green, *The Great American Adventure* (Boston, Beacon Press, 1984), p. 18.

the aristo-military caste, being a hunter in the American sense is in some ways not a caste activity, in that it takes place in a non-social space, outside the frontier of society. . . . Just for that reason, however, it represent more vividly the sacramental function of the man of violence. . . . Thus, if the hunter fails to represent the social aspect of caste, he nonetheless represents its religious aspect vividly.'[5] The religion in question is, I believe, 'natural,' the kind we sometimes see shimmer through the paintings of Thomas Cole, Frederick Edwin Church, Winslow Homer, or Albert Pinkham Ryder.

Spirit, then, is no stranger to violence, the violence of nature herself, the sacramental violence, too, of the hunter or primitive warrior who breaks the taboo against killing on behalf of his tribe. Indeed, some historians of the American frontier have come to consider the notion of 'sacramental violence' crux. Thus, for instance, Richard Slotkin claims that 'the myth of regeneration through violence became the structuring metaphor of the American experience.'[6] He continues: 'an American hero is the lover of the spirit of the wilderness, and his acts of love and sacred affirmation are acts of violence against that spirit and her avatars.'[7]

Slotkin's use of the feminine pronoun with reference to nature is instructive. The American hero loves nature but must also violate 'her', either profanely – exterminating the buffalo, wasting the land – or sacramentally. This ethos also affects the hero's attitude toward women, as Leslie Fiedler has famously argued in *Love and Death in the American Novel*. For quest always tempts the hero to abandon hearth, family, friends, leave society behind, a willed alienation aggravated by frontier conditions which released one kind of desire (freedom) only to constrain another (love).

Still, we can plausibly conclude that the historic experience of America proved singularly congenial to the spirit of quest. That experience conjoined energy and wonder, violence and sacrament, alienation and reverence, in unique measure. It is as if the 'complex fate' of which Henry James spoke at the turn of our century really entailed, more than a confrontation between Europe and America, a spiritual adventure into the uncharted wilderness of both the New World and of the Old Adam, Caliban, who Lawrence derisively invoked:

Ca Ca Caliban
Get a new master, be a new man.[8]

IV

Quests express our desires, betray our insufficiencies even more. For in

[5]Green, *Adventure*, p. 110.
[6]Richard Slotkin, *Regeneration Through Violence: The Mythology of the American Frontier* (Middletown, Conn., Wesleyan University Press, 1973), p. 5.
[7]Slotkin, *Violence*, p. 22.
[8]Lawrence, *American Literature*, p. 15.

quests, contemporary reality – personal or collective – finds a critique more stringent than in any Marxism.

We can commence with the solitary adventurer. What impels him to risk or seek? No single answer will do. Adventurers have adduced manhood, curiosity, rivalry, rage, the drive to excel, the need to experience extremity, the lure of things difficult and strange, the urge to confront death and master, if only for an instant, their own fate. Their motives may be ultimately, as we have seen, ontological: some profound affirmation of reality under the aspects of *both* harmony and strain, surrender and defiance. Chris Bonington reflects:

> The basic satisfaction of climbing is both physical and mental – a matter of coordination similar to any other athletic attachment. But in climbing there is the extra ingredient of risk. It is a hot, heady spice, a piquance that adds an addictive flavour to the game. It is accentuated by the fascination of pitting one's ability against a personal unknown and winning through. . . . It also gives a heightened awareness of everything around. The pattern of lichen on a rock, a few blades of grass, the dark still shape of a lake below, the form of the hills and cloud mountains above might be the same view seen by the passenger on a mountain railway, but transported to his viewpoint amongst a crowd, he cannot see what I, the climber, can. This is not an elitist ethic, but rather the deeper sensuous involvement that the climber has with the mountains around him, a feeling heightened by the stimulus of risk.[9]

There it all is: pride, risk, self-sufficiency, strenuous will, but also a 'coordination', some sensuous apprehension of being, beyond egoism. In its most intense awareness, the self opens, becoming everything that it is not.

Such solitary intuitions, however, scarcely exhaust the motives of quest. Men also venture in exclusionary groups, finding in male brotherhoods of power and peril alternatives to a society they contemn. Often, they avoid their own sahib-kind, drawn to 'natives', perhaps erotically, in associations that even racism may subtly excite. Often, they escape their own postindustrial societies, societies marked by bureaucratic chaos, collective alienation, immanent media, the deadly paradox of our time: 'unremitting [social] organization and the unleashing of vast destructive energies against civilization'.[10] In short, they flee the modern world itself, flee Western history, discovering another time in another place. Their quests, then, are as much judgements on the West as essays in utopia. Yet the best of them know that their intrusion on primitive 'utopias' alters them; their acts of exploration change the lands they explore. Applied to geopolitics, this Heisenbergian Principle – we affect what we observe – can be also called Colonialism.

[9]Chris Bonington, *Quest for Adventure* (New York, Clarkson N. Potter, Inc., 1982), pp. 11f.
[10]Ihab Hassan, *Radical Innocence: The Contemporary American Novel* (Princeton, N J, Princeton University Press, 1961), p. 14. See also Erich Kahler, *The Tower and the Abyss* (New York, George Braziller, 1967), pp. xiii, 9, 22–3.

This relates to what I term the adventurer's 'wound.' Frequently this is a literal, if obscure, infection, a mysterious disease almost like the Grail King's. Herman Melville suffers it in *Typee*, Francis Parkman in *The Oregon Trail*, Ernest Hemingway in *The Green Hills of Africa*. They all endure some debility, some 'pathetic' (the word is Melville's) flaw, a failure in their pampered immune systems. It is as if, in each seeker, two organic as well as social orders struggle more than meet. Call them Self and Other; call them the West and all *its* Others, those people it has discovered and deformed in the name of modernization. Thus 'the wound', secret agon of the blood, throbs also with the drama of colonial contamination. Is this the wound of postwar history, the revenge of the repressed, on an earth caught between enforced planetization and virulent retribalization? Khomeinis – and all their terrorists – believe they know the answer.

Yet 'the wound' is not only external, a gash in history, cicatrix of cultures. 'The wound' is also in the observer's mind, in his divided consciousness. It is in his enterprising gaze, a gaze without innocence, at once wounded and wounding. Encroaching on primal societies, the explorer finds, indeed *brings*, a serpent in every 'paradise'. Being human, he disturbs the pleroma of existence. Being, in addition, a Western seeker, adventurer, writer, he roils 'paradise' – it never was one – even more. Is this what the pathetic dis-ease of the adventurer conveys as it goads him on?

Note, though, who conveys, who speaks. It is not the wilderness nor its aborigines. Note who ventures and seeks. It is not the 'native'. In the Middle Ages, Arabs and Vikings raided the earth, roamed the seas. But since Renaissance voyagers, natives became 'natives' precisely because they remained where they had been born. They were dis-covered; like children, they were not meant to be heard, only seen. The winsome Bushmen and gentle Tasaday may have perfected an irenic mode of life. But they have not travelled far from the Kalahari Desert or rainforests of Mindanao – nor far from the Stone Age. It took another kind of curiosity, drive, aggression, ingenuity to speak them so that we all could hear. And as the Western explorers spoke them, everyone heard, everyone changed.

The adventurer/seeker, then, is a Westerner. Quest is the motive of his history and its deep wound. But it is the wound from which history flows, sometimes suppurates. His flight from modernity can not avail. His yearnings for desolations of sand or snow, in Arabia or Antarctica, lead him to an abandoned Coke can which rules that desolation more than Stevens's jar ever did the hills of Tennessee. Yet his will, malaise, disequilibrium, some radical asymmetry in his being, has made our world knowable, made the world we know.

V

We have reached the midway point; now abstractions must yield to selective examples. I have space for only five. Three would be labelled traditionally fiction, two non-fiction; all prove how fiction and fact, how quest, adventure, and autobiography, mingle in this avid genre.

Saul Bellow had never travelled in Africa when he wrote *Henderson the Rain King* (1959), possibly his best novel, no more than Defoe had visited the Americas when he wrote *Robinson Crusoe*. Bellow's book, we know, is a romance of ideas, a quest for reality, full of ordeals, initiations and rituals in the midst of mythic Africa. Its hero, Henderson, who speaks in the first person, is big, rich and strong, though past middle-age, with a face 'like an unfinished church', a truly exceptional 'amalgam of vehement forces'.

But Henderson's own heroes are not simply adventurers. They are men of universal service, like Albert Schweitzer and Wilfred Grenfel; they seek to give. For Henderson has grown weary of the voice within him that always cries: 'I want, I want, I want.' He wants to conjugate it: 'I want, you want, she wants.' In the end, he goes back to study medicine at the age of 55. Before that, however, he must find his truth, which always comes to him in blows; he must overcome his chaos, his fear of death, his raging desires.

The search takes him to the Dark Continent. This is not only an exotic and distant place; not only the land we exploit or colonize; but also the space where we meet our darker self or double. There his bungling adventures lead him finally to a kind of terrible self-knowledge, terrible and tranquil at the same time. Like Daniel, he enters a lioness's den, and lives deeply in her mysterious presence; an avoider all his life, he tries to become like her 'unavoidable'. He enters Being, which alone enables Love, and learns to move with the rhythms of things – no more *grun-tu-molani*, as huge Queen Willatale enjoins him – not against them. And incidentally, he fulfils the quotation he once read in his father's library, which has haunted him throughout his life: 'The forgiveness of sins is perpetual and righteousness first is not required.'[11]

Quest, here, requires temporary exile from civilization, with all its clutter and distractions; it also compels Henderson to desert Lily, his second wife, the only person with whom he has a vital, struggling relation. Hence the recurrent prophecy from the Book of Daniel: 'They shall drive you from among men, and thy dwelling shall be with the beasts of the field.' But this archetypal movement into the wilderness must complete itself in a return. Having learned self-acceptance at last, having slain the monsters within him and without, and overcome his own death (frozen image of an octopus), the hero goes back to society. Thus Bellow encompasses both 'Africa' and 'America', nature and society, with his multiple moral as well as increasingly mystic vision. Thus, too, he shows that the garrulous, querulous, greedy 'I' can learn to become, through risk, something other than itself. Here is the passage:

> The odor was blinding, for here, near the door where the air was trapped, it stank radiantly. From this darkness came the face of the lioness, wrinkling, with her whiskers like the thinnest spindles scratched with a diamond on the surface of a glass. She allowed the king to fondle

[11]Saul Bellow, *Henderson the Rain King* (New York, Viking, 1959), p. 3.

her, but passed by him to examine me, coming round with those clear circles of inhuman wrath, convex, brown, and pure, rings of black light within them. Between her mouth and nostrils a line divided her lip, like the waist of the hourglass, expanding into the muzzle. She sniffed my feet, working her way to the crotch once more and causing my parts to hide in my belly as best they could. She next put her head into my armpit and purred with such tremendous vibration it made my head buzz like a kettle.

Dahfu whispered, 'She likes you. Oh, I am glad. I am enthusiastic. I am so proud of both of you. Are you afraid?[12]

Here Henderson's wound – not literal though damaging enough – begins to heal. At least, so Henderson tells us in a fiction no less open than life.

Norman Mailer's *Why Are We in Vietnam?* (1967) is even more ambiguous as a fiction. Despite its title, the novel concerns Vietnam only obliquely. Ostensibly, the book relates a rousing hunt for grizzly in the Brooks Range of Alaska. Actually, it renders the initiation of a 16-year-old Texan, called D.J., into the violence within him and around him, a quest for manhood and identity, which will permit him to confront the war in Vietnam two years later.

D.J. is, of course, in the tradition of questing, adolescent heroes – Huck Finn (Twain), Henry Fleming (Crane), Nick Adams (Hemingway), Ike McCaslin (Faulkner), Holden Caulfield (Salinger) – whose initiation into reality also provides a critique of American society. Thus, in the remote wilderness of Alaska, under the Aurora Borealis, D.J. learns something about the betrayals of his father, the corruptions of America, the merciless laws of nature, the love and fear he harbours toward his friend, Tex – learns, above all, something about the intractable mystery of existence. Love, Power, Knowledge, Magic, Nature, and Death are all intimately bound; when their vital relations decay, we enter the universe of waste: cancer, excrement, money, Vietnam.

Once again, the hero learns from a beast. Here is the message in the grizzly's dying eyes:

At twenty feet away, D.J.'s little cool began to evaporate. Yeah, that beast was huge and then huge again, and he was still alive – his eyes looked right at D.J.'s like wise old gorilla eyes, and then they turned gold brown and red like the sky seen through a ruby crystal ball, eyes were transparent, and D.J. looked . . . and something in that grizzer's eyes locked into his, a message, fellow, an intelligence of something very fine and very far away, just about as intelligent and wicked and merry as any sharp light D.J. had ever seen in any Texan's eyes any time (or overseas around the world) those eyes were telling him something, singeing him, branding some part of D.J.'s future, and then the reflection of a shattering message from the shattered internal organs of that bear came twisting through his eyes in a gale of pain, and the head

[12]Bellow, *Henderson*, p. 261.

went up, and the bear now too weak to stand up, the jaws worked the pain.[13]

As in Bellow's novel, so in Mailer's, social criticism blends easily into the metaphysics of quest. Mailer's satire of America – this 'sweet beauteous land' which has allowed plastic to enter its soul (materialism) and bureaucratic violence to shape its policy (Vietnam) – can be savage as well as obscene. No one, nothing, is spared in the 'United Greedies of America', as its messages collect nightly in the E.M.F. of the North Pole, and an 'hour before sunrise' begin 'to smog the predawning air with their psychic glug, glut and exudations, not to mention all the funeral parlors cooling out in the premature morn. . . .'[14] In the end, though, Mailer slyly introduces a radical uncertainty into his account. We never really know who tells the story: D.J., the white, athletic son of Dallas millionaires, or some 'mad genius spade' up in Harlem, a crippled disc jockey? Who speaks for America? Mailer will not say, though clearly his prose sings, no less a critique of America than a paean to it. Or is the whole book, this breezy, hip, sarcastic, poetic 'I', the voice of some demiurge, more beast than man, yet immaterial enough to speak its warning to the whole world, not just about Vietnam, through the Aurora Borealis?

In contrast to Bellow's and Mailer's fictions, James Dickey's *Deliverance* (1970) seems less a quest than a brutal tale of survival. The reader may wonder: deliverance from what? From moral complacencies, social pieties, perhaps from civilization itself? The clues are scattered, and in one place they become nearly explicit. Making love to his wife on the morning of his fateful adventure, the narrator, Ed Gentry, imagines – he is on the whole steady, unimaginative – the golden eye of a girl, a studio model: 'The gold eye shone, not with the practicality of sex, so necessary to its survival, but the promise of it that promised other things, another life, deliverance.'[15] Another life, deliverance: there lies the book's knot which links its two heroes, Ed Gentry and Lewis Madlock, doubles.

Ed – all are called by their first names – is practical and forthright, given to the task at hand, as Lewis is visionary. Lewis seeks immortality, and learns finally to settle for death. Meantime he trains himself implacably, trains his instincts, will and powerful body, to survive an atomic holocaust in the Georgia woods. He insists on turning the canoe trip of four urban businessmen into a moral, a life principle, a way, a provocation to everything Western civilization has achieved in 3000 years. He wants to recover something absolutely essential, and in doing so perform some superhuman feat that beggars eternity. But Lewis breaks his leg early on the trip – again that wound – and it is Ed who pulls the survivors through, after two murders and one death by drowning.

The scene is perfectly set for the encounter between nature and civilization, instinct and law, *within* the West itself. An entire region of the north

[13]Norman Mailer, *Why Are We in Vietnam?* (New York, Putnam, 1967), pp. 146f.
[14]Mailer, *Vietnam*, p. 206.
[15]James Dickey, *Deliverance* (Boston, Houghton Mifflin), p. 28.

Georgia wilderness is about to drown, turned into a serviceable lake. The Cahulawassee River, with its horrendously beautiful whitewater rapids, must vanish. Ageless cemeteries of hillbillies must be moved to higher ground. Marinas and real estate developments will appear on the dammed lake. On the eve of their departure, the four white, married, middle-class men pore over a coloured map of the region, intuiting the secret harmonies of the land, thinking that, henceforth, a fragment of the American wilderness will survive only in archives and the failing memories of old woodsmen.

Excepting Lewis, though, these businessmen are unfit to venture; they have learned to meet existence mainly on legal, domestic, or social terms. Still, they sense obscurely an alternative to their humdrum lives. 'Up yonder', as Lewis tells them, life *demands* to be taken on other terms. This they discover in scene after harrowing scene, in encounters with the stupendous force of nature (the rapids) and malevolence of man (hillbilly outlaws). Yet, too, they experience a strange happiness at the heart of violence. Three of them survive, irrevocably altered.

Dickey's novel is a masterpiece in the poetry of action and menace. Relentlessly, it renders, in a prose at once tight, elusive, and earthy, the atavism and terror of two autumn days in the Georgia woods. The book spares us no detail in the struggle of life for itself. But the book also reveals instants of subtle intimacy, moments of pure being. Having climbed, with bare hands, the sheer face of a gorge to kill a man at daybreak, Ed suddenly exclaims:

> What a view. *What* a view. But I had my eyes closed. The river was running in my mind, and I raised my lids and saw exactly what had been the image of my thought. For a second I did not know what I was seeing and what I was imagining; there was such an utter sameness that it didn't matter; both were the river. It spread there eternally, the moon so huge on it that it hurt the eyes, and the mind, too, flinched like an eye. What? I said. Where? There was nowhere but here. Who, though? Unknown. Where can I start? . . . What a view, I said again. The river was blank and mindless with beauty. It was the most glorious thing I have ever seen. But it was not seeing, really. For once it was not just seeing. It was beholding. I *beheld* the river in its icy pit of brightness, in its far-below sound and indifference, in its large coil and tiny points and flashes of the moon, in its long sinuous form, in its uncomprehending consequence. What was there?[16]

Perhaps this is the 'selflessness' of every mountaineer, every adventurer, at his moment of truth, healing all wounds.

Dickey prefixes an epitaph from Georges Bataille, which proposes a 'principle of insufficiency' at the base of human existence. The radical lack may underlie all life *as perceived by man*. Something is always buried, hidden, lost to us: murdered bodies lying under forest leaves, the forest

---

[16]Dickey, *Deliverance*, pp. 170f.

itself flooded beneath a lake, hillbillies invisible, colonized within their own state, some part of our own nature, concealed and irreclaimable. Ed and Lewis – Ed *becomes* Lewis – manage to discover this perilous part of existence, and manage through great pain to reclaim it. But they must also face the ordinary world again, which Ed sees, at the end, in the image of a policeman: 'When we reached town he [the policeman] went into a cafe and made a couple of calls. It frightened me some to watch him talk through the tripled glass – windshield, plate glass and phone booth – for it made me feel caught in the whole vast, inexorable web of modern communication.'[17] The feeling passes, for Ed possesses the river permanently: 'Now it ran nowhere but in my head, but there it ran as though immortally.'[18] So ends his quest.

The transition from fiction to non-fiction seems almost imperceptible: the next two works share so many assumptions with the first three. Perhaps the authorial voice in the novels is less meddlesome; perhaps their interest in narrative, character, dialogue is more vivid or intense. Perhaps their imaginative freedom, a gaiety of reality, is more consciously felt. But these are matters of degree, conveyed in nuance more than in formal definition. In all, quest takes the language of the self to task and witness, and words walk in the shadow of death.

John McPhee's *Coming Into the Country* (1978) takes us to Alaska again, this time under the aspect of fact. As a reporter, an inspired essayist really, McPhee speaks in his own voice and gives us a luxuriance of precise detail, naming every flower, shrub, tree, bird, and beast in 'the last American frontier'. Yet the book often reads like a fable or romance because its characters are haunted by a dream of freedom, a stubborn intuition of possibility.

The Alaskan settlers – not the ones who go to make big bucks on the oil pipeline or a killing in real estate – all want space, independence, a chance to prove their worth. They seek a meaning in life, to which money, power, possession or celebrity is irrelevant. They want to live off the land, under the most exigent conditions, survive like Indian or Eskimo. They want to learn something about the final truths which civilization masks or distorts.

Their character, then, is solitary, anarchic, anti-authoritarian: no State or Federal interference, please! They are not socialists, not feminists, not joiners of any kind. But they obey the ecological ethic, without sentimentality or abstraction, like Cooper's Leatherstocking. Ecology? It is 'something eating something all the time out there', the wife of a settler says – eating out of need, without malice or waste. The voices of these uncommon men and women deserve to be heard in their own timbre:

> I want to change myself thoroughly 'from a professional into a bum' – to learn to trap, to handle dogs and sleds, to net fish. . . . It isn't easy to lower your income and raise your independence. . . . I've had to work twice as hard as most people.

[17]Dickey, *Deliverance*, p. 252.
[18]Dickey, *Deliverance*, p. 275.

I wanted to get away from paying taxes to support something I didn't believe in, to get away from big business, to get away from a place where you can't be sure of anything you hear or anything you read.

The czars exiled misfits to Siberia. The Soviets do that, too. . . . Alaskans are inheritors of determinative genes that took people out of Europe to the New World. [We're] doers. [We] don't destroy, we build.

The bush is so far beyond what anybody has been taught. The religious power here is beyond all training. There are forces here that a lot of people don't know exist.

Life and death are not a duality. They're just simply here – life, death – in the all-pervading mesh that holds things together.[19]

Does it all seem too literary? These pioneers, many of them college graduates, are articulate. McPhee himself joins them, drawn by their fierce vision. He knows that in their demesne, the grizzly stands as a symbol of freedom, the totem of all natural men who accept the rules of the wilderness, survival, death. (Like Faulkner's Ike McCaslin, McPhee doesn't carry a gun to see the grizzly.) But McPhee is also sufficiently clear-eyed to perceive their ineluctable contradictions. For the Alaskans end by reproducing the same conflicts they presume to leave behind. They bring with them alcoholism, envy, wife-stealing, even murder. And they dramatize the acute political dilemmas of our world in the four-way struggles between Federal Government, the State of Alaska, Corporate Enterprise, and the Individual, struggles that bush-planes and snow-mobiles carry to them at the edge of the Arctic.

In short, *Coming Into the Country* conveys tensions within both the Individual and American society – Freedom vs Equality, Progress vs Conservation, Libertarianism vs Liberalism, State vs Federal rights – tensions that even the immense Alaskan wilderness cannot resolve, dissolve. But the book also captures another persistent motive of the American Dream, the spirit of quest, an anarchic/religious impulse, still vibrant, still unappeased.

The motive in Peter Matthiessen's *The Snow Leopard* (1978) is explicitly religious, in fact Buddhist. Mathiessen tracks the rare, shy, nearly invisible snow leopard in the high fastness of the Inner Dolpo in Nepal. The animal becomes a symbol of spiritual knowledge or attainment, though Matthiessen never manages to see it. His Zen teacher had warned him before starting, in New York: 'Do not expect too much': that is, 'You may not be ready yet.' But in Zen, the admonition could also be taken to mean: to see or not see the leopard is the same, *satori* simply comes.

Matthiessen begins his journey in a troubled state. His young, beautiful wife, from whom he is about to be divorced, suddenly dies of cancer, leaving him a young son. The widower resolves to undergo the perilous

[19]John Mcphee, *Coming Into the Country* (New York, Bantam Books, 1979), pp. 177f., 178, 302, 255, 397.

journey nonetheless, as if to cleanse himself, come to terms with his guilt or pain. He gives us, in diary form, the record of his two-month mountain trek to the holy Crystal Monastery in the company of a professional biologist, George Schaller – who *does* see the leopard – as well as various Himalayan tribesmen and Sherpa guides.

The journey proceeds in several symbolic dimensions: horizontal (from Kathmandu to the Crystal Mountain), vertical (from valleys through mountain passes to unassailable peaks), temporal (present to past and back), cultural (West to East), generic (alternating between the forms of autobiography and didactic essay), and spiritual (a 'journey of the heart', toward enlightenment). The diary appears as a continuous dialogue of heterocosms, straining for peace between the One and the Many in all their manifestations.

This symbolic journey, however, is not without many complications and lapses. It confronts Matthiessen with the obdurate vanity of the self, its voracity, its tenacious fear of death. The journey also puts him in constant interactions with 'natives', including monks, lamas, and Sherpas, who form a loose caste system – lamas and Sherpas at the top. (Yet Tukten, the rogue Sherpa, a trickster figure and outsider, strikes Matthiessen as the most spiritually 'advanced'.) In them, he finds a tacit critique of his own society, its 'corrosive money rot', its 'retreat from wonder', its 'proliferations without joy'. Indirectly, he comments on race, sex, drugs, violence, illusion in America, with particular reference to the culture of the 60s, seen now from the austere, wholly essential – no dross there of any kind – perspective of the Himalayas.

How successful, finally, is this quest which subsumes the spirit of so many other quests? True to its moment, it seems ruled by ambiguities. Matthiessen relapses frequently into black moods; when he reaches the remote Crystal Monastery, he finds it empty; he never glimpses the snow leopard; he even begins to suspect that the willed act of searching may preclude the finding; he worries also that entrusting his experiences to the written word may falsify them irrevocably; and in Patan, after journey's end, he waits for Tukten at a Buddhist monastery in vain. Sometimes, even, he wonders if he has not been spared 'the desolation of success'. On the last day, he sees his face in the mirror: 'In the gaunt, brown face in the mirror – unseen since last September – the blue eyes in a monkish skull seem eerily clear, but this is the face of a man I do not know.'[20] Yet that stranger's face may also be the face of a being within us all, who neither error nor death can disfigure.

V

Quests have no conclusion; they are extreme enactments of our fate in the universe. Everything is gathered in them, from existential meetings with death to the geopolitical conditions of our epoch, from the mythic expe-

[20]Peter Matthiessen, *The Snow Leopard* (New York, Bantam Books, 1979), p. 328.

rience of America to the facticity of post-industrial societies, from the literary problems of autobiography to the nature of ultimate reality. As a symbolic option in the contemporary world, quests recover something essential to human life, often in encounters with animals (lion, grizzly, leopard), almost always in encounters with nature. However ravaging or equivocal, quests somehow pluck the nerve of human existence; they dispel the amnesia and anaesthesia, the complacent nihilism, of our cossetted lives. And they do so nowhere more vividly than in contemporary American and British letters. It is not clear that they change the world: Thor Heyerdahl burned his reed boat, *Tigris*, as a protest against the conditions of our world; a flaming signal of his disenchantment. But they may suggest a way for literature to renew itself, rise into bright forms from the ashes of postmodern ironies, parodies, pastiches, of all our vain verbal frolics. Perhaps Zweig will prove right, after all, when he says: 'The very movement inward, which undermined the traditional framework of adventure, created in its place the medium for a new exploit, and a new simplicity. Alongside our Proustian, our Freudian, and our existential complication, we have circled back to a level of primitive certainties.'[21]

But perhaps, too, all that will remain from quest is the indefectible perception of an individual alone, a perception that, in our best selves, speaks of us, speaks to us, all. Thus Matthiessen:

> In other days, I understood mountains differently, seeing in them something that abides. Even when approached respectfully (to challenge peaks as mountaineers do is another matter) they appalled me with their 'permanence', with that awful and irrefutable *rock*-ness that seemed to intensify my sense of my own transience. Perhaps this dread of transience explains our greed for the few gobbets of raw experience in modern life, why violence is libidinous, why lust devours us, why soldiers choose not to forget their days of horror; we cling to such extreme moments in which we seem to die, yet are reborn. In sexual abandon as in danger, we are impelled, however briefly, into that vital present in which we do not stand apart from life, we *are* life, our being fills us; in ecstasy with another being, loneliness falls away into eternity. But in other days, such union was attainable through simple awe.[22]

THE POLYTECHNIC OF WALES LIBRARY TREFOREST

[21]Zweig, *The Adventurer*, pp. 246f.
[22]Matthiessen, *Leopard*, pp. 256f.

Notes on Contributors

Malcolm Bradbury is Professor of American Studies at the University of East Anglia, Norwich, and has written widely on American literature and contemporary American fiction. He co-edited *The Penguin Companion to Literature, 3: America* and *An Introduction to American Studies*. He was formerly co-editor, with David Palmer, of Stratford-Upon-Avon Studies, and presently is co-editor of the Methuen *Contemporary Writers* series. He is author of many critical books, including *Saul Bellow* and *The Modern American Novel*. He is himself a well-known novelist, author of *Eating People is Wrong, Stepping Westward, The History Man* and *Rates of Exchange*.

Peter Currie lectures in English and American Studies for the Open University, Liverpool Institute of Higher Education, Edge Hill College, Ormskirk, and Liverpool Polytechnic.

Jerome Klinkowitz is Professor of English and University Distinguished Scholar at the University of Northern Iowa. Recent books are *Literary Disruptions* (University of Iowa Press, 2nd edn 1980), *The American 1960s* (Iowa State University Press, 1980), *The Practice of Fiction in America* (Iowa State University Press, 1980), *Kurt Vonnegut* (Methuen, 1982), *Peter Handke and the Postmodern Transformation* (University of Missouri Press, 1983), *The Self-Apparent Word: Fiction as Language / Language as Fiction* (Southern Illinois University Press, 1985) and *The New American Novel of Manners* (University of Georgia Press, 1986).

Warren French has retired from Indiana University and now spends part of each year in Swansea. He edits Twayne's Filmmakers series and contemporary titles in Twayne's United States Authors series. His principal books include *John Steinbeck, Frank Norris, J.D. Salinger, The Social novel at the End of an Era* and *Jack Kerouac*. He has also edited *The South in Film*.

Ihab Hassan is Vilas Research Professor of English and Comparative Literature at the University of Wisconsin in Milwaukee, and the author of many books, including *Radical Innocence* (1961), *The Literature of Silence* (1967), *The Dismemberment of Orpheus* (1971, 1982), *Paracriticisms* (1975), *The Right Promethean Fire* (1980), *Out of Egypt* (1986) and the forthcoming *Spirit of Quest*. He has also edited *Liberations* (1971) and, with Sally Hassan, *Innovation/Renovation* (1983).

Paul Levine is Professor of American Literature at Copenhagen University. He has published extensively in the field of contemporary American fiction. His study of E.L. Doctorow was published in 1985 by Methuen.

Keith Opdahl has written for such journals as *Commonweal, Nation, The Missouri Review, delta, Modern Fiction Studies* and *The Iowa Review*. A Professor of English at DePauw University, he is the author of *The Novels of Saul Bellow: An Introduction*. He has recently completed a study entitled *Imagination and Emotion: The Styles of Henry James, Mark Twain, Saul Bellow and John Updike*.

Sigmund Ro is Senior Lecturer in American Literature at the University of Trondheim, Norway. He is the author of *Rage and Celebration: Essays on Contemporary Afro-American Writing* (Oslo and New Jersey, Solum Forlag/Humanities Press, 1984).

Allan Lloyd Smith lectures in American literature at the University of East Anglia, Norwich. He is the author of two books on American fiction: *The Analysis of Motives: Early American Psychology and Fiction* (1980) and *Eve Tempted: Writing and Sexuality in Hawthorne's Fiction* (1984); and a forthcoming study of the uncanny in American literature, *Medusa's Face*.

Robert B. Stepto is Professor of English, Afro-American Studies, and American Studies at Yale University. He is the author of *From Behind the Veil: A Study of Afro-American Narrative* (1979) and the co-editor (with Michael S. Harper) of *Chant of Saints: A Gathering of Afro-American Literature, Art and Scholarship*. He has also re-edited (with Dexter Fisher) *Afro-American Literature: The Reconstruction of Instruction*. He is currently at work on a section of the Modern American Literature volume of the *Cambridge History of American Literature*.

Index

Please see under title for works discussed